THE ISLAMIC TRILOGY

VOLUME 11

THE SUBMISSION OF WOMEN AND SLAVES

ISLAMIC DUALISM

THE ISLAMIC TRILOGY SERIES

VOLUME 1

MOHAMMED AND THE UNBELIEVERS

VOLUME 2

THE POLITICAL TRADITIONS OF MOHAMMED

VOLUME 3

A SIMPLE KORAN

VOLUME 4

AN ABRIDGED KORAN

VOLUME 5

MOHAMMED, ALLAH AND THE JEWS

VOLUME 6

MOHAMMED, ALLAH, AND THE CHRISTIANS

VOLUME 7

MOHAMMED, ALLAH, AND HINDUISM

VOLUME 8

MOHAMMED, ALLAH, AND THE INTELLECTUALS

VOLUME 9

MOHAMMED, ALLAH, AND THE MIND OF WAR

VOLUME 10

MOHAMMED, ALLAH, AND POLITICS

VOLUME 11

THE SUBMISSION OF WOMEN AND SLAVES

WWW.CSPIPUBLISHING.COM

THE ISLAMIC TRILOGY

VOLUME 11

THE SUBMISSION OF WOMEN AND SLAVES

ISLAMIC DUALISM

CENTER FOR THE STUDY
OF POLITICAL ISLAM

CSPI PUBLISHING

WWW.CSPIPUBLISHING.COM

THE ISLAMIC TRILOGY
VOLUME 11

THE SUBMISSION OF WOMEN AND SLAVES

ISLAMIC DUALISM

ISBN 0-979794-0-6
ISBN13 978-0-9795794-0-0

V 6.04.07

PUBLISHED BY CSPI, LLC
WWW.CSPIPUBLISHING.COM

PRINTED IN THE USA

TABLE OF CONTENTS

THE CSPI MAXIM

Islam is a political system, a culture, and a religion based upon the Koran, Sira, and Hadith. To understand Islam, know the Trilogy.

PURPOSE

The Center for the Study of Political Islam is dedicated to:

- *Making the political doctrine of the Koran, Sira, and Hadith (the Trilogy) available to the world.*
- *Establishing authoritative/verifiable fact-based knowledge.*
- *Integrating knowledge—using primary sources to give the complete picture of Islam's political doctrine.*

OVERVIEW

All of the political and religious doctrine of Islam is found in three texts known as the Islamic Trilogy: the Koran, the Sira (the life of Mohammed) and the Hadith (the traditions of Mohammed). There is a very large problem, however: they are difficult to read. Who do you know who has read the entire Koran and understands it? Mohammed's life, the Sira, is eight hundred pages of academic text which, even in translation, is filled with Arabic names and terms. And the third text, the Hadith, contains seven thousand Traditions. There is a solution. If all three texts are woven together, each text supports and explains the rest. Taken as a whole, they become easier to understand.

RELIGIOUS AND POLITICAL ISLAM

Islam is a political system, a culture, and a religion. The religion of Islam is what a Muslim does to go to Paradise and avoid Hell. Political Islam determines the treatment of unbelievers and the governance of Muslims.

The chief features of the religion are charity to other Muslims, prayer to Allah, fasting during the month of Ramadan, pilgrimage to Mecca, and declaring that Mohammed is the prophet of the only god, Allah. The religion of Islam is important to Muslims, but the politics affect every non-Muslim.

Islam has a complete legal code, the Sharia. The foundation of Islam's legal and political system is clearly laid out in three texts—the Koran, the Sira, and the Hadith—the Islamic Trilogy. Every book of the Trilogy is both religious and political. More than half of the Koran focuses on the unbelievers. About three-quarters of the Sira (life of Mohammed) is political. The Hadith is filled with political statements and examples. Islam is a fully developed political system and the oldest form of politics active today.

The fundamental principle of Islam is that its politics are sacred, perfect, eternal, and universal. All other political systems are man-made and must be replaced by Islamic law.

Islam's success comes primarily from its politics. In thirteen years as a spiritual leader, Mohammed converted 150 people to his religion. When he became a political leader and warrior, Islam exploded, and Mohammed became king of Arabia in ten years.

THE ISLAMIC TRILOGY

The doctrine of Islam is found in the words of Allah (the Koran) and the words and actions of Mohammed (the Sunna). The words of Allah are found in the Koran, which is divided into two parts, the early part written in Mecca and the later part written in Medina.

The words and actions of Mohammed are contained in two collections of texts—the Sira and the Hadith. His words and actions are considered to be Allah's divine pattern for all humanity.

The Sira is Mohammed's biography; the two most widely known are by Ibn Ishaq and Al Tabari. Approximately three-quarters of the Sira relates to politics and war.

A hadith, which means ***tradition***, is a short story about what Mohammed did or said. A collection of hadiths is called a Hadith. There are many collections of hadiths, but the most authoritative are those by Bukhari and Abu Muslim.

So the Trilogy is:

The Koran
The Sira, or biographies, by Ishaq and Al Tabari
The Hadith, or Traditions, by Bukhari and Muslim

The Trilogy is the foundation and totality of Islam. Every one of the hundreds of biographies of Mohammed is based upon the Sira and Hadith. All of Islamic law, the Sharia, is based upon the Trilogy. Every statement and action of political and religious Islam comes from the Trilogy. The attack on the World Trade Towers, for example, was a political action based upon it. If you know the Trilogy, you can talk with an Islamic religious and political leader or critique an article written in a scholarly journal such as ***Foreign Affairs***. If you know the Trilogy, you will see every news report about Islam with new eyes.

THE KORAN

Islam believes that the Koran is the perfect, eternal, universal, final word of the only god, Allah. The Koran does not have the slightest error. It was brought to men by Mohammed who is the ideal pattern for all behavior of all peoples for all times, now and forever.

The Koran is written in classical Arabic. Many Muslims say that the Koran cannot be translated. But since very few Muslims can read classical Arabic, it has been translated many times.

The Koran is divided into suras or chapters. But unlike chapters, a sura has many different subjects that seem unrelated. So as you read, the subject matter jumps from one topic to the next.

The chapters are arranged in order of length, not in the order they were written. Imagine that you took a mystery novel and cut off the spine. Then you rebound the book starting with the longest chapter and so on down to the shortest chapter. As you read it you would jump back and forth in time and be completely confused. The story would be lost. Likewise, when you turn a page of the Koran, it could move forward or backward in time, and the reader is completely lost.

WHY THE KORAN IS NOT THE BASIS OF ISLAM

Most non-Muslims think Islam is based entirely upon the Koran. That is not true. There is not enough information in the Koran to form the religious and political system of Islam. For instance, there are apparent contradictions in the Koran that can be resolved only by knowing what was happening at that time, and that is known only by reading the Sira and Hadith. For that matter, a Muslim cannot even pray based upon the information in the Koran.

The Koran insists that it is the word of Allah, the only god. And it insists equally that Allah is pleased when the world imitates Mohammed in every aspect of his life, including religion. The Koran says more than seventy times that Mohammed is to be followed in every detail in every matter. And where is the only place that the ideal example of Mohammed can be found? Not in the Koran but in the Sira and the Hadith. The daily actions of a Muslim are governed far more by the Hadith than the Koran.

Therefore, the Islamic belief system is based upon and defined by the Sira, the Hadith, and the Koran.

No one text of the Trilogy can stand by itself; it is impossible to understand any one of the texts without the other supporting texts. The Koran, Sira, and Hadith are a seamless whole and speak with one voice. In order to understand the Koran, one must first understand the Sira and Hadith.

MAXIM

Islam is a political ideology. No action or statement by Islam can be understood without understanding its origins in the Trilogy. Any analysis, statement, or opinion about Islam is incomplete without a reference to the Trilogy. The Trilogy is the source and basis of all Islamic politics, diplomacy, history, philosophy, religion, and culture.

SCHOOLS OF SCHOLARSHIP

There are three schools of thought with regards to Islam. The first school is the Islamic school with its many subdivisions. All of its writings are by Muslims.

The second school is the Academic school. This is taught in universities. Courses of study include Islamic art, architecture, poetry, literature, Sufism (mystical Islam), history without jihad or victims. History and current events are described from a Western point of view using our political theory. The history of the victims of jihad is never mentioned. Islam is seen as a part of our civilization. The Trilogy source documents are not studied, only comments by other scholars.

The Academic school cannot connect the dots of Islamic current events, explain the "why" (the motivation, thinking or world-view) of Islamic history and can never predict the future of Islamic actions. All Islamic actions are explained as a reaction to the West. In a sense, the Academic school only references itself for explanations, never the Islamic texts.

The third school of thought is the Foundational school. The Foundational school uses the source documents of Islam to explain the world-view of Islamic civilization. It sees all Islam as motivated by the Koran and the Sunna of Mohammed. The history of Islam is interpreted as an expression of the political doctrine of Islam.

The Foundational school studies the history of the victims of Islam. This includes the history of slaves and ***dhimmis*** (semi-slaves).

The Foundational school can see the pattern (connect the dots) of Islamic current events, explain Islamic history and predict possible outcomes for the future. The reason is simple. The Foundational school studies the same texts that Islamic leaders use as a guide.

The Foundational school writing always quotes the Koran and Mohammed and includes the suffering of the victims. The Academic school does not reference the Trilogy and never includes any suffering of the victims.

There is a second major difference between the Academic school and the Foundational school. The Academic school accepts Islam as one of the world's great religions. As a result, the Academic school is respectful and does not find fault in Mohammed or Islam.

The Foundational school sees the Islamic texts as another set of doctrinal books. Every sentence, paragraph and verse can be divided into one of two categories that which is directed to Muslims and that which is about unbelievers (***kafirs***). The Foundational school concentrates on the kafir material.

Thus the Islamic school is written by believers. The Academic school is written by dhimmis (non-Muslims who serve and defer to Islam) and the Foundational school is written by kafirs.

REFERENCE NUMBERS

The information in this book can be traced back to the source by use of the reference numbers:

I234 is a reference to Ibn Ishaq's ***Sirat Rasul Allah***, translated by A. Guillaume as ***The Life of Muhammad***. This is a reference to margin note 234.

T123 is a reference to ***The History of al-Tabari*** by the State University of New York. The number refers to the margin note 123.

M234 is a reference to ***The Life of Mohammed*** by Sir William Muir, AMS Press, New York, NY, 1975. The number is page 234.

B2,3,45 is a reference to Bukhari's Hadith. The three example numbers are volume 2, book 3, and number 45, a standard reference system.

M2,345 is a reference to Muslim's Hadith. The example would be book 2, number 345.

12:45 is Koran chapter (sura) 12, verse 45.

The Hadith contain many versions of the same story. It is like getting different eye-witness accounts of a scene. When a hadith has a number such as [B6,61,572;B7,62,120] it means that all of those original hadiths have been condensed into one hadith. In this case two have been incorporated.

It is the present state of knowledge of the West about Islam that there is no standardized spelling of proper Arabic nouns. Examples: Muslim/Moslem, Mohammed/Muhammad, Koran/Quran.

SUBMISSION & DUALITY

CHAPTER 1

3:131 Obey Allah and His messenger so that you may receive mercy.

- Islam is a civilization based upon submission and duality.
- All of Islam is based upon the Koran and the Sunna.
- The Sunna is the words and deeds of Mohammed, the ideal Muslim.
- The Sunna is found in the Hadith and the Sira.

Islam means submission, submission in all things—religion, politics, culture, civilization and sexual roles. Duality means that everything is divided and submission means that one side of the duality must dominate the other. All Islamic doctrine follows from submission. Indeed, the opposite is true as well, without submission, there is no Islam. Dualism and submission are the very foundation of Islam.

Islam is about division and the power of one thing over another. Politically, it is about the dominance of the Islamic civilization over all non-Muslim civilizations. But inside of Islam, all Muslims are divided into male and female. And as we will see, one sex has dominance over the other.

Islam is not only a religion, but a complete civilization. It is a political system, legal system, ethical system, culture and a religion. Each of these categories is based upon a dualistic doctrine of submission. Only two of Islam's dualistic doctrines of submission will be dealt with in this book—women and slaves.

This book presents the doctrine of Islam; it is not about opinion or judgment. All of this work comes from Islam's three sacred texts (the Islamic Trilogy) that completely define Islam. The Trilogy is the Koran, the Hadith and the Sira. Every Muslim's life is ruled by the Trilogy. Every conquest of Islamic history is based upon the Trilogy.

Said another way, there is no Islam outside of the Trilogy. The Trilogy is the words of Allah and the Sunna of Mohammed.

THE SUNNA

Worshipping Allah does not make anyone a Muslim. Being a Muslim means worshipping Allah exactly in the same way that Mohammed did. But it goes much further than worship. Mohammed's words and actions are the perfect pattern for all social and personal conduct. Law, custom, business, art, literature, family, religion, history, knowledge, sex, and the smallest details of human behavior are patterned after what Mohammed did and said. Thus, Islam is a complete religion.

What Mohammed did and said is so important that it has a special name, Sunna. The Sunna is referred to in the Koran over 70 times. (This is the reason that each chapter starts with a quote from the Koran about the need to imitate Mohammed. For the same reason each chapter ends with the reminder that the chapter is sacred Islamic doctrine, Sunna.)

The Sunna is found in two sets of texts:

The life of Mohammed, the Sira
The Traditions of Mohammed, the Hadith

Without the Sunna there is no Islam, since the Koran does not contain enough information to form a political system or a religion. Indeed, the Koran contains only about 20% of the textual basis of Islam. Approximately 80% of the foundational Islamic texts are the Sira and the Hadith. So the Sunna is far more important to Islam than the Koran. We call the collection of the Koran, the Sira and the Hadith the Islamic Trilogy.

The Koran is so incomplete that it is a great error to call the Koran the "Islamic Bible." The Islamic Bible is the Trilogy—the Koran, Sira and Hadith.

There is a sureness in using the Trilogy for the study of Islam. All of the texts are foundational. They are the very source of all Islamic doctrine, law, custom and thought. The Trilogy is the only sound basis for judgment on doctrine.

WHAT YOU ARE GOING TO READ

The *Submission of Women and Slaves* is not about Islam. It is Islam. This book is not about opinion, but the actual doctrine that underlies each and every book ever written about Islam. Each paragraph has a number that relates to a Koranic verse or paragraph in the Sira or Hadith and allows you to verify any idea.

The first step in producing this book was an exhaustive computer search of the Trilogy—Koran, Sira and Hadith—for every verse, sentence, hadith and paragraph that included any mention of anything female. This gave the raw data. Female references such as she-camel and feminine poetic devices such as "Mecca, mother of cities" were dropped. There were also many references with female words where the woman was in the background or peripheral to the action; these were dropped. The organizing idea was to keep all references that developed the doctrine about women. Every reference to a woman being superior or equal was kept to present the best picture possible.

PERFECT, UNIVERSAL AND ETERNAL

Many of the references are from the Koran. For Islam, its words are not actually words. The Koran is the crystallized thoughts of the only god of the universe. The Koran is perfect and does not have the smallest flaw. It is universal. It is the destiny of every human being to be ruled by the Koran. It is eternal. There will never be any change in the Koran. It is final and complete. There is nothing else that needs to be known about religion, or politics, since the Koran is a political document, as well as a religious document.

Universal means that the Islamic civilization must dominate all other civilizations.

All of the Trilogy is eternal and unchangeable. The doctrine of Islam is permanent and complete. It cannot be reformed or altered.

KAFIR

The language of Islam is dualistic. As an example, there is never any reference to humanity as a unified whole. Instead there is a division into believer and ***kafir*** (unbeliever). Humanity is not seen as one body, but is divided into whether the person believes Mohammed is the prophet of Allah or not.

Kafir is what the Koran and Islam call the unbelievers. The Koran defines the kafir and says that the kafir is hated[1] and despised by Allah. A kafir can

1. 40:35 They who dispute the signs of Allah [kafirs] without authority having reached them are greatly hated by Allah and the believers. So Allah seals up every arrogant, disdainful heart.

be enslaved[2], raped[3], mocked[4], punished[5], beheaded[6], confused[7], plotted

2. B5,58,148 When some of the remaining Jews of Medina agreed to obey a verdict from Saed, Mohammed sent for him. He approached the Mosque riding a donkey and Mohammed said, "Stand up for your leader." Mohammed then said, "Saed, give these people your verdict." Saed replied, "Their soldiers should be beheaded and their women and children should become slaves." Mohammed, pleased with the verdict, said, "You have made a ruling that Allah or a king would approve of."

3. I759 On the occasion of Khaybar, Mohammed put forth new orders about forcing sex with captive women. If the woman was pregnant she was not to be used for sex until after the birth of the child. Nor were any women to be used for sex who were unclean with regard to Muslim laws about menstruation.

4. 83:34 On that day the faithful will mock the kafirs, while they sit on bridal couches and watch them. Should not the kafirs be paid back for what they did?

5. 25:77 Say to the kafirs: My Lord does not care for you or your prayers. You have rejected the truth, so sooner or later, a punishment will come.

6. 47:4 When you encounter the kafirs on the battlefield, cut off their heads until you have thoroughly defeated them and then take the prisoners and tie them up firmly.

7. 6:25 Some among them listen to you [Mohammed], but We have cast veils over their [kafirs] hearts and a heaviness to their ears so that they cannot understand our signs [the Koran].

against[8.], terrorized[9.], destroyed, deceived[10.], cut down, annihilated[11.], stolen from[12.], killed[13.], crucified[14.], made war on[15.], and humiliated[16.].

---

8. 86:15 They plot and scheme against you [Mohammed], and I plot and scheme against them. Therefore, deal calmly with the kafirs and leave them alone for a while.

9. 8:12 Then your Lord spoke to His angels and said, "I will be with you. Give strength to the believers. I will send terror into the kafirs' hearts, cut off their heads and even the tips of their fingers!"

10. B5,59,369 Mohammed asked, "Who will kill Ka'b, the enemy of Allah and Mohammed?"
Bin Maslama rose and responded, "O Mohammed! Would it please you if I killed him?"
Mohammed answered, "Yes."
Bin Maslama then said, "Give me permission to deceive him with lies so that my plot will succeed."
Mohammed replied, "You may speak falsely to him."

11. 6:45 So the kafirs were annihilated. All praise be to Allah, the Lord of the worlds!

12. B5,59,537 On the day of Khaybar, Allah's Apostle divided the spoils of war of Khaybar with the ratio of two shares for the horse and one share for the foot soldier.

13. 4:91 If they do not keep away from you or offer you peace or withdraw their hostilities, then seize them and kill them wherever they are. We give you complete authority over them.

14. 5:33 The only reward for those who war against Allah and His messengers and strive to commit mischief on the earth is that they will be slain or crucified, have their alternate hands and feet cut off, or be banished from the land. This will be their disgrace in this world, and a great torment shall be theirs in the next except those who repent before you overpower them. Know that Allah is forgiving and merciful.

15. 9:29 Make war on those who have received the Scriptures [Jews and Christians] but do not believe in Allah or in the Last Day. They do not forbid what Allah and His Messenger have forbidden. The Christians and Jews do not follow the religion of truth until they submit and pay the poll tax [jizya], and they are humiliated.

16. Ibid

A Muslim is not the friend of a kafir[17]. A kafir is ignorant[18], blind[19], arrogant[20], evil[21], a liar[22], disgraced[23], a partner of Satan[24], unclean[25], and cursed[26]. So says the Koran.

Christians and Jews are infidels, but infidels are kafirs, too. Polytheists are Hindus, but they are also kafirs. The terms infidel and polytheist are religious words. Only the word "kafir" shows the common political treatment of Christian, Jew, Hindu, Buddhist, animist, atheist and humanist.

The word kafir will be used in this book instead of "unbeliever", the standard word. Unbeliever is a neutral term. The Koran defines the kafir and kafir is not a neutral word. A kafir is not merely someone who does not agree with Islam, but a kafir is evil, disgusting, the lowest form of life. Kafirs can be tortured, killed, lied to and cheated. So the usual word "unbeliever" does not reflect the political reality of Islam.

SUBMISSION AND DUALITY

Dualism divides all of the universe into halves such as believer-kafir. But Islam never divides equals. One side must submit to the other. A believer is not equal to a kafir. The kafir must submit to the believer. Islam divides all Muslims into male/female. Males and females have different

---

17. 3:28 Believers should not take kafirs as friends in preference to other believers. Those who do this will have none of Allah's protection and will only have themselves as guards. Allah warns you to fear Him for all will return to Him.

18. 6:111 Even if We had sent down the angels to them [kafirs], the dead had spoken to them, and We had gathered all things before their eyes, they would not believe unless Allah had willed it, but most of them are ignorant.

19. 27:80 You can not make the dead listen or the deaf to hear, when they have turned to flee, nor can you guide the blind from their errors

20. 40:76 Enter the gates of Hell to live there forever. Evil is the abode of the arrogant ones.

21. 23:97 And say: Oh my Lord! I seek refuge with You from the suggestions of the evil ones [kafirs]. And I seek refuge with you, my Lord, from their presence.

22. 51:10 Cursed are the liars, who stumble along in the depths of ignorance!

23. 37:18 Tell them, "Yes! And you [kafirs] will be disgraced."

24. 25:55 And still they worship others besides Allah who can neither help nor hurt them. The kafir is Satan's ally against Allah.

25. 9:28 Oh, believers, only the kafirs are unclean.

26. 33:60 They [kafirs] will be cursed, and wherever they are found, they will be seized and murdered. It was Allah's same practice with those who came before them, and you will find no change in Allah's ways.

rules of conduct. The man may travel alone, but the woman must take a male relative with her. The woman must submit to the man.

Dualism divides and accepts contradictions in how to deal with issues. For instance, part of the Koran advocates good treatment of kafirs. Then a later verse will advocate harm. But this apparent contradiction is resolved by the fact that Allah gave both verses, so they are both true. The later verse is merely the stronger one. Duality allows both sides of a contradiction to be both true.

Submission assures that one side of the duality rules over the other.

Islam's doctrine regarding women and slavery are all based upon duality and submission. This ethical and political doctrine has one set of rules for Muslims and another set of rules for the slave. The doctrine says to treat slaves well, but sanctions the jihad that killed the slaves' defenders to take them slaves. This is a contradiction, but under duality, both sides are true. Good treatment and killing are both Islam.

Submission always involves a master and a slave. One thing must submit to another. Mohammed submitted to Allah. The Muslim must submit to Allah and Mohammed (the Sunna). The Muslim woman must submit to Muslim men. It is the goal of Islam that all kafirs submit to Islam. Submission is all about a master/slave relationship.

THE WOMAN

CHAPTER 2

5:92 Obey Allah, and obey the Messenger, and be on your guard.

- A woman's highest achievement is motherhood.
- Men and women will be judged equally on Judgment Day.
- The veil and clothing are to be used to conceal a woman's sexuality.
- A woman's behavior during her menstrual cycle must be controlled by men.
- Most of the people in Hell will be women.
- Women are less intelligent than men.
- Women have half the legal standing of a man.
- It is an insult to say that Allah has daughters.
- Islam forbids killing female children.

There is a major political division between Islam and the rest of the world. The political duality is:

dar al Islam (land of submission) and
dar al harb (land of war).

Islam's duality at the personal level is between the Muslim and the kafir.

The major duality inside Islam is male/female. There is one set of rules for men and another set of rules from women. If there were no submission, then there would need to be only one rule: men and women are treated the same. If they are not to be treated the same, then many more rules are needed.

There is only one area in which men and women are treated equally—both sexes will be judged on the basis of their lives on Judgment Day. This section of the book lays out the basis for doctrine that govern the rules, laws and customs for Muslim women.

There is not very much material in the Trilogy about females. Only about 9% of the Koran and about 12% of the Sira refers to females. The overwhelming amount of the doctrine is about men. But there is more than enough in the Trilogy to govern the smallest detail in the life of a woman from birth to death.

WOMAN AS MOTHER

There is only one way in which a woman is held to be superior to a man: if, and only if, a woman is a mother, is she held in higher esteem than a man.

> [B8,73,2;B8,73,4]
>
> *A man came to Mohammed and said, "O Allah's Apostle! Who should be my closest friend?" Mohammed said, "Your mother." The man said. "Who is next?" The Prophet said, "Your mother." The man asked again, "Who is next?" Mohammed said, "Your mother." The man asked for the fourth time, "Who is next?" Mohammed said, "Your father."*
>
> *Later Mohammed said. "It is one of the greatest sins that a man should curse his parents." The people listening asked, "O Allah's Apostle! How does a man curse his parents?" Mohammed said, "'The man abuses the father of another man and then that man abuses the first man's father and mother."*

> [B1,111,675;B1,111,676;B1,111,677;B1,111,678;B1,12,827]
>
> *Mohammed said, "When I start prayer, I intend for it to be long, but upon hearing the cries of a child I cut it short, as I dislike to trouble any child's mother."*

46:15 *We command man to show kindness to his parents. His mother bore and gave birth to him in pain. From birth to weaning is thirty months; when he reaches full strength at forty years of age, he says, "My Lord, open my heart so that I may be grateful for the favor You have given me and my parents and so that I will do the good works that please You. Be gracious to me in my offspring; I have turned to you and do surrender to Islam."*

4:1 *People! Fear your Lord who created you from one soul, and from that soul created its spouse, and from them He spread the earth with innumerable men and women. Fear Allah in whose name you claim your rights to one another and show reverence to the mother who gave birth to you. Allah is always watching you!*

EQUALITY

On Judgment Day both male and female will be judged on the basis of what they have done in their lives. However, as it will become clear from the following material, since a woman must submit to the man in all things, she will be judged by how well she submitted during her life.

> 16:97 *Whoever does good, whether male or female, and believes, We will certainly give a happy life, and We will certainly give them their reward for the best of their actions.*

> 40:40 *Whoever has committed evil will be paid back in like, while he who does things that are right, whether male or female, and is a believer will enter the Garden.*

> 4:32 *Do not covet the gifts Allah has given which have lifted up some among you. Men will be rewarded for their actions, and women will be rewarded for their actions. But ask Allah to give gifts to you of His bounty, for surely Allah knows all things.*

> 33:73 *Therefore, Allah will punish the hypocritical men and women. But as for the believing men and women, Allah will show them mercy, for Allah is forgiving and merciful!*

> 47:19 *Therefore, know that there is no god except Allah, and ask forgiveness for your sins and for the sins of the men and women who believe. Allah knows the places you go as well as your place of rest.*

> 57:18 *Those who give to charity, whether they are men or women, and those who loan generously to Allah, will be paid back double what they have given. They will receive a noble reward.*

> 4:124 *As for the believers who do good works, whether man or woman, they will enter Paradise, and they will not be treated unjustly in the least.*

> 48:5 *That He may bring the believing men and the believing women into Gardens, beneath whose trees the rivers flow, to dwell therein forever, and that He may cancel their evil deeds—this is the great bliss with Allah.*

This next verse is the high point of Islamic relations between the sexes. Women will be "rewarded by their actions," which must include submission to men.

> 9:71 *The faithful of both sexes are mutual friends. They command what is just and forbid what is evil. They observe regular prayer, contribute regularly to charity, and they obey Allah and His Messenger. Allah will*

> *show His mercy to these. Allah is mighty and wise. Allah promised the faithful, both men and women, Gardens beneath which the rivers flow in which they shall abide, and blessed mansions in the Gardens. The best, though, will be Allah's good pleasure in them. This is the supreme triumph. among you. Men will be rewarded for their actions, and women will be rewarded for their actions. But ask Allah to give gifts to you of His bounty, for surely Allah knows all things.*

This is not about Judgment Day, but there is equality in this good advice for all.

> 49:11 *Oh, believers, do not let men laugh at other men who may be better than themselves, nor let women laugh at women who may be better than themselves. Do not slander one another, nor call one another offensive names. It is bad to be called wicked after having professed the faith, and whoever does not repent of this does evil.*

THE VEIL

The veil has many manifestations, burka, purdah, hijab, but they are all methods of hiding and secluding the woman from society. In no case is there a choice for the woman.

Here we see that young girls and menstruating women were secluded in Mohammed's community.

> [B2,15,88;B2,15,91]
>
> *Um Atiya said that on the Day of Id [a festival], women were told to come out behind the men and say Takbir and invoke Allah with them. Also included were the menstruating women and young virgins who would normally be in seclusion.*

Mohammed's wives were all veiled. In the following hadith, Safiya is captured after her tribe has been beaten by the jihadists. She is the most beautiful captive and goes to Mohammed (he got the first pick of all war treasure, including the slaves).

> [B5,59,524]
>
> *[...]*
>
> *The Muslims said amongst themselves, "Will Safiya be one of the wives of the Prophet or just a slave-girl" Some of them said, "If the Prophet makes her observe the veil, then she will be one of the Prophet's wives, and if he does not make her observe the veil, then she will be his lady slave." So when he departed, he made a place for her behind him on his camel and made her observe the veil.*

[B1,8,395]

Narrated Umar: My Lord agreed with me in three things:

[...]

And as regards the veiling of the women, I said, 'O Allah's Apostle! I wish you ordered your wives to cover themselves from the men because good and bad ones talk to them.' So the verse of the veiling of the women was revealed.

[...]

[B1,4,148;B8,74,257]

The wives of the Prophet used to go to a large open place to answer the call of nature at night. Umar used to say to the Prophet "Let your wives be veiled," but Allah's Apostle did not do so. One night Sauda went out at night and she was a tall lady. Umar said, "I have recognized you, O Sauda."

He said he desired that the women might be veiled. So Allah revealed the verses of veiling.

A formal protocol began to surround Mohammed as he became more powerful. His wives spoke from behind a curtain. After Mohammed died all of his wives were still controlled.

33:53 *Believers! Do not enter the Messenger's house early for a meal unless you are given permission. When you are invited, enter, and when you have finished your meal, leave. Do not remain there hoping to start a conversation, for this would annoy the Messenger, and he would be ashamed to send you home, but Allah is not ashamed to tell you the truth. And if you should speak to his wives, do so behind a curtain. This will be purer for both their hearts and yours. And you should not cause Allah's Messenger any trouble nor ever marry any of his widows, for this would be a grievous sin in Allah's sight. Whether you do a thing in the open or in secret, truly Allah knows all things.*

A woman should be hidden from all men who might have sex with them. Only their relatives and slaves can know their private lives.

33:55 *There is no blame on the Messenger's wives if they speak unveiled with their fathers, sons, brothers, nephews on either their brother's or sister's side, their women, or their slave-girls. Women! Fear Allah, for Allah witnesses all things.*

24:30 *Tell the men who are believers that they should look away from that which tempts them and control their lustful desires. Therefore, they will be more pure. Allah is well aware of all they do. And tell the women who are believers that they should lower their eyes and guard their purity, and they should not display their beauty and adornments except that which is normally shown. They should cover their breasts with their veils and only show their adornments to their husband, father-in-law, sons, step-sons, brothers, nephews, or their female servants, eunuch slaves, and children who are innocent and do not notice a woman's nakedness. And do not let them stamp their feet so as to reveal their hidden adornments [ankle bracelets]. Believers, all of you turn to Allah and repent so that it will go well for you.*

The following account of an accident where the first order of business is to get Safiya's veil in place.

[B4,52,318;B4,52,319]

We were in the company of the Prophet while returning from Usfan, and Allah's Apostle was riding his she-camel keeping Safiya riding behind him. His she-camel slipped and both of them fell down. Abu Talha jumped from his camel and said, "O Allah's Apostle! May Allah sacrifice me for you." Mohammed said, "Take care of the lady."

So, Abu Talha covered his face with a garment and went to Safiya and covered her with it, and then he set right the condition of their she-camel so that both of them rode, and we were encircling Allah's Apostle like a cover. When we approached Medina, the Prophet said, "We are returning with repentance and worshipping and praising our Lord." He kept on saying this till he entered Medina.

[B1,8,368;B1,10,552;B1,12,826;B1,12,831]

Aisha said that some Muslim women would cover themselves with veiling sheets and attend the Fajr prayer with Mohammed. After the prayer, they would return home unrecognized because of the darkness.

Here we see that the seclusion of the veil is all about sex.

24:60 *As for the unmarried women past the age of childbearing, they will not be blamed it they take off their outer garments, as long as they do not show their adornments [jewelry]. It will be better for them if they do not take them off, for Allah hears and knows all.*

MENSTRUATION

A menstruating woman is unclean and is restricted as to what she can do.

[B1,6,311;B1,6,312;B9,92,456]

A woman asked Mohammed how to take a bath after finishing menses. He replied, "Take a piece a cloth perfumed with musk and clean the private parts with it thrice." Mohammed felt shy and turned his face.

[B1,4,227;B1,6,304;B1,6,305]

A woman came to Mohammed and asked, "If anyone of us gets menses in her clothes then what should she do?" He replied, "She should take hold of the soiled place, put it in water and rub it in order to remove the traces of blood and then pour more water over it. Then she can pray in it."

Menstruation makes a woman unclean.

2:222 *They ask you about women's menstrual cycle. Say: It is a discomfort. Therefore, keep away from them during this time and do not come near them until they are clean again. But when they are clean, you may lie with them as Allah has commanded. Allah loves those who turn to Him and seek cleanliness.*

THE STATUS OF WOMEN

It is the nature of females that most of those in Hell will be women.

[B1,4,184;B1,12,712;B2,18,154;B2,18,156;B2,18,157;B2,18,159;B2,18,161;B2,18,162;B2,18,164;B3;40,552;B4,54,423;B7,62,125;B9,92,390]

[...]

Mohammed's followers then told him that during his prayer they saw him reach out with his hands and grasp something, and later retreat in horror. Mohammed replied, "I saw Paradise and stretched my hands towards a bunch of fruit, and had I taken it, you would have eaten from it as long as this world remains. I also saw Hellfire, and I have never seen such a terrible sight. I saw that that the majority of the inhabitants were women." When asked why this was so, Mohammed replied, "They are ungrateful to their husbands and to good deeds. Even if you are good to one of them all of your life, whenever she sees some harshness from you she will say, 'I have never seen any good from you.'"

Mohammed also saw a woman in Hell being clawed by a cat. He learned that she had imprisoned a cat, neither feeding it nor allowing it to seek its own food, until it starved.

Women are less intelligent than men. They are also spiritually inferior to men.

[B1,2,28;B1,6,301;B2,24,541;B4,54,464;B7,62,124;B7,62,126;B7,76,456;B8,76,554;B8,76,555]

Once, after offering prayer at Musalla, Mohammed said to the women, "O women! Give alms, as I have seen that the majority of the dwellers of Hell were women." They asked, "Why is it so, O Allah's Apostle?" He replied, "You curse frequently and are ungrateful to your husbands. I have not seen anyone more deficient in intelligence and religion than you. A cautious sensible man could be led astray by some of you."

The women asked, "O Allah's Apostle! What is deficient in our intelligence and religion?" He replied, "Is not the evidence of two women equal to the witness of one man?" They agreed that this was so. He said, "This is the deficiency in her intelligence. Isn't it true that a woman can neither pray nor fast during her menses?" The women replied that this was so. He said, "This is the deficiency in her religion."

The religion of a women is controlled by the man.

[B6,61,572;B7,62,120]

Mohammed once said "A woman should not engage in optional fasts without her husband's permission if he is at home."

Women are an affliction to men.

[B4,52,111;B7,62,30;B7,62,31;B7,62,33;B7,62,32;B7,71,649;B7,71,666]

Mohammed said, "If at all there is a bad omen, it is in the horse, the woman and the house."

On another occasion, he had said, "I have not left any affliction after me more harmful to men than women."

Women cannot help their flaws, so be nice to them.

[B4,55,548;B7,62,113;B7,62,113]

Mohammed said, "Treat women nicely, for a women is created from a rib, and is much like one. If you try to straighten a rib, it will break, so I urge you to take care of the women."

A woman, a donkey or a dog can nullify prayers.

[B1,9,486;B1,9,490]

When told that a prayer is annulled if the praying ones are passed by a dog, a donkey, or a woman, Aisha said,

Do you make us women equal to dogs and donkeys? While I used to lie in my bed, the Prophet would sometimes come to pray facing the middle of the bed. I felt like it was wrong of me to remain in front of him while he prayed, so I would slip away slowly and quietly from the foot of the bed until I stopped feeling guilty.

Female leadership will lead to political failure.

> [B9,88,219]
>
> *During the battle of Al-Jamal, Mohammed heard the news that the people of Persia had made the daughter of Khosrau their ruler. On this, he said, "A nation that makes a woman their ruler will never succeed."*

Women are not to be involved in jihad.

> [B2,26,595;B3,29,84;B4,52,43;B4,52,127;B4,52,128;B4,52,295]
>
> *When Aisha requested of Mohammed that she be allowed to participate in a jihad, he said that a woman's jihad is the performance of the Hajj pilgrimage. It is even important for a husband to forsake a jihad campaign to accompany his wife on a Hajj.*

LEGAL

The longest verse in the Koran is about contract law. The general principle in Islamic law is that it takes two women to equal one man.

> 2:282 *Believers! When you contract a loan for a certain period, write it down, or to be fair, let a scribe write it down. The scribe should not refuse to write as Allah has taught him; therefore, let the scribe record what the debtor dictates being mindful of his duty to Allah and not reducing the amount he owes. If the debtor is ignorant and unable to dictate, let his guardian do so with fairness. Call two men in to witness this, but if two men cannot be found, then call one man and two women whom you see fit to be witnesses. Therefore, if either woman makes an error, the other can correct her. Witnesses must not refuse to give testimony if they are called upon to do so; therefore, do not forget to record your debts in writing, whether they are little or much, along with the date on which they were paid. This is more fair in Allah's sight, as it ensures accuracy in proof and is the best way to avoid doubt. If, however, the transaction is one that occurs on the spot, you are not to blame if it is not recorded in writing. And have witnesses when you sell, and do not let harm come to the scribe or witnesses for it will be a sin for you if this occurs. And fear Allah and Allah will give you knowledge for He has knowledge of all things.*

In this verse about estates, we have another application of the principle that a woman is half of a man.

> 4:7 *Men will have a share in what their parents and relatives leave, and women will have a share in what their parents and relatives leave. Whether the amount is small or large, they are entitled to equal shares. But when the inheritance is divided, if other relatives, orphans, or the poor are present, give them a part of it and speak kindly to them.*

4:11 *It is in this manner that Allah commands you concerning your children: A male should receive a share equal to that of two females, and if there are more than two females, they should receive two-thirds of what the deceased has left. If there is only one female, she will inherit half. The father and mother of the deceased will each receive a sixth of what is left if he has a child, but if he has no children, his parents are his heirs, and his mother should receive a third. If he has brothers, his mother will only receive a sixth, after paying his inheritances and debts. You may not know whether your parents or your children are more useful, but this is Allah's law. Allah is knowing and wise!*

4:176 *When they ask you for guidance say: Allah directs you about your distant relatives who die with neither parents nor children. If a man dies without children, but he has a sister, she will inherit half of his estate, and if she dies without children, then he will inherit half of her estate. If a woman dies without children, then her brother will be her sole heir. If a man without children has two sisters, then they will inherit two-thirds of his estate, but if he has both brothers and sisters, the brothers will receive the same amount as two sisters. Allah directs you clearly so that you will not sin; Allah knows all things.*

4:127 *When they ask your advice regarding women say: Allah has instructed you concerning them, and His will is laid out for you in the Scriptures concerning female orphans to whom you have not given their legal due but whom you refuse to marry. In regard to helpless children, He has commanded you to deal fairly with orphans. Allah knows all the good that you do.*

POETIC IMAGES

The Koran has several uses of female imagery:

83:10 *Woe on that day to those who deny Our signs, who regard the Judgment Day as a lie! No one regards it as a lie except the transgressor or the criminal, who, when Our signs are recited to him, says, "Old wives tales!" No! Their habits have become like rust on their hearts. Yes, they will be veiled from their Lord's light that day. Then they will be burned in Hell. They will be told, "This is what you called a lie."*

42:7 *So We have revealed to you an Arabic Koran so that you may warn the mother-city [Mecca] and all around it, and warn them of that day of the gathering, of which there is no doubt, when some will be in Paradise and some in the Flame.*

91:1 *By the sun and its midday brightness! By the moon when she follows him! By the day when it reveals his [the sun's] glory! By the night when it [the moon] covers him [the sun]! By the heaven and Him who built it! By the earth and Him who spread it! By the soul and by Him who formed it, and breathed into it its perception of right and wrong. Blessed is he who has kept it pure, and cursed is he who has corrupted it!*

92:1 *By the night when she spreads her veil, by the day when it shines bright and by Him who made man and woman – certainly you strive for many goals!*

99:4 *On that day she will tell her news, because your Lord inspired her. On that day men will come forward in droves to witness their deeds, and whoever has done even an atom's weight of good will see it, and whoever has done even an atom's weight of evil will see it.*

16:92 *Do not be like a woman who unravels her yarn after it is spun and strong. Do not use your oaths to deceive anyone lest one group becomes more numerous than another. Allah will test you, and on the Judgment Day, He will resolve your arguments.*

Here is use of feminine imagery in the Hadith:

[B9,87,161;B9,87,162;B9,87,163]

Mohammed said, "I saw in a dream a black woman with unkempt hair going out of Medina and settling at Mahaia. I interpreted that as a symbol of the epidemic of Medina being transferred to another town."

THE DAUGHTERS OF ALLAH

In the Koran of Mecca, there are five references to Allah's denial of having daughters. The background is that there were three goddesses who were part of the worship at the Kabah of Mecca. The Meccans also said that angels were females.

43:16 *What? Has Allah adopted daughters from among His creations [the Meccans said that angels were the daughters of Allah] and chosen sons for you? Allah's face darkens and He becomes filled with anger when He hears that one of His servants is set up as His likeness.*
43:18 *What? Can they say that a being, brought up among trinkets [the idols were bedecked with jewelry] and unreasonably contentious, is the child of Allah? And they say that the angels that personally serve Allah are females. Did they witness their creation?*

53:19 *Do you see Al-Lat and Al-Ozza, and Manat [Arabic deities] the third idol? What? Do you have male children and Allah female children [Arabs called angels the daughters of Allah]? That is an unfair division!*

> 53:23 *These are mere names. You and your fathers gave them these names. Allah has not acknowledged them. They follow only their own conceits and desires, even though their Lord has already given them guidance.*
> 53:24 *Will man have everything he desires? The future and the present are in Allah's hands. No matter how many angels are in the heavens, their intercession will do no good, until Allah has permitted entry to whom He pleases and whom He will accept.*
> 53:27 *Surely, the ones who give female names to the angels are the ones who do not believe in the hereafter, but of this they have no knowledge. They are following a guess, and a guess can not replace the truth.*

> 6:100 *They make the jinn [spirits] equal to Allah, though He created them, and they falsely attribute to Him, in ignorance, sons and daughters. Praise and glory be to Him, for He is above their imaginations.*

It is evil to suggest that Allah has any partners, but it is even worse to imply that Allah has daughters.

> 16:57 *Glory be to Him! They wish for sons, and they say that Allah has daughters [the Meccans considered the angels to be the daughters of Allah]. If they receive news that they have a daughter, their face darkens and they are filled with anguish. They hide themselves from their people in shame. Should they keep the child in shame or simply bury it? What an evil choice they make for themselves.*

> 17:40 *What? Has your Lord honored you by giving you sons while He has taken for Himself daughters from among the angels? Truly, you say a dreadful thing.*

BURYING DAUGHTERS

Islam claims to have greatly improved women's rights. Whatever improvement Islam made was a limited improvement since the Trilogy is eternal, universal and perfect. In short, whatever improvement Islam made in the condition of women 1400 years ago, is done. No more improvement to be done. "Eternal' and "perfect" do not allow for improvement.

We can see what female life was like before Islam by looking at Mohammed's wife Khadija. Before she met Mohammed, she was independently wealthy, ran her own business, owned slaves and other property, proposed her own marriage, inherited property, loaned money and was not secluded behind a curtain.

One of the ways that Islam claims to have improved the status of women is to prevent the "burying of daughters". The Koran states that very poor Arabs would bury female babies alive. Both the Koran and the Hadith condemn this practice.

[B3,41,591;B8,73,6;B8,76,480;B9,92,395]

According to Al-Mughira, Mohammed used to forbid idle talk, asking too many questions about religion, wasting money, not giving what should be given in charity, and asking others for something (except in great need), extravagance, being undutiful to mothers, and burying one's little daughters alive.

81:1 *When the sun ceases to shine and the stars fall; when the mountains fall to pieces; when the she-camels are abandoned; when the wild animals are herded together; when the seas boil; when souls are rejoined with their bodies; when the female child that had been buried alive is asked for what crime was she killed; when the books are opened; when the sky is torn away; when Hell is ignited; when Paradise is brought near, every soul will know what it has done.*

This is the Sunna of Mohammed

MARRIAGE

CHAPTER 3

4:59 Believers! Obey Allah and obey His Messenger and those among you with authority.

- A Muslim woman has many regulations as to whom she can marry.
- The woman receives a dowry.
- The main element a woman brings to marriage is sex.
- A woman must have sex whenever a man wants it.
- Divorce is determined by the man.
- A man may have up to four wives.

The marriage in Islam is not like that of Western civilization. Marriage is a civil contract exactly like any business contract. There does not even have to be a religious ceremony.

One of the great strengths of Islam is how it makes marriage and having children a center of Islamic civilization. Not only is marriage encouraged, but celibacy is condemned. Marriage is called half of a Muslim's religion. To be healthy and unmarried is to be a brother of Satan. When a Muslim reaches puberty he should marry.

[B7,62,7]

Ibn Abbas asked Said if he was married. When Said said that he was not, Ibn Abbas said, "Marry, for the best person of this Muslim nation had the largest number of wives of all other Muslims."

[B7,62,173]

Mohammed said to Jabir, "If you enter your town at night after coming from a journey, do not enter upon your family till your wife shaves her pubic hair and combs her hair. O Jabir! Seek to have offspring, seek to have offspring!"

QUALIFICATIONS

A Muslim woman may not marry whomever she may choose. The Trilogy is very specific about whom a woman may and may not marry.

[B7,62,44;B7,62,45]

Mohammed forbade any woman to marry a man who was also married to one of her aunts, either maternal or paternal.

The following hadith comes from the Arabic custom of fostering a child or using a wet nurse. The relations from having a common fosterage or common wet nurse lead to the same restrictions about sex and marriage as blood kinship.

[B3,48,808;B7,62,41;B7,62,42]

Uqba married the daughter of Abu Ihab, and then a woman came and said, "I suckled you and your wife." Uqba said to her, "I do not know that you have suckled me, and you did not inform me." He then sent someone to the house of Abu Ihab to enquire about that but they did not know that she had suckled their daughter. Then Uqba went to Mohammed in Medina and asked him about it. Mohammed said to him, "How can you keep your wife after it has been said that both of you were suckled by the same woman?" So, he divorced her and she was married to another husband.

On a different occasion, Um Habiba asked her husband Mohammed if he would like to marry her sister. He replied, "Even if she were not my stepdaughter, she should be unlawful for me to marry, for Thuwaiba suckled me and her father, Abu Salama. So you should present neither your daughters, nor your sisters, to me to marry."

A Muslim woman cannot be married against her will.

[B9,85,78;B9,86,99;B7,62,69]

Khansa was given in marriage by her father when she was a matron and she disliked the marriage. She complained to Mohammed and he declared that marriage invalid. This event was used by Abdur-Rahman and Mujammi to comfort another woman forced to marry against her will.

[B7,62,67;B7,62,68;B9,85,79;B9,86,98]

Aisha asked Mohammed, "O Allah's Apostle! Should women be asked for their consent to their marriage?" When he replied that they should, Aisha said, "A virgin, if asked, feels shy and keeps quiet." He said, "Her silence expresses her consent."

A Muslim woman may not marry a non-Muslim. Pagan (not a Jew or Christian) women may not be married to a Muslim male.

2:221 *You will not marry pagan women unless they accept the faith. A slave girl who believes is better than an idolatress, although the idolatress may please you more. Do not give your daughters away in marriage to kafirs until they believe, for a slave who is a believer is better than an idolater, though the idolater may please you more.*

24:32 *And marry those among you who are single, or an honorable male or female slave. And if they are poor, then Allah will give them riches from His own bounty. Allah is bountiful and all-knowing.*

4:25 *If any of you is not wealthy enough to marry a free, believing woman, then allow him to marry a believing slave-girl. Allah knows your faith well, and you come from one another. Marry them with their master's permission, and give them a fair dowry, given that they are chaste, honorable, and have not had lovers. If the slave you marry commits adultery after you are married, then their punishment should be half of that commanded for a free woman. This is a law for those among you who fear sinning, but it will be better for you if you abstain. Allah is forgiving and merciful!*

4:22 *And do not marry the women your fathers have married, though in the past it was allowed, for this is an evil act, shameful and abominable. Forbidden to you for marriage are your mothers, daughters, sisters, your parents' sisters, nieces on both your brother's and sister's side, foster-mothers, foster-sisters, mothers-in-law, step-daughters in your care who were born to women you have slept with, (but if you have not slept with their mothers, it is not wrong to marry them), and your biological sons' wives. You are also forbidden to marry two sisters at the same time, with the exception of those whom you have already married [married before the Koran]. Truly Allah is forgiving and merciful! Also forbidden to you are married women unless they are your slaves. This is the command of Allah. Other than those mentioned, all other women are lawful to you to court with your wealth and with honorable intentions, not with lust. And give those you have slept with a dowry, as it is your duty. But after you have fulfilled your duty, it is not an offense to make additional agreements among you. Truly Allah is knowing and wise!*

THE CONTRACT

The marriage dowry is not refundable.

4:4 *And give the women you marry their dowries as free gifts, but if they freely give it up to you, then you are free to absorb it into your wealth.*

And do not entrust the feeble-minded with the land Allah has given to support them; instead, feed and clothe them with the proceeds you make from it, and speak kindly to them.

4:20 *If you want to exchange one wife for another, do not take anything away from the dowry you have given her. Would you take it by slandering her and doing her obvious wrong? How could you take it back when you have slept with one another and entered into a firm covenant?*

Marriage always includes the business of the dowry (mahr) paid to the bride.

A man may have from one to four wives and as many slave-girls as he wishes.

4:3 *If you fear that you will not be able to deal with orphan girls fairly, marry other women of your choice, two, or three, or four; but if you fear that you cannot treat them equally, then marry only one, or any of the slave-girls you have acquired. This will prevent you from being unjust.*

MARITAL SEX

The most important thing that a woman brings to the marriage is her vagina.

[B3,31,129;B7,62,81]

Mohammed said:

He who can afford to marry should marry, because it will help him refrain from looking at other women, and save his private parts from looking at other women, and save his private parts from committing illegal sexual relations; and he who cannot afford to marry is advised to fast, as fasting will diminish his sexual power.

He also said, "The stipulations of the marriage contract most entitled to be abided by are those with which you are given the right to enjoy a woman's private parts."

Allah curses the woman who resists sex.

[B4,54,460;B7,62,121;B7,62,122;]

Mohammed said, "If a husband calls his wife to his bed for sex and she refuses and causes him to sleep in anger, the angels will curse her till morning."

This next hadith and verse clearly give the status of a Muslim woman. A Muslim wife is always ready to have sex upon demand. It is her husband's right. Plowed fields is an Islamic term for the vagina, an interesting agricultural image.

M008,3363

Jabir said that the Jews had an expression which said, "When a man has sex with his wife from behind, their child will have squinty eyes." Consequently, the verse was revealed,

2:223 Your women are your tilth (plowed fields, vagina): go into your fields when you like, but do some good deed beforehand and fear Allah. Keep in mind that you will meet Him. Give good news to the believers.

M008,3365

Mohammed: "It is all right if a man wants to enter his wife from behind or from on top, but he should enter the vagina."

THE HOME

When a woman is out of the house, she should be accompanied by a relative. And the woman cannot have a man in her house who is not related to her if her husband is not at home. The sexuality of a woman is to be controlled at all times. Absolute control of a woman's sexuality in all of its forms is part of a man's ghira (pride, honor, self-respect and sacred jealousy).

[B2,20,192;B2,20,193;B3,29,85;B3,31,215]

Mohammed said that a woman is forbidden from traveling for two or more days without her husband or a Dhi-Mahram (a man she cannot marry by Islamic law).

It is the husband or father who determines who comes into the house. It is not allowed for a wife or daughter to exercise this choice. Exercising this power is part of a man's ghira (see next section, Jealousy and Honor).

[B1,2,53;B2,24,506;B2,24,518;B2,24,520;B2,24,521;B2,24,546;B3,34,279;B3,34,280;B7,62,123;B7,64,273]

Mohammed said, "You will be rewarded for whatever you spend for Allah's sake even if it were a morsel which you put in your wife's mouth." As Mohammed told the wife of Abu Salama, this also counts for what one spends to feed one's own children: "Spend on them and you will get a reward for what you spend on them."

"If a lady gives meals (in charity) from her husband's house without spoiling her husband's property," Mohammed added, "she will get a reward and her husband will also get a reward

likewise, as will the storekeeper. The husband will get a reward because of his earnings and the woman because of her spending. The reward of one will not decrease the reward of the others."

Also, Mohammed said that if a wife gives some of her husband's property without his permission, he will receive half of the reward.

She may not fast without his permission if he is at home, and she must not allow anyone to enter his house without his permission.

The wife should always be allowed to go the mosque.

[B1,12,824;B2,13,22;

Mohammed said, "If your women ask permission to go to the mosque at night, allow them."

If a man brings a new wife into the home, here is the law for the new wife.

[B7,62,140;B7,62,141]

It is Mohammed's tradition that if someone marries a virgin and he already has a matron wife then he should stay for seven days with the virgin and then alternate between the two; conversely, if someone marries a matron and he already has a virgin wife then he should stay with the matron for three days and then alternate the two.

JEALOUSY AND HONOR—GHIRA

In this hadith we have the basis for a Muslim's sense of honor and pride. The man rules the woman, and his status in the community depends upon how his women conduct themselves. Ghira is sacred jealousy, even Allah has ghira. Ghira is also self-respect and is the basis of honor killings. Notice that Saed's threat to kill a man with his wife is not condemned, but supported. Violence in defence of a Muslim's ghira is pure Islam.

[B8,82,829;B9,93,512]

Saed bin Ubada said, "If I saw a man with my wife, I would strike him with the blade of my sword." This news reached Mohammed, who then said, "You people are astonished at Saed's ghira (self-respect). By Allah, I have more ghira than he, and Allah has more ghira than I, and because of Allah's ghira, He has made unlawful shameful deeds and sins done in open and in secret.

And there is none who likes more that the people should repent to Him and beg His pardon than Allah, and for this reason He sent the admonishers and the givers of good news. And there is

none who likes to be praised more than Allah does, and for this reason, Allah promised to grant Paradise to the doers of good."

THE RIGHTS OF A WOMAN

Islam is very clear on a woman's rights. Mohammed talked about this in his last sermon at Mecca. If a woman obeys her husband and never acts in a sexual manner towards another man (including being alone with another male), then she must be given food and shelter. [All quotes with the number starting with I are from Ishaq, the Sira.]

> I969 Mohammed also told them men had rights over their wives and women had rights over their husbands. The wives were never to commit adultery or act in a sexual manner toward others. If they did, they were to be put in separate rooms and beaten lightly. [Stoning is the penalty in other hadiths.] If they refrained from what was forbidden, they had the right to food and clothing. Men were to lay injunctions on women lightly for they were prisoners of men and had no control over their persons.

Again, from the Sira, we have some more about a husband's rights:

> I957 Mohammed sent Muadh to Yemen to proselytize. While he was there he was asked what rights a husband has over the wife. He replied to the woman who asked, "If you went home and found your husband's nose running with pus and blood and you sucked it until it was cleaned, you still would not have fulfilled your husband's rights."

The husband rules over the wife and family. This hadith gives the hierarchy of rights in Islam.

> [B2,13,18;B3,41,592;B7,62,128]
> ***Ruzaiq wrote to Ibn Shihab saying, "Shall I lead the Jumua prayer?" Ruzaiq was working on the land and there was a group of Sudanese people and some others with him; Ruzaiq was then the Governor of Aila.***
> ***Ibn Shihab wrote back to Ruzaiq ordering him to lead the Jumua prayer and telling him that Mohammed had said, "All of you are guardians and responsible for your wards and the things under your care.***
> ***The Imam (i.e. ruler) is the guardian of his subjects and is responsible for them and a man is the guardian of his family and is responsible for them.***

A woman is the guardian of her husband's house and is responsible for it. A servant is the guardian of his master's belongings and is responsible for them."

Umar also believed Mohammed had said, "A man is the guardian of his father's property and is responsible for it. All of you are guardians and responsible for your wards and the things under your care."

DIVORCE, DEATH AND REMARRIAGE

Before there is a divorce, the families should try to resolve the problem.

4:35 *If you fear a breach between a man and wife, then send a judge from his family, and a judge from her family. If they both want to come to a reconciliation, Allah will bring them back together. Truly Allah is all-knowing and wise!*

There is a period of time called *iddah* that a woman must wait after the divorce before she can remarry.

[B7,63,256]

Ibn Abbas interpreted the Koranic verse 2.240 as a cancellation of the order that a woman must spend the period of iddah (mourning for one's husband) in her husband's house. He must provide for her to stay at his house for one year in his will, but if she leaves, his family is no longer obligated to care for her.

[B5,59,326;B6,60,52;B6,60,54;B6,60,55;B7,62,61;B7,63,239;B7,63,240;B7,63,241;B7,63,248]

Allah proclaimed that a woman separated from her husband by his death must wait for a period of four months and ten days (or three menstrual cycles) before she could marry again. This period, also required after a woman is divorced, is called the iddah, and was revealed in the verse:

2:232 When you have divorced a woman and she has fulfilled the period of waiting, iddah, do not interfere with her marrying a new husband if it has been agreed between them honorably. This is commanded for everyone who has faith in Allah and the Last Day; this course of action is more virtuous and pure. Allah knows and you do not.

Subaia, whose husband Sad died while she was pregnant, gave birth soon afterward and prepared herself for suitors. Abu As-Sanabil said to her, "I see you dressed up for the people to ask you in marriage. Do you want to marry? By Allah, you are not allowed to marry unless four months and ten days have elapsed." That evening, Subaia went to Mohammed and asked him about this problem. He said that she was free to marry because she had already given birth to her child.

The sister of Maqil was married to a man who divorced her and remained away until she had completed her iddah. He then sought to marry her again, and this angered Maqil, who refused to allow the marriage. Then Allah revealed the Iddhah verse. Mohammed recited this verse to Maqil, and so he yielded to Allah's command.

The mahr is the dowry. It does not have to be returned, but here the wife returns the garden (mahr), and she gets to have her divorce.

[B7,63,197;B7,63,198;B7,63,199]

The wife of Thabit came to Mohammed and said, "O Allah's Apostle! I do not blame Thabit for defects in his character or his religion, but I am afraid I would behave in un-Islamic manner and become unthankful for Allah's blessings." On that Mohammed said, "Will you give back the garden which your husband has given you as mahr?" She said, "Yes." Then the Prophet said to Thabit, "O Thabit! Accept your garden, and divorce her at once."

A woman's menstrual period determines when a divorce may be granted.

[B7,63,178;B7,63,179;B7,63,184;B7,63,249;B7,63,250;B9,89,274]

Abdullah divorced his wife during her menses, and his father Umar mentioned that to Mohammed, who became angry and said, "He must take her back and keep her with him until she becomes clean from her menses and then to wait till she gets her next period and becomes clean again from it and only then, if he wants to divorce her, may he do so."

This hadith gives an option of a semi-divorce. The "wife" has no sexual rights, but has a roof and food. Mohammed had two wives who "gave up their turn" in order to remain in the household, but had no sex with him. In their case, they also got an assured seat in Paradise along with all of Mohammed's wives.

[B3,43,630;B3,49,859;B6,60,125;B7,62,134]

Aisha explained the meaning of the Koran verse:

4:128 And if a wife fears cruelty or desertion from her husband, then they are not to blame for coming to a mutual agreement between themselves, for peace is best, although people are often prone to greed. But if you do good and fear Allah, Allah knows all that you do. As hard as you try to treat all your wives equally, you cannot. Do not abandon one of them altogether, so as to leave her hanging in suspense. If you come to a mutual agreement and fear Allah, then truly Allah is forgiving and merciful. But if they separate, Allah will provide for the both of them from His abundance; Allah is vast and wise.

She said that it concerns the woman whose husband does not want to keep her with him any longer, but wants to divorce her and marry some other lady, so she says to him: "Keep me and do not divorce me, and then marry another woman, and you may neither spend on me, nor sleep with me."

This next hadith is a short story. Lian is a swearing contest. Both parties swear a public oath on Allah that they are telling the truth. Usually, a divorce follows the lian process.

[B1,8,415;B3,48,837;B7,63,180;B7,63,185;B7,63,226;B7,63,227;B7,63,228;B7,63,229;B7,63,230;B7,63,232;B7,63,233;B7,63,234;B7,63,235;B7,63,236;B7,63,262;B8,82,837;B8,82,839;B9,89,278;B9,89,279;B9,92,407]

Uwaimir came to Asim and asked, "If a man found another man with his wife and killed him, would you sentence the husband to death in qisas (i.e., equality in punishment)? O Asim! Please ask Allah's Apostle about this matter on my behalf." Asim asked Mohammed but he disapproved of the question and considered it disgraceful. Asim returned and informed Uwaimir that Mohammed disliked that type of question. Uwaimir said, "By Allah, I will not give up on this matter until I ask the Prophet about it." So Uwaimir proceeded until he came to Mohammed in the midst of a crowd and asked him the question.

So Mohammed said to Uwaimir, "Allah has revealed to me regarding you and your wife." The Prophet then called for them, and they came and carried out the order of lian, during which he proclaimed that one of the two was a liar before Allah. Then Uwaimir said, "O Allah's Apostle! Now if I kept her with me, I would be accused of telling a lie." So Uwaimir divorced her although the Prophet did not order him to do so. Later on this practice of divorcing became the tradition of couples involved in a case of lian. Mohammed has said that a man is not entitled to get his property back from the wife in the case of lian, because if he was telling the truth, then his property acts as payment for having sexual relations with her; if he was lying, then he would be less entitled to the property.

The Prophet said to the people. "If she delivers a red small child like a wahra (a short red animal) then I will be of the opinion that Uwaimir has told a lie, but if she delivered a black big-eyed one with big buttocks, then I will be of the opinion that he has told the truth about her." Ultimately she gave birth to a child that proved the accusation.

There is an extensive amount of the Koran devoted to divorce.

33:49 *Believers! If you marry a believing woman and divorce her before consummating the marriage, you do not have to wait out the prescribed term. Provide for her and dismiss her with honor.*

These verses abolish an old method of Arabic divorce, telling her, "Be to me as my mother's back." This phrase is considered evil. Whereas, the husband telling his wife, "I divorce you" three times is good.

58:1 *Allah has heard the words of the woman who pleaded with you against her husband and made her complaint to Allah. [Khawlah was divorced by the old Arab custom of her husband saying, "Be to me as my mother's back."] Allah has heard both sides of the conversation, for Allah hears and sees everything.*
58:2 *Those who divorce their wives by saying, "Be to me as my mother's back," should know that they are not. The only ones who are their mothers are those who gave birth to them. Their words are certainly hateful and untrue, but surely Allah is forgiving and merciful. Those who divorce their wives in this manner, and afterwards recant their words, must free one of their slaves as a penalty before they can touch one another again. You are commanded to do this. Allah is aware of all you do. And as for those who do not have a slave to free, they must fast for two consecutive months before they can touch each other. Those who are unable to fast must feed sixty poor people. This is commanded so that you may show your faith in Allah and His Messenger. These are the limits set by Allah, and dreadful punishment awaits the kafirs.*

The prescribed legal period is the iddah, the amount of time measured by her period.

65:1 *Prophet! When you or the believers divorce a woman, divorce them at the end of the prescribed legal period. Calculate carefully the number of days and fear Allah your Lord. Do not put them out of their homes or let them leave on their own unless it is proven they have committed adultery. These are the boundaries Allah has imposed, and those who overstep these boundaries wrong their own souls. You do not know if Allah will cause something to occur that will reunite the two of you.*
65:2 *When they have waited out the prescribed period, either keep them in kindness or part with them honorably. Find two honest men as witnesses from among you, and testify before Allah. This is a warning to those who believe in Allah and the Last Day. For those who fear Allah,*

Allah will provide a means of salvation and provide for them from sources which were never imagined. For those who put their trust in Him, Allah is All-Sufficient. Allah will surely accomplish that which He has planned. Allah has an appointed time for everything.

This next verse allows for marriage to girls who have not reached puberty. The pregnant woman must wait until her child is born to get a divorce.

65:4 *If you have doubt about your wives who have ceased to menstruate, the prescribed waiting period is three months. This length of time is also prescribed for young girls [wives] who have not yet menstruated. As for women who are pregnant, they must wait until they have given birth. Allah will make His command easy for those who fear Him. This is Allah's command which He has sent down to you. Whoever fears Allah will be forgiven of his sins and He will increase his reward.*
65:6 *Keep your divorced wives in your home according to your means, and do not injure them so as to make life unbearable for them. If they are pregnant, keep them until they give birth. After that, if they breast-feed their children, pay them and seek mutual guidance together. But if you cannot agree, hire a wet-nurse for the child.*

2:226 *Those who abandon their wives on oath must wait four months. If they decide to return, Allah is forgiving and merciful. If, however, they decide to divorce them, remember that Allah hears and knows all.*

Men are a degree above women in legal rights.

2:228 *Divorced women must keep themselves from men for three menstrual periods. It is not lawful for them to hide what Allah has created in their wombs if they believe in Allah and the Last Day. If they are in that state, it is better for their husbands to take them back if they want reconciliation. Women have rights similar to those of men in regard to justice, but men are a degree above them. Allah is mighty and wise.*
2:229 *You may divorce your wives twice; afterwards, you must retain them with honor or release them in kindness. It is not lawful for you to take back any of the gifts you have given her unless both fear they may be unable to keep the limits set by Allah. In such a case it is not a sin for either if the wife ransoms herself. These are the limits set up by Allah, so do not exceed them, and whoever exceeds them are evil-doers.*

The history behind the following verse is not known. After the third divorce the woman must marry a second man and have sex with him. Then she and the second man get a divorce and then she can remarry the first husband.

> 2:230 *If a husband divorces his wife for a third time, it is not lawful for him to take her back until she has married and divorced another husband. Then if they return to each other, it will not be a sin for either if they can keep within the limits set by Allah. Such are the limits set by Allah. He makes them clear for those who understand. But if you have divorced a woman and she has fulfilled the period of waiting, then either keep her honorably or let her leave with kindness. You must not keep her to do her evil or take advantage for if anyone does that, he harms his soul. Do not mock Allah's revelations, but remember the grace He has shown you and the Scriptures and the wisdom He has sent down as a warning. Fear Allah and know that Allah is all-knowing.*

It is the man who determines how long the baby will nurse the mother.

> 2:233 *Divorced mothers should breast-feed their children for two full years if the father wishes for the child to nurse that long. They should be cared for and clothed by the father during this time. No one should pay more than they can afford. A mother should not have to suffer for her child's sake nor should the father, and these duties are the same for the father's heir. But if it is agreed upon that the child should be weaned, they should not be blamed. If you decide to have a wet-nurse for your children, there is no blame if you pay her fairly. Fear Allah and know that Allah sees everything you do.*

> 2:236 *You will not be blamed if you divorce your wife before you consummate the marriage or receive the dowry. Provide for her according to your means, whether rich or poor; this is a duty of the righteous. If you decide to divorce her before you consummate the marriage but after you have received the dowry, then she is entitled to half the dowry unless she or the husband agrees to relinquish it. Do not forget to show kindness to one another. Allah sees all you do.*

> 2:240 *If you should die and leave behind a wife, you should leave her at least enough to live a year in the home; but if she leaves on her own, you are not to blame for her lawful actions. Allah is mighty and wise. Reasonable provisions must also be made for women you divorce; this is the duty of righteous men. It is in this manner that Allah makes His signs clear to you so that you will understand.*

MORE ABOUT MARRIAGE

There is one way that Islam resembles the rest of the world world—wedding feasts.

[B7,62,105;B7,62,111;B7,62,112;B7,69,495;B7,69,502;B8,78,676]

Abu invited Mohammed to his wedding party and they were served by his new bride. She gave Mohammed a drink that she made by soaking dates in water overnight.

Temporary marriage still exists today with the Shia Muslims.

[B7,62,52;B9,86,90]

Mohammed told the men in this army that they were allowed to engage in a muta marriage, which allows a man and a woman to agree to marry temporarily. During such, the marriage would last for three nights, and if they want it to continue, it can, or they can separate.

Not long thereafter, Mohammed decreed that the muta marriage was unlawful. Mohammed also forbade shingar marriage, which is when a man marries the daughter of a man in exchange for marrying his daughter to the man, without exchange of property (a dowry). It is also called shingar when such a marriage occurs with an exchange of sisters.

There is an implication in this hadith that husbands do not betray their wives.

[B4,55,547;B4,55,611]

Mohammed said, "If it were not for Eve, wives would never betray their husbands."

Both the Koran and the Hadith show concern for the female orphan.

[B3,44,674;B4,51,25;B6,60,97;B6,60,98;B6,60,124;B7,62,2;B7,62,29;B7,62,59;B7,62,62; B7,62,70;B7,62,71;B9,86,95]

Aisha's nephew Urwa asked her about the meaning of the Koranic verse:

4:3 If you fear that you will not be able to deal with orphan girls fairly, marry other women of your choice, two, or three, or four; but if you fear that you cannot treat them equally, then marry only one, or any of the slave-girls you have acquired. This will prevent you from being unjust.

She said, "It is about an orphan girl in the custody of her guardian, who was attracted by her wealth and beauty and wanted to marry her with a mahr (bridal gift) less than that of other women of her status. So, such guardians were forbidden to marry such orphan girls unless they treated them justly and gave them suitable mahr; otherwise they were ordered to marry any other woman."

Aisha further said, "After that verse the people again asked the Prophet about marriage with orphan girls, so Allah revealed the following verses:

4:127 When they ask your advice regarding women say: Allah has instructed you concerning them, and His will is laid out for you in the Scriptures concerning female orphans to whom you have not given their legal due but whom you refuse to marry. In regard to helpless children, He has commanded you to deal fairly with orphans. Allah knows all the good that you do.

When the Meccans came to Medina, they were poor and the Medinans had to care for them. Mohammed made each Meccan a brother to a fellow Medinan. Here we see how generous one of the Medinans was. Sad gives away one of his wives like a piece of property.

[B3,34,264;B5,58,124;B5,58,125;B7,62,47;B8,75,395]

When Mohammed made a bond of fraternity between Abdur-Rahman and Sad, who was a rich man, Sad said, "The Ansar know that I am the richest of all of them, so I will divide my property into two parts between me and you. I have two wives; see which of the two you like so that I may divorce her and you can marry her after she becomes lawful to you by her passing the prescribed period of divorce. Abdur-Rahman said, "May Allah bless your family for you."

While he was trading in the market, Abdur-Rahman encountered Mohammed bearing the traces of yellow scent over his clothes. Mohammed asked him, "What is this scent?" He replied, "I have married a woman." Mohammed asked, "How much mahr (marriage gift) have you given?" Abdur-Rahman replied that he had given either gold amounting to the size of a date-stone or an actual golden date-stone; the sources are unsure. Mohammed told him, "Arrange a marriage banquet, even if just with a sheep."

Since Mohammed married both virgins and matrons, he had practical advice to give on the matter of which type was good for what service. We have another reference of her shaving the pubic hair.

[B3,41,589;B4,52,211;B7,62,16;B7,62,17;B7,62,174;B7,64,280;B8,75,396]

Jabir was riding back toward Medina with Mohammed following a jihad battle and Mohammed asked why he was in such a hurry. Jabir said that he was newly married. Mohammed asked, "A virgin or a matron?" Jabir replied, "A matron." Mohammed said, "Why didn't you marry a young girl so that you could play with her and she with you?" Jabir said, "My father died and I have some young sisters, so I have married a matron so that she may serve them and teach them manners." On that Mohammed said, "May Allah bless you. That is good."

When they neared Medina and were going to enter it, Mohammed said, "Wait till you enter your home early in the night so that the lady whose hair is unkempt may comb her hair and that the lady whose husband has been away may shave her pubic hair."

Here is more about jihad and sex.

[B4,53,353]

When Mohammed was about to carry out a holy military expedition (jihad), he said to his followers, "Anyone who has married a woman and wants to consummate the marriage, and has not done so yet, should not accompany me; nor should a man who has built a house but has not completed its roof; nor a man who has sheep or she-camels and is waiting for the birth of their young ones."

Mohammed then carried out the expedition. When he reached the town he was going to attack, it was almost sunset. Mohammed then called upon Allah to stop the sun from setting. It stopped until Allah made him victorious.

This Islamic law improved the status of a widow.

[B6,60,103]

In the Pre-Islamic Period, if a man died, his relatives used to have the right to inherit his wife; if they wished, one of them could marry her or give her in marriage. If they did not give her away in marriage, they would be entitled to treat her as they saw fit. Addressing this, Allah revealed the following verse:

4:19 Believers! It is not allowed for you to inherit the wives of your deceased family members against their will, or to prevent the wives from re-marrying in order to take away part of the dowry you have given them unless they are guilty of flagrant indecency. Treat them kindly for if you hate them, it may be that you hate that in which Allah has placed abundant goodness.

2:234 *As for widows, they should keep apart from men for four months and ten days after their husband's death. When they have fulfilled the waiting period, there will be no blame if they choose another and act in a decent way. Allah knows all that you do. You will not be blamed for openly proposing to widows or for holding them close to your hearts; Allah knows that you will not forget them. Do not arrange a secret meeting with them, and if you do meet, treat them honorably. You should not consummate the marriage until her waiting period is over.*

A MARRIAGE STORY

There are many of these stories of how a Muslim used jihad for the purpose of getting the money for the mahr, the marriage dowry.

> 1990 A Muslim, Ibn Hadrad, was to marry and had proposed a dowry of 200 dirhams. He went to Mohammed and asked if he had such an amount. Mohammed said no. A man named Rifa was the head of the Jusham clan and was an enemy of Allah. So Mohammed sent Ibn Hadrad and two other men to get information about the tribe.
>
> 1990 The Muslims sneaked upon the Jusham camp and waited. To their good fortune Rifa left the camp to look for a lost shepherd. Ibn Hadrad shot him through the heart and the three Muslims then shouted, "Allah akbar," and charged into the camp with swords and the tribe fled. Ibn Hadrad cut off Jusham's head, took the livestock, and went back to Mohammed.
>
> 1991 Ibn Hadrad was given some of the livestock to sell and pay his dowry so he could consummate the marriage.

THE TEMPTATIONS OF FAMILY

The Trilogy holds the family in highest regard. However, it has warnings about family as well.

> 64:14 ***Believers! You certainly have enemies among your wives and children, so beware of them! If you forgive and bear with them, then Allah too will be forgiving and merciful. Your riches and your children are only a source of temptation! But with Allah is the great reward!***

> 3:13 ***Tempting is the lure of women and children, of stored up treasures of gold and silver, of well-bred horses, cattle and farmland. These are the pleasures of this world, but a more excellent home is found with Allah.***

THE SHARIA LAW

The Sharia system of Islamic law is the practical conclusion of political Islam. It is also a way for the non-Muslim to see how the Trilogy forms the basis of not only for a religion but also for the most powerful political system in history. The Trilogy is both a political theory and a complete, detailed code of law that covers contract law, banking, family law, insurance, criminal law, and foreign policy.

The following is a summary from a thirteen-hundred-year-old classic text, *The Reliance of the Traveller.*[1] Due to the fact that the Koran is considered to be unchangingly perfect and final, this legal code is unchanging and is still used today. Once you have read the Koran and the Hadith, you will recognize all of these laws. They are nothing more than a codified summary of both texts. The Sharia is the fruit of the doctrine of political Islam.

THE WIFE'S MARITAL OBLIGATIONS

It is obligatory for a woman to let her husband have sex with her immediately when he asks her; at home; and if she can physically endure it.

If sex will harm her, she does not have to comply.

THE HUSBAND'S RIGHTS

A man has all rights to his wife's body. He is entitled to take her with him when he travels.

PERMITTING ONE'S WIFE TO LEAVE THE HOUSE

A husband may permit his wife to leave the house for religion and to see her female friends, or to go to any place in the town. A woman may not leave the city without her husband or a member of her unmarriageable kin accompanying her. All other travel is unlawful.

The husband may forbid his wife to leave the home because the Prophet said, "It is not permissible for a woman who believes in Allah and the Last Day to allow someone into her husband's house if he is opposed, or to go out if he is averse".

THE CONDITIONS THAT ENTITLE A WIFE TO SUPPORT

The husband is only obliged to support his wife when she does not refuse him sex at any time of the night or day. She is not entitled to support from her husband when she does not obey him, even if for a moment or travels without his permission.

This is the Sunna of Mohammed

---

1. Ahmad Ibn Naqib Al-Misri, ***The Reliance of the Traveller, A Classic Manual of Islamic Sacred Law*** (Amana Publications, 1994).

SEX

CHAPTER 4

4:69 Those who obey Allah and His Messenger will live with the messengers and the faithful and the martyrs and the righteous. What wonderful company!

- Adultery is a capital offense.
- Mohammed allowed female genital mutilation as an acceptable practice.
- A woman should not enhance her appearance.
- A woman should never be alone with any man who could be a sexual partner.

Sex outside marriage with another Muslim has serious consequences. Sex with a kafir female does not have any strictures. Under no circumstances, including marriage, is a Muslim female to ever have sex with a kafir.

[B1,10,504;B2,23,413;B6,60,209]

A man told Mohammed that he had kissed a woman. Through his Prophet, Allah revealed:

11:114 Observe prayer at early morning, at the close of the day, and at the approach of night, for good deeds drive away evil deeds. This is a warning for the mindful. Be patient, for Allah will not let the reward of the righteous perish.

The man asked Mohammed, "Is this instruction for me?" He said, "It is for all my followers."

When Maiz came to the Mohammed to confess adultery, the Prophet said to him, "Probably you have only kissed the lady, or winked, or looked at her?" He said, "No, O Allah's Apostle!" Mohammed said, using no euphemism, "Did you have sexual intercourse with her?" After he confessed to his crime, the Prophet ordered that he be stoned to death.

On another occasion, the Jew brought before Mohammed a man and woman who had committed adultery. He ordered both

of them to be stoned to death near the place where the funeral prayers are offered beside the mosque.

[B6,60,4;B8,73,30;B8,82,802;B9,83,1;B9,93,611;B9.93,623]

Abdullah asked Mohammed, "What is the greatest sin in the sight of Allah?" He replied, "To set up a rival unto Allah though He alone created you." Abdullah asked what was next, and Mohammed said, "To kill your son lest he should share your food with you." Abdullah asked what was next, and Mohammed said, "To commit illegal sexual intercourse with the wife of your neighbor."

SEXUAL MUTILATION

It is unfortunate that the term circumcision is applied to both the removal of the foreskin of the male and the removal of the clitoris of the woman. There is no comparison as to the effects. Circumcision does not destroy sexual pleasure for the man. However, removal of the clitoris of the female is akin to removal of the entire penis of the man.

[B7,72,777;B7,72,778;B7,72,779]

Mohammed said, "Five practices are characteristics of the ancient prophets: circumcision, shaving the pubic hair, cutting the moustaches short, clipping the nails, and depilating the hair of the armpits."

This hadith refers to the circumcision of female genitalia. It assumes that both the man and the woman are circumcised.

M003,0684

An argument arose in Medina between a group of Helpers and Immigrants concerning bathing. The Helpers believed that bathing after sex was obligatory only if there is an ejaculation. The Immigrants believed that a bath is always obligatory after sex. Abu Musa said, "Let me settle the matter."

He went to Aisha and asked and received her permission to speak. He said, "Aisha, beloved of the prophet, I want to question you about an embarrassing matter." Aisha said, "Do not be shy. Speak to me as you would your mother." Abu Musa then said, "When is a bath obligatory?" Aisha responded, "You have asked the right person. Mohammed has said that a bath is obligatory when a man is encompassed by a woman and their circumcised genitalia touch."

Circumcision is part of the Sharia law. Here we have both the translation and an argument about the translation.

e4.3 Circumcision is obligatory for both men and women. For men it consists of removing the prepuce from the penis, and for women, removing the prepuce of the clitoris (not the clitoris itself, as some mistakenly assert). [1]

However what the Arabic actually says is:

"Circumcision is obligatory (for every male and female) by cutting off the piece of skin on the glans of the penis of the male, but circumcision of the female is by cutting out the clitoris (this is called Hufaad)."

This deceptive translation obscures the Sharia law. It is a deception is called ***taqiyya***, a form of sacred deception.

At the battle of Badr, we have a reference to the custom of removing the clitoris.

I564 Hamza fought until he killed Arta who was one of those who were carrying the standard. Then Siba passed by him, and Hamza said, '***Come here, you son of a female circumciser.***' Now his mother was Umm Anmar, ***a female circumciser in Mecca.*** Then Hamza smote him and killed him.

The Sunna of Mohammed is that he never forbade the removal of the clitoris, a common custom of his day.

Even dreaming about sex makes a Muslim unclean.

[B1,3,132;B1,5,249;B1,5,276;B1,5,280;B1,5,291;B1,5,292;B4,55,545;B8,73,113;B8,73,142

Um Sulaym came to Mohammed and said, "Truly, Allah does not feel shy to tell the truth. If a woman has a wet dream, is it essential for her to take a bath?" He replied, "Yes, if she notices a discharge." Um Salama laughed and said, "Does a woman get a discharge?" He said, "How then does her son resemble his mother?"

When questioned about a man who engages in sex with his wife but does not discharge, Mohammed said, "He should wash the parts which came in contact with the private parts of the woman, perform ablution (ritual bathing) and then pray."

This next hadith gives an insight into Arabian community life.

[B6,60,203;B6,60,204]

When asked about the meaning of the Koranic verse,

---

1 Ahmad Ibn Naqib Al-Misri, ***The Reliance of the Traveller, A Classic Manual of Islamic Sacred Law*** (Amana Publications, 1994).

11:5 Surely they fold up their hearts to hide their thoughts from Him, but even when they cover themselves in their garments, He knows what they conceal and what they make public. He knows what is in the secrets of their hearts.

Ibn Abbas said, "Some people used to hide themselves while answering the call of nature in an open space lest they be exposed to the sky, and also when they had sex with their wives in an open space lest they be exposed to the sky, so the above revelation was sent down from Allah."

Sex is used to tell the doctrine of predestination. Islam has a dualistic theory about predestination. There is support for predestination and there is support for free will. Which is right? Both are right, that is the nature of duality.

[B1,6,315;B4,54,430;B4,55,550;B8,77,593;B8,77,594;B9,93,546]

Mohammed said:

Each one of you collected in your mother's womb for forty days, and then turned into a clot for forty days, and turned into a piece of flesh for a similar period of forty days.

Then Allah sends an angel and orders him to write four things upon you: your livelihood, deeds, age, and whether you will be of the wretched or the blessed in the Hereafter. Then the soul was breathed into you.

And by Allah, a man may do the evil deeds of the people of Hell until he is within arm's reach of Hell, but then that writing which Allah has ordered the angel to write takes precedent, and he will do the deeds of the people of Paradise and enter it. Conversely a man may do the good deeds of the people of Paradise until he is within arm's reach of Paradise, and then that writing takes precedent and he will do the deeds of the people of the Hell and enter it.

In Islam, the only males that a female should be alone with are those she cannot marry. This limits her male relationships to family members. School, sports, career, friendships, are all determined by this hadith. Islam always assumes that if a man and a woman are alone, it is about sex.

[B4,52,250;B7,62,160]

Mohammed said, "It is not permissible for a man to be alone with a woman, and no lady should travel except with her husband or a person whom she could not possibly marry." Then a man got up and said, "O Allah's Apostle! I have enlisted in the army for jihad and my wife is proceeding for the Hajj pilgrimage to Mecca." Mohammed said, "Go, and perform the Hajj with your wife."

Although this hadith is not about the sex act, it is about sexual attractiveness.

[B7,62,133;B7,72,815;B7,72,816;B7,72,817;B7,72,818;B7,72,819;B7,72,822;B7,72,826;B7,72,829;B7,72,830;B7,72,832]

Mohammed said, "Allah has cursed the lady who artificially lengthens hair and the one who gets her hair lengthened, as well as the one who tattoos and the one who gets herself tattooed." Mohammed has also said that Allah curses women who remove hair from their faces, those who space their teeth on purpose for beauty, or any woman who changes features created by Allah.

Before sex, a Muslim should always pray for protection from Satan.

[B1,4,143;B4,54,493;B4,54,503B7,62,94;B8,75,397;B9,93,493;]

Mohammed said that when having sex with one's wife, he should say, "'In the name of Allah. O Allah! Protect us from Satan and prevent Satan from approaching our offspring that you are going to give us." If the man and his wife have a child as a result of that encounter, Satan will not harm it.

[B4,52,74i;B4,55,635;B4,55,637]

Mohammed said, "Once Solomon, son of David, said, 'Tonight I will have sexual intercourse with ninety-nine women, each of whom will give birth to a knight who will fight in Allah's cause [jihad].' But he did not say, 'Allah willing.' Therefore, only one of those women conceived and gave birth to a half-man. If he had said, 'Allah willing', he would have begotten sons, all of whom would have been knights striving in Allah's cause."

[...]

Homosexuality between women is treated more seriously than between men.

4:15 *If any of your women are guilty of lewdness [lesbianism], then bring in four of you as witnesses against them. If they admit their guilt, then shut them up in their houses until they die or until Allah makes some other way for them. If two of your men are guilty of an indecent act [homosexuality], punish both of them. If they ask for forgiveness and change their ways, then leave them alone, for Allah is forgiving and merciful!*

This is the Sunna of Mohammed

BEATING THE WIFE

CHAPTER 5

8:13 This was because they opposed Allah and His messenger. Ones who oppose Allah and His messenger will be severely punished by Allah.

- Men are superior to women.
- Men can lightly beat their wives.
- Mohammed hit one of his wives.
- Sharia law supports beating the wife.
- A wife should not be struck in the face.

If the detailed rules of marital conduct are not followed by the wife, there is sacred force. Here we have the words of the Koran:

> 4:34 ***Allah has made men superior to women because men spend their wealth to support them. Therefore, virtuous women are obedient, and they are to guard their unseen parts as Allah has guarded them. As for women whom you fear will rebel, admonish them first, and then send them to a separate bed, and then beat them. But if they are obedient after that, then do nothing further; surely Allah is exalted and great!***

When Mohammed gave his last sermon, he mentioned beating the wife:

> I969 He also told them men had rights over their wives and women had rights over their husbands. The wives were never to commit adultery or act in a sexual manner toward others. If they did, they were to be put in separate rooms and ***beaten lightly***. If they refrained from what was forbidden, they had the right to food and clothing. Men were to lay injunctions on women lightly for they were prisoners of men and had no control over their persons.

Beating the wife is sacred because both Allah and Mohammed sanction it. The Hadith is filled with examples that establish the Sharia law about how to go about beating the wife.

In this hadith, a wife has her face bruised from being hit by her husband and goes to see Mohammed for his judgment on a marital problem.

[B3,48,807;B7,63,186;B7,63,187;B7,63,190;B7,63,238;B7,72,684;B7,72,715;B8,73,107]

Rifa divorced his wife, who then married Abdur-Rahman. The lady came to Aisha, wife of Mohammed, wearing a green veil and complained to Aisha of her husband and showed her a green spot on her skin caused by beating. It was the habit of ladies to support each other, so when Mohammed came, Aisha said, "I have not seen any woman suffering as much as Muslim women. Look! Her skin is greener than her clothes!"

When Abdur-Rahman heard that his wife had gone to Mohammed, he came with his two sons by another wife. The wife in the green veil said, "By Allah! I have done no wrong to him but he is impotent and is as useless to me as this," holding and showing the fringe of her garment, Abdur-Rahman said, "By Allah, O Allah's Apostle! She has told a lie! I am very strong and can satisfy her but she is disobedient and wants to go back to Rifa." Mohammed said to her, "If that is your intention, then know that it is unlawful for you to remarry Rifa until you have consummated your marriage with Abdur-Rahman."

Then the Prophet saw two boys with Abdur-Rahman and asked (him), "Are these your sons?" After Abdur-Rahman replied that this was so, Mohammed said to the woman, "You claim that he is impotent? But by Allah, these boys resemble him as a crow resembles a crow."

Several things should be noticed. Aisha, the favorite wife of Mohammed, calls attention to the common mistreatment of Muslim wives by their husbands. Mohammed does not condemn the beating, nor even mention it. The wife may want a divorce, but before she can get it, she must have sex with the husband she wants to leave.

In the next hadith Mohammed does not condemn the fact that Abu Jahm beats his wives.

Muslim 009, 3527;3512;3526

...She said: Muawiya and Abul-Jahm were among those who had given me the proposal of marriage. Thereupon Allah's Apostle said: Muawiya is destitute and in poor condition and Abul-Jahm beats women, you should take Osama b. Zaid as your husband.

Not only did Abul Jahm beat women, this hadith shows that using a stick to beat the wife is not disapproved by Mohammed.

M009,3512

[...] She said: When my period of iddah was over, I mentioned to him that Muawiya and Jahm had sent proposals of marriage to me, whereupon Allah's Messenger said: As for Abu Jahm, he does

not put down his staff from his shoulder, and as for Muawiya, he is a poor man having no property; marry Osama. I objected to him, but he again said: marry Osama; so I married him. Allah blessed me and I was envied by others.

In the next hadith we have part of the code for beating. A woman may be beaten, but not on the face. This contradicts the earlier hadith where Mohammed did not condemn the husband bruising his wife's face.

Abu Dawud 11, 2137

Narrated Muawiyah al-Qushayri:

Muawiyah asked: Apostle of Allah, what is the right of the wife of one of us over him? He replied: That you should give her food when you eat, clothe her when you clothe yourself, do not strike her on the face, do not revile her or separate yourself from her except in the house.

At first Mohammed said that Muslims should not beat their wives.

Abu Dawud 11, 2138; 2139

Muawiyah said: Apostle of Allah, how should we approach our wives and how should we leave them? He replied: Approach your tilth (tilth is a plowed field, a term for the vagina) when or how you will, give her (your wife) food when you take food, clothe when you clothe yourself, do not revile her face, and do not beat her.

But the men complained about wives who were not submissive enough, and had to be put in their place. When the Muslim women came to his house to complain about their beating, he condemned them, not the husbands who beat them. Physical force is always an option in Islam.

Abu Dawud 11, 2141:

Mohammed said: Do not beat Allah's handmaidens, but when Umar came to Mohammed and said: Women have become emboldened towards their husbands, Mohammed gave permission to beat them. Then many women came round the family of Mohammed complaining against their husbands.

So Mohammed said: Many women have gone round Mohammed's family complaining against their husbands. They are not the best among you.

Here we have an example of Mohammed striking his favorite wife.

Muslim 004, 2127

...When it was my turn for Allah's Messenger to spend the night with me, he turned his side, put on his mantle and took off

his shoes and placed them near his feet, and spread the corner of his shawl on his bed and then lay down till he thought that I had gone to sleep. He took hold of his mantle slowly and put on the shoes slowly, and opened the door and went out and then closed it lightly.

I covered my head, put on my veil and tightened my waist wrapper, and then went out following his steps till he reached Baqi'. He stood there and he stood for a long time. He then lifted his hands three times, and then returned and I also returned. He hastened his steps and I also hastened my steps. He ran and I too ran. He came (to the house) and I also came (to the house). I, however, preceded him and I entered (the house), and as I lay down in the bed, he (the Holy Prophet) entered the (house), and said: Why is it, O Aisha, that you are out of breath? I said: There is nothing.

He said: Tell me or Allah would inform me. I said: Messenger of Allah, may my father and mother be ransom for you, and then I told him the whole story. He said: Was it the darkness of your shadow that I saw in front of me? I said: Yes. He struck me on the chest which caused me pain, and then said: Did you think that Allah and His Apostle would deal unjustly with you?...

Mohammed did not complain when Abu Bakr hit his daughter, Mohammed's wife.

[B5,57,21;B5,57,117;B6,60,131;B7,62,93;B7,72,770,B8,82,828;B6,60,132;B8,82,828;B1,7,330;B1,7,330]

Mohammed was on one of his journeys when Aisha lost her necklace, and so he stopped to look for it. The people who had stopped to look with Mohammed had no water, nor was there any water in this place. They complained to Abu Bakr (Aisha's father) that Aisha had caused them to stop in this place with no water. Abu Bakr came while Mohammed was sleeping with his head on Aisha's thigh, admonished her and struck her with his fist, but she did not move because she did not want to rouse Mohammed.

When Mohammed woke the next morning, Allah revealed the verse of purifying with dust. Later, they moved Aisha's camel and found her necklace beneath it.

Usaid said to Aisha, "May Allah reward you handsomely. Whenever you have a difficulty, Allah takes you out of it and brings with it a blessing for the Muslims."

This hadith determines Islamic social custom and family law about wife beating.

Abu Dawud 11, 2142

Mohammed said: A man will not be asked as to why he beat his wife.

This hadith equates camels, slaves and women.

Abu Dawud 11, 2155

Mohammed said: If one of you marries a woman or buys a slave, he should say: "O Allah, I ask You for the good in her, and in the disposition You have given her; I take refuge in You from the evil in her, and in the disposition You have given her." When he buys a camel, he should take hold of the top of its hump and say the same kind of thing.

More advice about slaves and women:

[B7,62,132]

The Prophet said, "None of you should flog his wife as he flogs a slave and then have sexual intercourse with her in the last part of the day."

Here we have another sacred example of beating the wife. It is not wrong to beat the woman, but compassion dictates making this beating symbolic. Job swore to beat his wife with one hundred blows. Later he softened, and, to fulfill his oath, he put one hundred small twigs in his hand and hit her once.

38:44 ***And We gave him back his family and doubled their number as an example of Our mercy and as a reminder for men of understanding. We said to him, "Take up in your hand a branch and strike her with it, and do not break your oath." Truly, We found him to be full of patience and constant. He was an excellent servant, because he constantly turned toward Us in repentance.***

SHARIA LAW

The Hadith, the Sira and the Koran are all the basis of Islamic law, the Sharia. Here we see how Islamic law follows from the previous material.

DEALING WITH A REBELLIOUS WIFE[1]

m10.12 When a husband notices signs of rebelliousness in his wife whether in words as when she answers him coldly when she used to do so politely. or he asks her to come to bed and she refuses,

1. Ahmad Ibn Naqib Al-Misri, *The Reliance of the Traveller, A Classic Manual of Islamic Sacred Law* (Amana Publications, 1994).

contrary to her usual habit; or whether in acts, as when he finds her averse to him when she was previously kind and cheerful), he warns her in words without keeping from her or hitting her, for it may be that she has an excuse.

The warning could be to tell her,

"Fear Allah concerning the rights you owe to me,"

or it could be to explain that rebelliousness nullifies his obligation to support her and give her a turn amongst other wives, or it could be to inform her,

"Your obeying me is religiously obligatory".

If she commits rebelliousness, he keeps from sleeping (having sex) with her without words, and may hit her, but not in a way that injures her, meaning he may not bruise her, break bones, wound her, or cause blood to flow. It is unlawful to strike another's face. He may hit her whether she is rebellious only once or whether more than once, though a weaker opinion holds that he may not hit her unless there is repeated rebelliousness.

To clarify this paragraph, we mention the following rulings:

(1) Both man and wife are obliged to treat each other kindly and graciously.

(2) It is not lawful for a wife to leave the house except by the permission of her husband, though she may do so without permission when there is a pressing necessity. Nor may a wife permit anyone to enter her husband's home unless he agrees, even their unmarriageable kin. Nor may she be alone with a non-family-member male, under any circumstances.

(3) It is obligatory for a wife to obey her husband as is customary in allowing him full lawful sexual enjoyment of her person. It is obligatory for the husband to enable her to remain chaste and free of want for sex if he is able. It is not obligatory for the wife to serve her husband; if she does so, it is voluntary charity.

(4) If the wife does not fulfill one of the above mentioned obligations, she is termed "rebellious", and the husband takes the following steps to correct matters:

(a) admonition and advice, by explaining the unlawfulness of rebellion, its harmful effect on married life, and by listening to her viewpoint on the matter;

(b) if admonition is ineffectual, he keeps from her by not sleeping in bed with her, by which both learn the degree to which they need each other;

(c) if keeping from her is ineffectual, it is permissible for him to hit her if he believes that hitting her will bring her back to the right path, though if he does not think so, it is not permissible. His hitting her may not be in a way that injures her, and is his last recourse to save the family;

Examples of rebelliousness are when a wife gives a cold answer or does not submit to sex when he asks. He should not hit her but tell her, "Fear Allah concerning the rights you owe to me,"

He can explain that rebelliousness means that he does not need to support her or it could be to inform her, "Your obeying me is a religious obligation."

If she commits rebelliousness, he may hit her but not in a way that injures her, meaning he may not bruise her, break bones, wound her, or cause blood to flow. It is unlawful to strike another's face. He may hit her whether she is rebellious only once or whether more than once.

THE PRACTICAL RESULTS

Here is a quote from a Muslim apostate about the practical state of Islamic marriage that results from the doctrine in this chapter. Every point about this perfect Islamic wife is based upon the eternal, perfect, universal doctrine of Islam.

> A woman who is ***baari*** is like a pious slave. She honors her husband's family and feeds them without question or complaining. She never whines or makes demands of any kind. She is strong in service, but her head is bowed. If her husband is cruel, if he rapes her and then taunts her about it, if he decides to take another wife, or beats her, she lowers her gaze and hides her tears. And she works hard, faultlessly. She is a devoted, welcoming, well-trained work animal. This is baari.
>
> If you are a Somali woman you must learn to tell yourself that Allah is just and all-knowing and will reward you in the Hereafter.

Meanwhile, everyone who knows about your patience and endurance will applaud your father and mother on the excellence of your up-bringing. Your brothers will be grateful to you for preserving their honor (ghira). They will boast to other families about your heroic submission. And perhaps, eventually, your husband's family will appreciate your obedience, and your husband may one day treat you as a fellow human being.

If in the process of being baari you feel grief, humiliation, fatigue, or a sense of everlasting exploitation, you hide it. If you long for love and comfort, you pray in silence to Allah to make your husband more bearable. Prayer is your strength. Nomadic mothers must try to give their daughters this skill and strength called baari.[2]

This is the Sunna of Mohammed

2 Ayaan Hirsi Ali, ***Infidel***, Free Press-Simon and Shuster, NY, NY 10020, 2007, pg.12.

MOHAMMED'S WIVES

CHAPTER 6

47:33 Believers! Obey Allah and the messenger, and do not let your effort be in vain.

- Khadija was his favorite wife.
- Aisha was the favorite wife in his harem.
- Mohammed started having sex with Aisha when she was nine.
- One of Mohammed's favorite sexual partners was a Christian slave girl.
- Aisha was the most scholarly of his wives.
- Two of Mohammed's wives were captive booty in jihad.

The best estimate of the number of Mohammed's wives is eleven and he had two sex slaves.

KHADIJA

Khadija married Mohammed when she was forty and he was twenty-five. She was a wealthy widow and was his only wife for twenty-five years. She died at age sixty-five, when Mohammed was fifty. They had six children, with only their daughter, Fatima, surviving Mohammed.

[B4,55,605;B9,88,111;B427,19]

[...]

The angel came to him and asked him to read. The Prophet replied, "I do not know how to read.

The Prophet added, "The angel caught me (forcefully) and pressed me so hard that I could not bear it any more. He then released me and again asked me to read and I replied, 'I do not know how to read.' Thereupon he caught me again and pressed me a second time till I could not bear it any more. He then released me and again asked me to read but again I replied, 'I do not know how to read (or what shall I read)?' Thereupon he caught me for the third time and pressed me, and then released me and said,

96:1 Recite: In the name of your Lord, Who created man from clots of blood.
96:3 Recite: Your Lord is the most generous, Who taught the use of the pen and taught man what he did not know.

Then Allah's Apostle returned with the Inspiration and with his heart beating severely. Then he went to Khadija and said, "Cover me! Cover me!" They covered him till his fear was over and after that he told her everything that had happened and said, "I fear that something may happen to me." Khadija replied, "Never! By Allah, Allah will never disgrace you. You keep good relations with your friends and relatives, help the poor and the destitute, serve your guests generously and assist those in trouble."

[...]

[B5,58,166;B5,58,164;B5,58,165;B5,58,167;B8,73,33;B9,93,576;B9,93,588]

Narrated Aisha:

I did not feel jealous of any of the wives of the Prophet as much as I did of Khadija. I did not ever see her, but the Prophet used to mention her very often, and when ever he slaughtered a sheep, he would send some to the women friends of Khadija.

When I sometimes said to him, "You treat Khadija as if there is no woman on earth except Khadija." He replied "Khadija was such-and-such, and from her I had children."

Gabriel told Mohammed to tell Khadija she had a palace of precious stones in Paradise.

[B5,58,163;B4,55,642]

Mohammed said, "The best of the world's women is Mary (in her lifetime), and the best of the world's women is Khadija (in her lifetime)."

SAUDA

Mohammed married Sauda, a Muslim widow, two months after Khadija's death. About seven years later, she gave up her turn with Mohammed to Aisha, his favorite wife.

[B2,26,740;B2,26,740]

Sauda asked the permission of the Prophet to leave early from Al Muzdalifa since she was a fat and very slow woman. The Prophet gave her permission.

[B3,47,766;B3,48,853]

Whenever Mohammed wanted to go on a journey, he would draw lots as to which of his wives would accompany him. He used to fix for each of them a day and a night. But Sauda gave up her turn day and night to Aisha to please Allah's Apostle.

AISHA

Aisha was the daughter of Abu Bakr. She was engaged to Mohammed when she was six and Mohammed started having sex with her when she was nine and he was fifty-three. She was Mohammed's favorite wife and was eighteen when he died. She was two years old at the time of this dream.

[B5,58,35;B7,62,15;B7,62,57;B9,87,139;B9,87,140]

Mohammed dreamed of Aisha twice before they met. In his dream, an angel carried a picture on a piece of silk, and the angel said to him, "This is your wife." When he uncovered the picture, and saw that it was Aisha's, he said, "If this is from Allah, it will be done."

Mohammed was the one who proposed marriage to Aisha when she was six years old.

[B7,62,18]

When Mohammed asked Abu Bakr for Aisha's hand in marriage, Abu replied, "But I am your brother." Mohammed said, "You are only my brother in Allah's religion and His Book, so it is lawful for me to marry her."

Aisha's wedding night:

[B5,58,234;B5,58,236;B7,62,64;B7,62,65;B7,62,88;B7,62,90]

Mohammed became engaged to Aisha when she was six years old. She then went to Medina and stayed at the home of Bani-al-Harith, where she got ill and lost her hair. After her hair grew back by the age of nine, her mother handed her to the care of some women, who prepared her for her marriage to Mohammed. He consummated his marriage with her when she was nine years old and she remained with him for nine more years until his death.

Aisha brought her dolls into the harem. Since Mohammed hated images this was a big favor to her.

[B8,73,151]

Aisha used to play with dolls in front of Mohammed even though such acts were forbidden. She was allowed to do so before she reached the age of puberty. Her friends who played with her would hide when Mohammed entered the room, but he would call them back to resume playing with Aisha.

[B1,6,298;B1,6,299;B1,6,300;B3,33,247;B3,33,262;B9,93,639]

During the menses, Mohammed used to order Aisha to put on a dress worn below the waist and he fondled her. While in religious retreat in the mosque, he used to bring his head near her and she would wash it while she used to be in her periods

[B1,6,302;B2,26,712;B7,68,466]

Aisha set out with Mohammed for the Hajj and when they reached Sarif she got her menses. When Mohammed came to her, she was weeping. He asked, "Why are you weeping?" Aisha said, "I wish I had not performed Hajj this year." He asked, "Is this because you got your menses?" She replied, "Yes." He then said, "This is the thing which Allah has ordained for all the daughters of Adam. So do what all the pilgrims do except do not perform the Tawaf round the Kabah until you are clean."

Once Mohammed thought he was bewitched and did not know that he was not sleeping with his wives.

[B7,71,660;B8,73,89]

Magic was worked on Mohammed so that he imagined that he had slept with his wives, when in fact he had not. One day he said to his wife Aisha:

"Allah has instructed me regarding this matter, about which I had asked Him. There came to me two men, one of them sat near my feet and the other near my head. The one near my feet, pointing at me, asked the one near my head, "What is wrong with this man?" The latter replied, "He is under the effect of magic." The first one asked, "Who had worked magic on him?" The other replied, "Lubaid, who was an ally of the Jews and a hypocrite." The first one asked, "What material did he use?" The other replied, "The skin of the pollen of a male date tree in combination with a comb and the hair stuck to it, kept under a stone in the well of Dharwan."

Then Mohammed went to that well and said, "This is the same well which was shown to me in the dream. The tops of its date-palm trees look like the heads of the devils, and its water looks reddish brown"

Then Mohammed ordered that those things be taken out. Aisha said, "O Allah's Apostle! Won't you disclose the magic object?" Mohammed said, "Allah has cured me and I hate to circulate the evil among the people."

Many men have reached high perfection, but very few women.

[B4,55,643;B4,55,623]

Mohammed said that this superiority of Aisha to other ladies is like the superiority of tharid (a dish of meat and bread) to other meals. He added that many men have reached this level of perfection, but no women except for Mary, the daughter of Imran (the mother of Jesus), and Asia, the wife of Pharaoh."

Allah never inspired Mohammed when he was with his other wives, but only when he was with Aisha.

[B3,47,754;B3,47,755;B5,57,119]

The people used to send gifts to Mohammed on the day it was Aisha's turn to be with him. The other wives of Mohammed gathered and complained about it, for they too liked to enjoy the gifts. Um Salama brought this issue before Mohammed, but he remained silent. She asked him about this a second time, and again he was silent. On the third time, Mohammed said, "O Um Salama! Don't trouble me by harming Aisha, for the Divine Inspiration never came to me while I was under the blanket of any woman amongst you except her."

Aisha commented on the Koran and related many of the hadiths.

[B6,61,515]

A man from Iraq asked Aisha if he could see her copy of the Koran so that he could arrange his suras in the proper order. On this, she said,

What does it matter which part of it you read first? The first thing that was revealed thereof was a Koran chapter, wherein heaven and hell were mentioned. After the people embraced Islam, the verses regarding legal and illegal things were revealed. If the first thing to be revealed was: 'Do not drink alcoholic drinks,' the people would have said, 'We will never leave alcoholic drinks,' and if there had been revealed, 'Do not commit illegal sexual intercourse,' they would have said, 'We will never give up illegal sexual intercourse.'

Then Aisha took out her copy of the Koran and told the man the proper order of the suras (chapters).

[B2,26,595;B3,29,84;B4,52,43;B4,52,127;B4,52,128;B4,52,295]

When Aisha requested of Mohammed that she be allowed to participate in a jihad, he said that a woman's jihad is the performance of the Hajj pilgrimage. It is even important for a husband to forsake a jihad campaign to accompany his wife on a Hajj.

[B1,11,644;B7,64,276;B8,73,65]

When Aisha was asked what Mohammed did at home, she said that he kept busy by serving his family whenever it was not time for prayer.

Mohammed chastised Aisha for decorations. He disliked art and music, so to this day, there is little music and representative art in the Islamic world.

[B3,34,318;B7,62,110;B7,72,844]

Aisha, the wife of Mohammed, bought a cushion with pictures on it. When Mohammed saw it, he stood in the doorway without entering the house. When she saw the look of disgust and hatred on his face, she said, "O Allah's Apostle! I repent to Allah and His Apostle! What sin have I committed?" Allah's Apostle said, "Those who make these pictures will be punished on the day of resurrection, and it will be said to them, 'Put life in what you have created.'" Mohammed added, "The angels do not enter a house where there are pictures."

[B3,43,659;B4,54,449;B7,72,841;B7,72,842]

Aisha, Mohammed's wife, had a thick curtain embroidered with pictures on her cupboard. Mohammed said to her, "Take it away from my sight, for its images come into my mind in my prayers." Aisha turned it into two cushions, which remained in the house for Mohammed to sit on.

Zaid told Said and Busr that Mohammed had said, "The Angels do not enter a house with pictures in it."

[...]

Aisha remained Mohammed's favorite wife up until his last day on earth.

[B5,57,118]

While Mohammed was suffering from his fatal illness and was visiting his various wives he would ask, "Where will I be tomorrow?" He was anxious to be in Aisha's home. When it was his day to be with Aisha, he would not ask that question.

[B8,80,722]

After Mohammed died, his wives wanted to send Uthman to Abu Bakr asking him for their share of the inheritance. Aisha said to them, "Didn't Allah's Apostle say that whatever he leaves behind should not be inherited, but spent in charity?"

[B2,23,474]

Aisha dictated some of her will to Abdullah, saying, "Do not bury me with the Prophet and his companions, but instead bury me with my companions, the other wives of the Prophet in Al-Baqi. I would not like to be looked upon as better than I really am."

JUWAIRIYA

Juwairiya was a captive when Mohammed attacked her tribe. She was beautiful and Mohammed paid her ransom to the jihadist who owned her. He then married her. As a result, the rest of the captives of her tribe were now related to Mohammed by marriage. They were then freed as a result. The attack was a sneak attack, a favorite of Mohammed.

[B3,46,717]

Ibn Aun wrote a letter to Nafi and Nafi wrote in reply that Mohammed had suddenly attacked the Bani Mustaliq tribe without warning while they were heedless and their cattle were being watered at the places of water. Their fighting men were killed and their women and children were taken as captives. Mohammed got Juwairiya on that day.

HAFSA

Hafsa was a widow and the daughter of Umar, later to be the second caliph.

[B7,62,145]

Umar entered upon Hafsa and said, "O my daughter! Do not be misled by the manners of Aisha who is proud of her beauty because of the love of Allah's Apostle for her." He added, "Then I told that to Allah's Apostle and he smiled on hearing that."

ZAINAB, DAUGHTER OF KHUZAIMAH

This Zainab was the widow of Mohammed's cousin, killed at the battle of Badr. She was called the "Mother of the Poor" for her charity work. She died before Mohammed.

UMM SALAMA

Umm Salama was the widow of a jihadist killed at the battle of Uhud.

[B1,6,297;B1,6,319]

While Um Salama was laying with Mohammed under a single woolen sheet, she got her menses. She slipped away and put on the clothes for menses. Mohammed asked, "Have you got menses?" I replied, "Yes." He then called me and made me lie with him under the same sheet.

ZAINAB BINT JAHSH

Zainab was the beautiful wife of Mohammed's adopted son, Zaid. The Koran changed the Arabian incest laws so that Mohammed could marry her. She bragged to the other wives that Mohammed had chosen them, but she was chosen by Allah for Mohammed. [Her story is also in the chapter, Mohammed's Family Life.]

[B7,62,84;B7,62,92m;B7,62,95;B7,62,97;B7,62,100;B8,74,255;B8,75,374]

When Mohammed married Zainab, he gave a finer banquet for this marriage than for any of his others. After the meal, he went out to the houses of his other wives, as was his custom on marrying, invoking good on them, and they were invoking good on him. When he returned, some men had remained and were conversing, so Mohammed left again. When he again returned, some men still remained, and so Mohammed recited:

33:53 Believers! Do not enter the Messenger's house early for a meal unless you are given permission. When you are invited, enter, and when you have finished your meal, leave. Do not remain there hoping to start a conversation, for this would annoy the Messenger, and he would be ashamed to send you home, but Allah is not ashamed to tell you the truth.

[B2,24,501;B2,24,501]

Narrated Aisha:

Some of the wives of the Prophet asked him, "Who amongst us will be the first die after you?" He said, "Whoever has the longest hand." So they started measuring their hands with a stick and Sauda's hand turned out to be the longest. When Zainab bint Jahsh died first of all in the caliphate of Umar, we came to know that the long hand was a symbol of practicing charity, so she was the first to follow the Prophet and she used to love to practice charity.

SAFIYA

Safiya was a beautiful Jew of Khaybar. Her husband and father were killed by Mohammed's jihad. After the battle Mohammed married her.

[B1,8,367;B2,14,68;B3,34,431;B3,34,437;B4,52,143,B5,59,512;B5,59,513;B5,59,522;B5, 59,523;B875,374]

Anas said, 'When Allah's Apostle invaded Khaybar, we offered the Fajr prayer there yearly in the morning when it was still dark. The Prophet rode and Abu Talha rode too and I was riding behind Abu Talha. The Prophet passed through the lane of Khaybar quickly and my knee was touching the thigh of the Prophet. He uncovered his thigh and I saw the whiteness of the thigh of the Prophet.

When he entered the town, he said, 'Allahu Akbar! Khaybar is ruined. Whenever we approach near a nation to fight then evil will be the morning of those who have been warned.' He repeated this thrice. The people came out for their jobs and some of them said, 'Mohammed has come with his army.' We conquered Khaybar, took the captives, and the booty was collected.

Dihya came and said, 'O Allah's Prophet! Give me a slave girl from the captives.' He took Safiya. A man came to the Prophet and said, 'O Allah's Apostle! You gave Safiya to Dihya and she is the chief mistress of the Jews and she befits none but you.' So the Prophet said, 'Bring him along with her.' So Dihya came with her and when the Prophet saw her, he said to Dihya, 'Take any other slave girl from the captives.'

Her husband had been killed by the Muslims while she was a bride. Mohammed then proposed that she marry him. Since she was a captive she needed to be ransomed to be freed. On the other hand, Mohammed owed her a dowry. So the dowry was set equal to the ransom.

The Prophet stayed with Safiya for three days on the way from Khaybar. After three days her period was over and Um Sulaym dressed her for marriage and at night she sent her as a bride to the Prophet.

Safiya was amongst those who were ordered to use a veil.

So the Prophet was a bridegroom and he said, 'Whoever has any food should bring it.' He spread out a leather sheet for the food and some brought dates and others cooking butter. So they prepared a dish. And that was the marriage banquet of Allah's Apostle."

[B3,33,254;B3,33,251;B3,33,255;B4,53,333;B4,54,501;B8,73,238]

The wives of Mohammed were with him in the mosque and then they departed. Mohammed said to Safiya, "Don't hurry away, for I shall accompany you," The Prophet went out and in the meantime two men met him and they looked at the Prophet and hurried away. The Prophet said to them, "Come here. She is my wife." They replied, "Subhan Allah, How dare we think of evil. O Allah's Apostle, we never expect anything bad from you." The Prophet replied, "Satan circulates in the human being as blood circulates in the body, and I was afraid that Satan might insert an evil thought in your minds."

UMM HABIBA

Umm Habiba was the daughter of Abu Sufyan, an enemy of Mohammed. She was a widow when Mohammed married her.

[B1,8,419;B2,23,425;B5,58,213]

When the Prophet became ill, some of his wives talked about a church which they had seen in Ethiopia. Um Salma and Um Habiba talked about the Church's beauty and the pictures it contained. The Prophet raised his head and said, "Those are the people who, whenever a pious man dies amongst them, make a place of worship at his grave and then they make those pictures in it. Those are the worst creatures in the Sight of Allah."

[B1,6,324]

Um Habiba got bleeding in between the periods for seven years. She asked Mohammed about it. He ordered her to take a bath after the termination of actual periods and added that it was from a blood vessel. So she used to take a bath for every prayer.

MAIMUNA

Maimuna was a widow of 51 when Mohammed married her.

[B2,22,289;B6,60,96;B1,12,818;B1,16,106;B6,60,93;B6,60,94;B1,3,117;B1,4,173;B1,11,665;B1,11,666;B1,11,667]

Abdullah said that he had passed a night in the house of Maimuna, the mother of the faithful believers, who was his aunt. He said, "I slept across the bed, and Allah's Apostle, along with his wife, slept lengthwise. Allah's Apostle slept till mid-night or slightly before or after it. Then he woke up, sat, and removed the traces of sleep by rubbing his hands over his face. Then he recited ten verses of the Koran. Then he went towards a hanging leather water-container and performed a perfect ablution and then stood up for prayer." Abdullah bin Abbas added, "I got up and did the same as Allah's Apostle had done and then went and stood by his side. He then put his right hand over my head and caught my right ear and twisted it. After prayer he lay down until Bilal came and waked him. Then he prayed the early morning prayer."

[B3,47,765]

Maimuna manumitted a slave-girl without taking the permission of the Prophet. On the day when it was her turn to be with the Prophet, she said, "Do you know, O Allah's Apostle, that I have manumitted my slave-girl?" He said, "Have you really?" She replied in the affirmative. He said, "You would have got more reward if you had given the slave-girl to one of your maternal uncles."

MARY, THE COPT

Mary was a Christian slave used for sex by Mohammed. Mary was fair skinned with wavy hair. She was the cause of a revolt of Mohammed's wives when he spent too much time with her. She had a son by him, who died at an early age.

RIHANA

Riahana was a beautiful Jewish slave used for sex by Mohammed. She became his after he executed her husband, along with eight hundred other Jewish males.

MOHAMMED AND MARRIAGE

A health issue:

[B1,6,306;B1,6,307;B3,33,253]

One of the wives of Mohammed noticed blood and a yellowish discharge from her private parts, and so the other wives would put a dish beneath her when she prayed.

These are some interesting "failed" romances:

[B7,63,181]

The daughter of Al-Jaun was brought to Mohammed as his bride. When he went near her, she said, "I seek refuge from you with Allah." Mohammed said, "You have sought refuge with The Great; return to your family."

[B7,69,541]

An Arab lady was mentioned to Mohammed, and he sent for her to meet him at the castle of Bani Saida. He entered upon her bed chambers, but she was sad and said, ""I seek refuge from you with Allah." He said, "I grant you refuge from me."

Later, when she was told that he was Allah's Apostle and had sought her hand in marriage, she regretted losing such a chance.

[B3,38,505;B6,61,547;B6,61,548;B7,62,24;B7,62,53;B7,62,54;B7,62,58;B7,62,66;B7,62,72;B7,62,79;B7,62,760;B8,73,144]

A woman came to Mohammed and said, "O Allah's Apostle! I have come to give myself to you in marriage." Mohammed looked at her carefully and fixed his glance on her and then lowered his head. When the lady saw that he did not say anything, she sat down.

A man from among his companions got up and said, "O Allah's Apostle! If you are not in need of her, then marry her to me." Mohammed said, "Have you got anything to offer?" The man said, "No, by Allah!" Mohammed said to him, "Go to your family and see if you have something." The man went and returned, saying, "No, by Allah, I have not found anything." Allah's Apostle said, "Go again and look for something, even if it is an iron ring." He went again and returned, saying, "No, by Allah! I could not find even an iron ring, but this is my waist sheet. I give half of it to her." Mohammed said, "What will she do with your waist sheet? If you wear it, she will be naked, and if she wears it, you will be naked."

So that man sat down for a long while and then got up to depart. When Mohammed saw him going, he called him back. Mohammed said, "How much of the Koran do you know?" The man listed the suras (chapters of the Koran) he knew. Mohammed asked, "Do you know them by heart?" He replied, "Yes." Mohammed said, "Go, I have married her to you for what you know of the Koran."

When Anas told his daughter of this event, she commented, "How shameless that woman was!" On that Anas said, "She is better than you, for she presented herself to Allah's Apostle for marriage."

One of Islam's favorite references is Mohammed's sexual capacity.

[B1,5,268;B1,5,282]

Anas once said, "The Prophet used to visit all his wives in turn, during the day and night and they were eleven in number." When asked if Mohammed had the strength for such activity, Anas replied, "We used to say that the Prophet was given the strength of thirty men."

Said said that Anas had told him that Mohammed had only nine wives during such occasions.

This is the Sunna of Mohammed

JEALOUSY

CHAPTER 7

61:11 Believe in Allah and His messenger and fight valiantly for Allah's cause [jihad] with both your wealth and your lives. It would be better for you, if you only knew it!

- Mary, Mohammed's sex slave, caused jealousy in the harem.
- Mohammed abandoned his wives for a month over an argument.
- The wives competed with each other over Mohammed's attention.
- All Muslims know about Mohammed's favorite wife.

A natural question arises: how did Mohammed live with all of his wives without jealousy, tension, arguments and bad feelings? The answer is that there were jealousy, tension, arguments and bad feelings. The family quarrels are reflected in all of the Trilogy.

MARY, THE COPTIC SLAVE OF PLEASURE

M425 Mohammed was given two Coptic (Egyptian Christian) slaves. One he gave to another Muslim but he kept Mary, fair of skin with curly hair. He did not move her into the harem, but set up an apartment in another part of Medina. Mary gave something in sex that none of his wives could—a child and it was a male child, Ibrahim. Mohammed doted on him.

M426 The harem was jealous. This non-Arab slave had given Mohammed his best gift. One of his wives, Hafsa, was away and Mohammed took Mary to Hafsa's apartment in the harem. Hafsa returned and there was a scene. The harem was incensed. A slave in one of their beds was an outrage and a scandal. The wives banded together and it was a house of anger and coldness.

M427 Mohammed withdrew and swore he would not see his wives for a month and lived with Mary. Omar and Abu Bakr were appalled as Mohammed, their son-in-law had abandoned their daughters for a slave. But at last Mohammed relented and said that Gabriel had spoken well of Hafsa and he wanted the whole affair to be over.

The Koran:

> 66:1 *Why, Oh, Messenger, do you forbid yourself that which Allah has made lawful to you? Do you seek to please your wives? [Mohammed was fond of a Coptic (Egyptian Christian) slave named Mary. Hafsa found Mohammed in her room with Mary, a violation of Hafsa's domain. He told a jealous Hafsa that he would stop relations with Mary and then did not. But Hafsa was supposed to be quiet about this matter.] Allah is lenient and merciful. Allah has allowed you release from your oaths, and Allah is your master. He is knowing and wise.*
> 66:3 *When the Messenger confided a fact to one of his wives, and when she divulged it, [Hafsa had told Aisha (Mohammed's favorite wife) about Mary and the harem became embroiled in jealousy.] Allah informed Mohammed of this, and he told her [Hafsa] part of it and withheld part. When Mohammed told her of it, she said, "Who told you this?" He said, "He who is knowing and wise told me."*
> 66:4 *"If you both [Hafsa and Aisha] turn in repentance to Allah, your hearts are already inclined to this, but if you conspire against the Messenger, then know that Allah is his protector, and Gabriel, and every just man among the faithful, and the angels are his helpers besides. Perhaps, if he [Mohammed] divorced you all, Allah would give him better wives than you—Muslims, believers, submissive, devout, penitent, obedient, observant of fasting, widows, and virgins."*

This next hadith is one of the longest. It goes into great detail about "the secret that Hafsa told Aisha." The secret was about Mohammed's being in Hafsa's bed with the slave, Mary.

> [B3,43,648;B13,89;Bj7,72,734,B7,62,119]
> *Narrated Ibn Abbas:*
> *I had been eager to ask Umar about the two ladies from among the wives of the Prophet mentioned in the Koran.*
> *If you two (wives of the Prophet namely Aisha and Hafsa) turn in repentance to Allah your hearts are indeed so inclined (to oppose what the Prophet likes) (66.4),*
> *On our way back from Mecca Umar went to answer the call of nature and I also went aside along with him carrying a tumbler of water. When he had answered the call of nature and returned, I poured water on his hands from the tumbler and he performed ablution. I said, "O Chief of the believers! ' Who were the two ladies from among the wives of the Prophet mentioned in the Koran. He said, "I am astonished at your question, O Ibn Abbas. They were Aisha and Hafsa."*

Then Umar said. "I and neighbor of mine used to visit the Prophet in turns. He used to go one day, and I another day. When I went I would bring him the news of what had happened that day regarding the instructions and orders and when he went, he used to do the same for me.

We, the people of Mecca used to have authority over women, but when we came to live in Medina, we noticed that the Medinan women had the upper hand over their men, so our women started acting like them. Once I shouted at my wife and she shouted back at me. She said, 'Why do you take it ill that I shout at you? By Allah, the wives of the Prophet shout at him, and some of them may not speak with him for the whole day till night.' What she said scared me and I said to her, 'Whoever amongst them does so, will be a great loser.' Then I dressed myself and went to Hafsa (Umar's daughter and a wife) and asked her, 'Does any of you keep Allah's Apostle angry all the day long till night?' She replied in the affirmative. I said, 'She is a ruined losing person and will never have success! Doesn't she fear that Allah may get angry for the anger of Allah's Apostle and thus she will be ruined? Don't ask Allah's Apostle too many things, and don't talk back to him in any case, and don't desert him. Demand from me whatever you like, and don't be tempted to imitate Aisha in her behavior towards the Prophet, for she is more beautiful than you, and more beloved to Allah's Apostle.

In those days it was rumored that the Ghassan, (a tribe living in Sham) was getting prepared to invade us. My companion went to the Prophet and returned to us at night and knocked at my door violently, asking whether I was sleeping. I was scared by the hard knocking and came out to him. He said that a great thing had happened. I asked him: What is it? Have the Ghassan come? He replied that it was worse and more serious than that, and added that Allah's Apostle had divorced all his wives.

I said, 'Hafsa is a ruined loser! I expected that would happen some day.' So I dressed myself, went to the mosque and offered the Fajr prayer with the Prophet. Then the Prophet entered an upper room and stayed there alone. I went to Hafsa and found her weeping. I asked her, 'Why are you weeping? Didn't I warn you? Has Allah's Apostle divorced you all?' She replied, 'I don't know. He is there in the upper room.'

I then went out and came to the pulpit and found a group of people around it and some of them were weeping. Then I sat with them for some time, but could not endure the situation. So I went to the upper room where the Prophet was and requested to a black slave of his: "Will you get the permission for Umar to enter? The slave went in, talked to the Prophet about it and came out saying, 'I mentioned you to him but he did not reply.' So, I went and sat with the people who were sitting by the pulpit, but I could not bear the situation, so I went to the slave again and said: "Will you get permission for me? He went in and brought the same reply as before. When I was leaving, behold, the slave called me saying, "Allah's Apostle has granted you permission."

So, I entered upon the Prophet and saw him lying on a mat without bedding on it, and the mat had left its mark on the body of the Prophet, and he was leaning on a leather pillow stuffed with palm leaves. I greeted him and while still standing, I said: "Have you divorced your wives?' He raised his eyes to me and replied in the negative. And then while still standing, I said, chatting: "Will you heed what I say, 'O Allah's Apostle! We, the people of Mecca used to have the upper hand over our wives, and when we came to the people whose women had the upper hand over them.."

Umar told the whole story about his wife. "On that the Prophet smiled." Umar further said, "I then said, 'I went to Hafsa and said to her: Do not be tempted to imitate Aisha for she is more beautiful than you and more beloved to the Prophet.' The Prophet smiled again. When I saw him smiling, I sat down and cast a glance at the room, and by Allah, I couldn't see anything of importance but three hides. I said to Allah's Apostle "Invoke Allah to make your followers prosperous for the Persians and the Byzantines have been made prosperous and given worldly luxuries, though they do not worship Allah?' The Prophet sat up straight and said, 'O Umar! Do you have any doubt that the Hereafter is better than this world? These people have been given rewards of their good deeds in this world only.'

I asked the Prophet, "'Please ask Allah's forgiveness for me." The Prophet did not go to his wives because of the secret which Hafsa had told to Aisha, and he said that he would not go to his wives for one month as he was angry with them. Allah admonished him for his oath that he would not approach his slave Mary, the Copt. When twenty-nine days had passed, the Prophet went to Aisha first of all. She said to him, 'You took an oath that you would not come to us for one month, and today only twenty-nine days have passed, as I have been counting them day by day.' The Prophet said, 'The month is also of twenty-nine days.' Aisha said, 'When the Divine revelation of Choice was revealed, the Prophet started with me, saying to me, 'I am telling you something, but you needn't hurry to give the reply till you can consult your

parents." Aisha knew that her parents would not advise her to part with the Prophet. The Prophet said that Allah had said:

33:28 Messenger! Say to your wives, "If you desire a life of this world and all its glittering adornment, then come. I will provide for you and release you with honor. If, however, you seek Allah and His Messenger and the world to come, then know that Allah has prepared a great reward for those of you who do good works.

Aisha said, 'Am I to consult my parents about this? I indeed prefer Allah, His Apostle, and the Home of the Hereafter.' After that the Prophet gave the choice to his other wives and they also gave the same reply as Aisha did."

Mary, the Copt, may have been a slave who was looked down upon by the wives, but she had the advantage of giving Mohammed a son. Soon that was lost.

M429 Ibrahim became a favorite of Mohammed. But when the child was fifteen months old, he fell sick. Mary and her slave sister attended the child during his illness. Mohammed was there at his death and wept mightily. Mohammed was to suffer the Arabic shame of having no living male children to succeed him. Mary, the Copt, disappears from the Trilogy after the death of Ibrahim.

HADITH OF JEALOUSY

This hadith is humorous. Aisha's jealousy of Hafsa causes a plot to be hatched.

[B9,86,102;B7,63,193;B8,78,193]

Narrated Aisha:

Allah's Apostle used to like sweets and also used to like honey, and whenever he finished the Asr prayer, he used to visit his wives and stay with them. Once he visited Hafsa and remained with her longer than the period he used to stay, so I enquired about it. It was said to me, "A woman from her tribe gave her a leather skin containing honey as a present, and she gave some of it to Allah's Apostle to drink."

I said, "By Allah, we will play a trick on him." So I mentioned the story to Sauda (a wife of the Prophet) and said to her, "When he enters upon you, he will come near to you whereupon you should say to him, 'O Allah's Apostle! Have you eaten bad tasting food?' He will say, 'No.' Then you say to him, 'What is this bad smell? ' And it would be very hard on Allah's Apostle that a bad smell should be found on his body. He will say, 'Hafsa has given

me a drink of honey.' Then you should say to him, 'Its bees must have sucked from a foul smelling flower.' I too, will tell him the same. And you, O Safiya, say the same."

So when the Prophet entered upon Sauda she said, "I was about to say to him what you had told me to say while he was still at the gate because of fear from you. But when Allah's Apostle came near to me, I said to him, 'O Allah's Apostle! Have you eaten bad tasting food?' He replied, 'No.' I said, 'What about this smell?' He said, 'Hafsa has given me a drink of honey.' I said, 'Its bees must have sucked a foul smelling flower.' " When he entered upon me, I told him the same as that, and when he entered upon Safiya, she too told him the same.

So when he visited Hafsa again, she said to him, "O Allah's Apostle! Shall I give you a drink of honey?" He said, "I have no desire for it." Sauda said, "Subhan Allah! We have deprived him of honey." I said to her, "Be quiet!"

Here the jealousy is between Aisha and Hafsa.

[B3,47,766;B3,48,853;B4,52,130;B7,62,138;B7,62,139]

Whenever Mohammed was preparing for a journey, he would draw lots to see which of his wives would accompany him. Also, he would fix a day and a night for each of his wives. Sauda gave her day and night to Aisha so the she might please Mohammed with this action.

During one of his journeys, the lot fell on Aisha and Hafsa, and at night Mohammed would ride beside Aisha and talk with her. One night Hafsa asked Aisha to switch camels with her, and she agreed. After Mohammed rode beside Hafsa on Aisha's camel, Aisha missed him, and when they dismounted she put her legs in the grass and said, "Oh Allah! Send a scorpion or snake to bite me for I am not to blame the Prophet."

The fact that Aisha was Mohammed's favorite wife was known by all the Muslims. Aisha was special even to Allah. The Koran was never revealed in any of the other wive's company.

[B3,47,755]

The wives of Mohammed were in two groups. One group consisted of Aisha, Hafsa, Safiya and Sauda; and the other group consisted of Um Salama and the other wives of Allah's Apostle. The Muslims knew that Allah's Apostle loved Aisha, so if any of them had a gift and wished to give to Allah's Apostle, he would delay it, till Allah's Apostle had come to Aisha's home and then he would send his gift to Allah's Apostle in her home.

The group of Um Salama discussed the matter together and decided that Um Salama should request Mohammed to tell the people to send their gifts to him in whatever wife's house he was. Um Salama told Allah's Apostle of what they had said, but he did not reply. Then those wives asked Um Salama about it. She said, "He did not say anything to me." They asked her to talk to him again. She talked to him again when she met him on her day, but he gave no reply. When they asked her, she replied that he had given no reply. They said to her, "Talk to him till he gives you a reply." When it was her turn, she talked to him again. He then said to her, "Do not hurt me regarding Aisha, as the Divine Inspirations do not come to me on any of the beds except that of Aisha." On that Um Salama said, "I repent to Allah for hurting you."

Then the group of Um Salama called Fatima, the daughter of Allah's Apostle and sent her to Allah's Apostle to say to him, "Your wives request you to treat them and the daughter of Abu Bakr on equal terms." Then Fatima conveyed the message to him. The Prophet said, "O my daughter! Don't you love whom I love?" She replied in the affirmative and returned and told them of the situation. They requested her to go to him again but she refused.

They then sent Zainab bint Jahsh (another wife) who went to him and used harsh words saying, "Your wives request you to treat them and Aisha on equal terms." On that she raised her voice and abused Aisha to her face so much so that Allah's Apostle looked at Aisha to see whether she would retort. Aisha started replying to Zainab till she silenced her. The Prophet then looked at Aisha and said, "She is really the daughter of Abu Bakr."

Mohammed had to deal with jealousy among his wives.

[B7,62,152]

While Mohammed was in the house of one of his wives, one of his other wives sent a meal in a dish. The wife he was visiting at the time struck the hand of the slave, causing the dish to fall and break. Mohammed gathered the broken pieces of the dish and then started collecting on them the food which had been in the dish and said, "My wife felt jealous." Then he detained the slave until an unbroken dish was provided by the wife he was visiting. He gave the sound dish to the wife who had sent the meal and left the broken one at the house where it had been broken.

It is implied that Aisha was jealous of all the other wives.

> [B4,55,642;B5,58,164;B5,58,165;B5,58,166;B5,58,168;B7,62,156;B8,73,33]
> *Aisha never felt so jealous of any of Mohammed's wives as she did of Khadija, who died three years before he was engaged to Aisha. He would mention Khadija often, praising her as the best woman of this nation, and whenever he slaughtered a sheep, he would send some of its parts to her friends. The angel Gabriel once told Mohammed to inform Khadija that in heaven she would have a palace made precious stones and pearls.*

Mohammed said that he looked like Abraham. If so, he also had the same problems of jealousy.

> [B3,40,556;B4,55,582;B4,55,583;B4,55,584]
> *Abraham had a son, Ishmael, by Hagar, his wife's slave. Abraham's wife, Sarah, was jealous of Hagar so he took Ishmael and his mother and went to Mecca. During those days there was nobody in Mecca, nor was there any water. Abraham made them sit in the Kabah mosque and placed near them a leather bag containing some dates, and a small waterskin containing some water, and set out homeward.*
>
> *Hagar followed him saying, "O Abraham! Where are you going, leaving us in this valley where there is no person whose company we may enjoy, nor is there anything to eat or drink?" She repeated that to him many times, but he did not look back at her. Then she asked him, "Has Allah ordered you to do so?" He said, "Yes." She said, "Then He will not neglect us," and returned while Abraham proceeded onwards. Ishmael's mother went on suckling Ishmael and drinking from the water she had.*
>
> *When the water in the waterskin had all been used up, she became thirsty and her child also became thirsty. She went to the top of the mountain Safa to see if she could see anyone, but could not. She descended and climbed the Marwa mountain, but in vain. She repeated this seven times. When she reached Marwa the last time, she saw an angel stamping his feet until water flowed at the site of the future Zam-zam well. Ishmael's mother started to make something like a basin around it, and started filling her waterskin with water with her hands. Ishmael's mother started drinking from the water and her milk increased for her child.*
>
> *Mohammed has said, "May Allah bestow mercy on Ishmael's mother! Had she not scooped from that water to fill her waterskin, Zam-zam well would have been a stream flowing on the surface of the earth."*

This next hadith shows how the wives were in competition.

> [B3,33,249;B3,33,250;B3,33,257]
>
> *Aisha said, "the Prophet used to practice Itikaf [retirement to the mosque and prayer] in the last ten days of Ramadan and I used to pitch a tent for him. After offering the morning prayer, he used to enter the tent." Hafsa asked the permission of Aisha to pitch a tent for her and she allowed her and she pitched her tent. When Zainab (another wife) saw it, she pitched another tent. In the morning the Prophet noticed the tents. He said, 'What is this?" He was told of the whole situation. Then the Prophet said, "Do you think that they intended to do righteousness by doing this?" He therefore abandoned the Itikaf in that month and practiced Itikaf for ten days later.*

Mohammed is on his death bed. Here we have a record of a lifelong tension between Aisha and Hafsa.

> [B1,11,647;B1,11,684;B9,92,406]
>
> *Narrated Aisha:*
>
> *When Mohammed was in his illness said, "Tell Abu Bakr to lead the people in prayer." I said to him, "If Abu Bakr stands in your place, the people would not hear him owing to his excessive weeping. So please order Umar to lead the prayer."*
>
> *Aisha added, I said to Hafsa, "Say to him: If Abu Bakr should lead the people in the prayer in your place, the people would not be able to hear him owing to his weeping; so please, order Umar to lead the prayer." Hafsa did so but Allah's Apostle said, "Keep quiet! You are verily the Companions of Joseph [a betrayer]. Tell Abu Bakr to lead the people in the prayer. " Hafsa said to Aisha, "I never got anything good from you."*

Since a verse of the Koran related to Zainab, she lorded this over the other wives.

> [B9,93,517]
>
> *The Verse of Al-Hijab (veiling of women) was revealed in connection with Zainab bint Jahsh. On the day of her marriage with the Prophet, he gave a wedding banquet with bread and meat; and she used to boast before other wives of the Prophet and used to say, "Allah married me to the Prophet in the Heavens."*

The next hadith reflects how jealousy plays a part in polygamy.

[B8,77,598;B7,62,82]

Mohammed said, "No woman should ask for the divorce of her Muslim sister in order to take her place, but she should marry the man without compelling him to divorce his other wife, for she will have nothing but what Allah has written for her."

This is the Sunna of Mohammed

MOHAMMED'S FAMILY LIFE

CHAPTER 8

48:13 We have prepared a blazing Fire for these kafirs who do not believe in Allah and His Messenger.

- Mohammed's favorite wife, the young Aisha, was left behind during a jihad raid and she wound up being in the company of a young Muslim man for a day. Gossip raged and accusations were whispered. The Koran finally settled the issue.
- Mohammed did not like to spend money on his family and his wives complained.
- Mohammed's devotion to his new favorite sexual partner, a Christian slave, caused an uproar among his wives.
- Mohammed fell in love with his daughter-in-law. The Koran changed Islamic marriage law so he could marry her.

Mohammed had many wives. He is the perfect model for the Muslim husband, except other Muslims are limited to four wives at a time. The Koran goes into detail about his romances.

THE LIE

When Mohammed went on his missions to attack those who resisted Islam, he took one of his wives with him. Which one got to go was determined by lots. Mohammed took Aisha with him on this trip to fight in Allah's cause in attacking the Mustaliq tribe.

I731 Now there was a problem in taking one of Mohammed's wives on an expedition and that was privacy. By now the veil had been prescribed for his wives. So the wife was not supposed to be seen or heard. To accomplish this a light cloth-covered howdah was used. Basically this was a box with a seat that could be mounted on a camel's saddle. On the way back on the expedition Aisha had gone out in the morning to relieve herself. When she got back she discovered that she had lost a necklace and went back to find it. The tent had been struck and the men in charge loaded the howdah on the camel and off they went without Aisha.

I732 When Aisha got back the entire group had moved on. She returned on a camel lead by a young Muslim who had lagged behind the main body and brought her back to Medina.

I732 Tongues began to wag, imaginations worked overtime and gossip spread. Aisha fell ill and was bedridden for three weeks.

I734-5 Tempers flared and men offered to kill the gossips. Something had to be done. Mohammed asked for advice from Ali, who said, "Women are plentiful and you can easily exchange one for the other. Ask the slave girl, she will tell the truth." So Mohammed called in the slave girl and stood by while Ali severely beat her. Ali said, "Tell the apostle the truth." The slave said that she knew of nothing bad about Aisha except she could be lazy about house work.

In the end the innocence or guilt of Aisha was determined by revelation in the Koran which to this day is the Sharia (Islamic law) about adultery.

> 24:1 *A sura [chapter] which We have sent down and ordained, and in which We give you clear signs so that you will take warning. The man and woman who commit adultery should each be beaten with a hundred lashes, and do not let your pity for them prevent you from obeying Allah. If you believe in Allah and the Last Day, then allow some of the believers to witness their punishment. An adulterer can only marry an adulteress or a kafir, and a adulteress cannot marry anyone other than an adulterer or a kafir. Such marriages are forbidden for believers.*
> 24:4 *Those who make accusations against honorable women and are unable to produce four witnesses should be given eighty lashes. Thereafter, do not accept their testimony, for they are terrible sinners, except those who repent afterwards and live righteously. Allah is truly forgiving and merciful.*
> 24:6 *If a husband accuses his wife of adultery but he has no witnesses other than himself, his evidence can be accepted if he swears by Allah four times that he is telling the truth and then calls down Allah's curse upon him if he is lying. If, however, the wife swears by Allah four times that she is innocent and calls Allah's curse down upon herself if she is lying, then she should not be punished.*
> 24:10 *If it were not for Allah's grace and mercy towards you and that Allah is wise, this would not have been revealed to you.*
> 24:11 *Truly there is a group among you who spread that lie, but do not think of it as a bad thing for you for it has proved to be advantageous for you. Every one of them will receive the punishment they have earned. Those who spread the gossip will receive a torturous punishment.*
> 24:12 *Why did the believing men and women, when they heard this, not think better of their own people and say, "This is an obvious lie"? Why*

did they not bring four witnesses? And because they could not find any witnesses, they are surely liars in Allah's sight.

24:14 *If it were not for Allah's goodness towards you and His mercy in this world and the world to come, you would have been severely punished for the lie you spread. You [the Muslims] gossiped about things you knew nothing about. You may have thought it to be only a light matter, but it was a most serious one in Allah's sight. And why, when you heard it, did you not say, "It is not right for us to talk about this. Oh, Allah! This is a serious sin." Allah warns you never to repeat this if you are true believers. Allah makes His signs clear to you, for Allah is all-knowing, wise. Those who take pleasure in spreading foul rumors about the faithful will be severely punished in this world and the world to come. And Allah knows, while you do not.*

24:20 *If it were not for Allah's grace and mercy towards you, you would have been punished long ago, but know that Allah is kind and merciful.*

24:21 *Believers, do not follow in Satan's footsteps for those who do so will be commanded to commit shameful and evil acts. If it were not for Allah's grace, not one of you would be pure. And Allah purifies those He pleases, and Allah is all-hearing.*

24:22 *And do not allow those among you who are wealthy and have many possessions to swear that they will not give to their family, the poor, and those who have fled their homes for Allah's cause [jihad]. Instead, let them be forgiving and indulgent. Do you not want Allah to show you forgiveness? Allah is forgiving and merciful.*

24:23 *Truly, those who carelessly slander believing women will be cursed in this world and the world to come. Their own tongues, hands, and feet will one day testify against them concerning their own actions. On that day Allah will give them what they have earned, and they will know that Allah is the clear truth.*

Since there were not four witnesses, then there was no adultery and the gossips got eighty lashes.

I736 But the scandal did not end here. One of those who got flogged for gossip was a poet and propagandist for the Muslim cause. The young warrior who led Aisha's camel was in a poem written by the poet and was offended. So he took his sword and cut the poet badly. The poet and his friends managed to bind the young warrior and take him to Mohammed. Mohammed wanted this to all go away. He gave the wounded poet a nice home and a Christian slave girl of pleasure as compensation for the sword blow.

FINANCIAL ARGUMENTS

Islam was no longer poor, indeed, the money from jihad poured in. But Mohammed was a simple man and had no attraction to money. Hence, his household was poor and the wives complained.

[B6,60,10]

When Umar heard that Mohammed was upset with some of his wives, he came to them and said, "You should stop troubling the Prophet or else Allah will give His Apostle better wives than you." After this, the Koranic verse 66.5 was revealed.

33:28 *Messenger! Say to your wives, "If you desire a life of this world and all its glittering adornment, then come. I will provide for you and release you with honor. If, however, you seek Allah and His Messenger and the world to come, then know that Allah has prepared a great reward for those of you who do good works.*

33:30 *Wives of the Messenger! If any of you are proven guilty of public indecency, then you will be doubly punished; that is easy for Allah. But those of you who obey Allah and His Messenger and do good works will be doubly rewarded. We have prepared honorable provisions for you.*

33:32 *Wives of the Messenger! You are not like any other women. If you fear Allah, then do not be too lax in your speech for fear that lecherous-hearted men will lust after you. Stay in your homes and do not go out in public dressed in your fine clothes as they did in the time of ignorance [all non-Islamic history, civilization and customs are of the time of ignorance], but pray regularly, pay the poor tax and obey Allah and His Messenger. It is Allah's desire to remove all that is unclean from you, People of His House, and to make you pure. And remember what is said to you in your homes of Allah's revelations and wisdom, for surely Allah knows all mysteries and is aware of all.*

33:35 *Allah has prepared forgiveness and a great reward for the men and women who submit to Him and believe, who are devout, truthful, patient, humble, generous, and pure; who fast, are modest, and always remember Allah.*

33:50 *Messenger! We allow you your wives whose dowries you have paid, and the slave-girls Allah has granted you as spoils of war, and the daughters of your paternal and maternal uncles and aunts who fled with you to Medina, and any believing woman who gives herself to the Messenger, if the Messenger wishes to marry her. This is a privilege for you only, not for any other believer. We know what We have commanded the believers concerning wives and slave-girls. We give you this privilege so you will be free from blame. Allah is forgiving and merciful!*

> 33:51 *You may turn away any of them that you please, and take to your bed whomever you please, and you will not be blamed for desiring one you had previously set aside for a time. Therefore, it will be easier for you to comfort them and prevent their grief and to be content with what you give each of them. Allah knows what is in your hearts, and Allah is all-knowing and gracious.*
> 33:52 *It will be unlawful for you to marry more wives after this or to exchange them for other wives, even though you are attracted by their beauty, except slave-girls you own. Allah watches over all things.*

Mohammed's wives were declared by the Koran to be the "mothers of Islam". Being every Muslim's mother meant they could not marry after Mohammed's death.

> 33:6 *The Messenger is more closely related to the believers than they are to themselves, and his wives are like their mothers. Allah decrees that those who are related by blood are closer to each other than other believers, and are closer than those who have fled their country [left Mecca to come to Medina] for Islam, but showing kindness to fellow believers is decreed by Allah.*

MARRIAGE TO HIS DAUGHTER-IN-LAW

M290 Mohammed had an adopted son, Zaid, and went by his house. Zaid was not there and Mohammed went on in the house. He wound up seeing his daughter-in-law, Zeinab, in a thin dress, and her charms were evident. Mohammed was smitten and said, "Gracious Lord! Good Heavens! How thou dost turn the hearts of men!"

M290 Well, Zeinab, had turned the head of the future king of Arabia and she told her husband what Mohammed said. The step-son went to Mohammed and said that he would divorce Zeinab so he could have her. Mohammed said no. But Zaid went ahead and divorced her anyway. In Arabia a union between a man and his daughter-in-law was incest and forbidden. But while Mohammed was with Aisha, he had a revelation and said, "Who will go and congratulate Zeinab and tell her that Allah has blessed our marriage?" The maid went right off to tell her of the good news. So Mohammed added another wife.

> 33:4 *Allah has not given any man two hearts for one body, nor has He made your wives whom you divorce to be like your mothers, nor has He made your adopted sons like your real sons. [Previous to this verse, an Arab's adopted children were treated as blood children. This verse relates to verse 37 of this sura.] These are only words you speak with your mouths, but Allah speaks the truth and guides to the right path. Name your*

adopted sons after their real fathers; this is more just in Allah's sight. But if you do not know their fathers' names, call them your brothers in the faith and your friends. There will be no blame on you if you sin unintentionally, but that which you intend in your heart will be held against you. Allah is forgiving and merciful.

33:36 *And it is not the place of a believer, either man or woman, to have a choice in his or her affairs when Allah and His Messenger have decided on a matter. Those who disobey Allah and His Messenger are clearly on the wrong path. And remember when you said to your adopted son [Zaid], the one who had received Allah's favor [converted to Islam], "Keep your wife to yourself and fear Allah," and you hid in your heart what Allah was to reveal, and you feared men [what people would say if he married his daughter-in-law], when it would have been right that you should fear Allah. And when Zaid divorced his wife, We gave her to you as your wife, so it would not be a sin for believers to marry the wives of their adopted sons, after they have divorced them. And Allah's will must be carried out.*

33:38 *The Messenger will not be blamed for anything that Allah has given him permission to do. This was Allah's way with the messengers who came before you, and Allah's commands are absolute. The messengers fulfilled Allah's mission and feared Him, and feared no one but Allah. Allah takes sufficient account. Mohammed is not the father of any man among you. He is Allah's Messenger and the last of the messengers. Allah knows all things.*

Since Zaid was adopted, he was not really a son, so there was no incest.

[B9,93,516]

Zaid, Mohammed's step-son, came to Mohammed complaining about his wife. The Prophet kept on saying to him, "Be afraid of Allah and keep your wife."

Aisha said, "If Allah's Apostle were to conceal anything of the Koran he would have concealed this verse [33:36, above]."

Zainab used to boast before the wives of the Prophet and used to say, "You were given in marriage by your families, while I was married to the Prophet by Allah from over seven Heavens."

FATIMA

Mohammed had several children, but none of them survived him except for Fatima, the daughter of his first wife, Khadija.

[B1,4,228;B1,6,303;B1,6,322;B1,6,324]

Fatima asked the Prophet, "I have persistent bleeding in between the periods and do not become clean. Shall I give up prayers?" He replied, "No, this is from a blood vessel. Give up the prayers only for the days on which you usually get the menses and then take a bath and offer your prayers."

[B3,47,783]

Once, Mohammed refused to enter Fatima's house because he saw a decorated curtain on her door, saying, "I am not interested in worldly things." Following Mohammed's instruction, Fatima sent the curtain to some needy people.

[B5,57,55;B8,75,330]

When Fatima requested that Mohammed give her a servant to relieve her of hand-mill duties, he said to her, "When you go to bed, say, 'Allahu-Akbar' thirty-four times, and 'Subhan Allah thirty-three times, and 'Alhamdu-lillah thirty-three times, for that is better for you than a servant."

[B4,56,819;B4,56,819;B5,57,62]

When Mohammed was in the midst of his fatal illness, he called his daughter Fatima and told her a secret that made her weep. Then he called her and told her another secret, and she started laughing. When asked what made her weep and laugh, she replied, "The Prophet told me that he would die in his fatal illness, and so I wept, but then he secretly told me that from amongst his family, I would be the first to join him, and so I laughed."

The hadith above is touching, but after Mohammed died, Fatima was very angry that Mohammed did not leave her any inheritance. She stayed angry until she died.

[B4,53,325;B5,57,60;B5,59,546;B8,80,718]

After Mohammed died, his daughter Fatima asked Abu Bakr to give her a share of Mohammed's estate. Abu Bakr explained that Mohammed had ordered that his property be donated to charity, so Fatima became angry and stopped speaking to him. She kept this attitude until she died six months later.

This is the Sunna of Mohammed

WOMEN OF THE BIBLE

CHAPTER 9

24:52 It is such as obey Allah and His Apostle, and fear Allah and do right, that will win (in the end).

There are stories in the Koran with the same cast of characters as those of the Jewish Torah. However, the stories do not have the same purpose or objective. According to Islam, the stories in the Jewish scriptures are different because they are corrupt and in error. The Koran gives the correct version of the stories.

JOSEPH

One of the Jewish stories is that of Joseph. It contains the theme of the power of woman as a deceiver and sexual predator. Islamic law is designed to keep women's sexuality under control.

Joseph's brothers were jealous of him and by deceit managed to get him sold as a slave into Egypt. Joseph wound up as a servant in an Egyptian's home. The Egyptian's wife was sexually attracted to Joseph.

> 12:23 ***The mistress of his home developed a passion for Joseph, and she shut the doors and said, "Come here." He said, "Allah keep me! Your husband has given me a good home and treated me honorably no good comes to wrongdoers." Still, she desired him, and he would have longed for her if he had not seen the signs from his Lord. So We ordered that We might turn him away from all evil and indecency for he was one of Our sincere servants.***
>
> 12:25 ***They both raced to the door, and she tore his shirt from behind, and they met her husband at the door. She said, "What is the punishment to him who would do evil to your wife? Prison or a painful doom?"***
>
> 12:26 ***Joseph said, "It was she who asked me to commit an evil act." One from her own family bore witness: "If his shirt is torn in front, then she speaks truth, and he is a liar. But if his shirt be torn behind, she lies and he is true."***
>
> 12:28 ***So when his lord saw his shirt torn behind, he said, "This is a device of you women. Your devices are great, "Joseph, leave this affair. Wife, ask pardon for your crime, for you have sinned."***

> 12:30 *The women in the city said, "The wife of the Prince is trying to seduce her servant. He has inspired her with his love, but we clearly see she is going astray." And when she heard of their spiteful talk, she sent for them and prepared a banquet for them and gave each one of them a knife. She said, "Joseph, show yourself." When they saw him, they were amazed and cut their hands and said, "Allah keep us. This is no man. This is a noble angel." She said, "This is the man about whom you blamed me. I tried to seduce him from his true self, but he stood firm. Now, if he does not obey my command, he will surely be cast into prison and become one of the despised."*

Joseph is unjustly imprisoned but is released when he is able to interpret the Pharaoh's disturbing dream. The wife is then revealed as the liar and a temptress.

> 12:50 *The King said, "Bring him to me." And when the messenger returned, Joseph said, "Go back to your lord, and ask him what is the case of the women who cut their hands, for my lord well knows the snare they laid."*
>
> 12:51 *The King sent for the women and asked, "What happened when you tried to seduce Joseph?" They said, "Allah keep us. We do not know any evil against him." The wife said, "Now the truth appears. It was I who tried to seduce him. He is most surely one of the truthful ones."*

SOLOMON

This is a story about Solomon and the queen of Saba (Sheba). Solomon had magical powers. He could understand the birds' language, had power over the jinns (spirits of good and bad) and work iron like it was clay. These powers play a part in this story.

The story starts with Solomon calling the birds together.

> 27:20 *He reviewed the birds and said, "Why do I not see the lapwing [hoopoe]? Is he one of those absent? I will certainly punish him severely or even kill him if he does not have a good excuse." But the lapwing was not far behind, and he said, "I have discovered something you are unaware of, and I come to you from Saba [a kingdom of South Arabia] with good news. I have found out that they are ruled by a woman, and she has been given great wealth and has a mighty throne. I discovered her and her peoples worshipping the sun instead of Allah. Satan has made their actions seem pleasing in their minds and has prevented them from finding the true path so they receive no guidance. They do not worship Allah, Who brings forth what is hidden in the heavens and the earth, and Who knows what you hide and what you admit. There is no god, but Allah! Lord of the glorious throne!"*

27:27 *Solomon said, "We shall soon see whether you are telling the truth, or not. Take and deliver my letter to them; then turn away from them and wait for their answer."*
27:29 *The queen said, "My chiefs, a noble letter has been delivered to me. It is from Solomon and it says, "In the name of Allah, most gracious, most merciful. Do not be arrogant against me, but instead come and submit to me."*
27:32 *She said, "My counselors, give me advice. I never decide an issue without your advice."*
27:33 *They said, "We are strong, willing, and brave, but the power is in your hands. Tell us what you want us to do."*
27:34 *She replied, "Typically, when kings enter a city, they pillage and humiliate its leading citizens. These people will do the same. I will send them a gift and wait until my ambassadors return with their response."*

While the queen is visiting Solomon, he has her throne magically brought to his palace. "Disguising her throne", means that her religious symbols were removed from it. He tricks her into showing her legs, a sexual provocation, and causes her to sin. It is the act, not the intention that counts in Islam.

27:41 *He said, "Disguise her throne so that it is unrecognizable. We will see whether or not she has guidance."*
27:42 *When she arrived, she was asked, "Is this your throne?" She replied, "It seems to be the same." Solomon said, "We received knowledge long before she, and we have submitted to Allah." And he persuaded her from worshiping others besides Allah because she came from a people who had no faith.*
27:44 *It was said to her, "Enter the palace." When she saw it, she thought it was a pool of water, and she pulled up her garment and bared her legs. Solomon said, "It is a palace paved with glass." She said, "Lord, I have sinned against my soul. I submit with Solomon to the Lord of the worlds."*

Here we have more about Solomon and magic. There is a deep undercurrent of magic in the religious doctrine of Islam. Mohammed warned about the evil eye and demons harming humans. The Koran speaks at length about jinns. Jinns have a soul and are made of fire. They can work to help or harm humans.

The Hadith has a story about magic being worked against Mohammed's sexuality. Here we have a Koran verse about how magic can be worked against a husband and wife.

2:102 *They followed what the evil ones read against the kingdom of Solomon. It was not Solomon who was a kafir, but the evil ones teaching people sorcery and that which was revealed in Babylon to the angels Harut and Marut [The angels Harut and Marut were sent down from heaven to be tempted. They sinned and will be punished on Judgment Day. Until then they teach magic]. But neither of them instructed the people without first saying, "Truly we are only sent to tempt you; therefore, do not become disbelievers." And from the two angels they learned how to create animosity between husbands and wives, although they cannot cause harm unless it is Allah's will, and they learned what would harm them and what did not benefit them. And surely they know that those who bought into the sorcery would have no part in the life to come! And the price for which they sold their souls was vile; if they had only known! If they had kept their faith and guarded against evil, their reward from Allah would certainly have been better, if they had only realized!*

LOT'S WIFE

Lot's wife was destroyed by the decree of Allah. The Koran is very clear that Allah can, and will, arbitrarily punish people.

27:54 *And remember what Lot said when We sent him to his people, "What? Will you act wickedly even though you see that it is wrong? Will you really lust after men rather than women? You are certainly an ignorant people." And the only answer that his people gave was: "Expel Lot and his family from your city. They wish to remain pure!" But We saved him and his family except his wife. We decreed that she would be one of those who lingered behind. And We rained down a shower of brimstone upon the others, and this rain was fatal for those who had been warned, but who did not take heed.*

RELIGIOUS LAW & CUSTOM

CHAPTER 10

72:23 Those who rebel against Allah and His apostle have the fire of Hell, and they will remain there forever!

- In Paradise men will have perfect sexual partners called houris as well as their wives.
- A woman's religious practice depends upon her menstrual cycle.
- How long a woman may morn for the dead is regulated.
- The virginity of a Muslim woman is sacrosanct.

HOURIS

Since ***houris*** are the female companions in Paradise, the houri could be considered the ideal woman. A houri is a companion of sexual pleasure, with large dark eyes, a perpetual virgin, same age, chaste (won't ever be with another man), voluptuous, beautiful, light-skinned, modest and won't look you in the eye. A houri will never say no and men will have more than one of them. Houris are not intellectual; they only serve. A houri is perfect for a Muslim man's *ghira* (honor, self respect, sacred jealousy). There is no such thing as a male houri as an ideal companion for women.

> 52:17 ***But those who have feared Allah will live pleasantly amid Gardens, rejoicing in what their Lord has given them, and what their Lord has protected them from, saying, "Eat and drink in health as a reward for your good deeds." They will recline on arranged couches, and We will marry them to dark-eyed houris [beautiful companions of pleasure].***

> 56:10 ***The people who were foremost on earth [the first to follow Mohammed], they will be foremost in the hereafter. A large number of those who lived before are the people who will be brought close to Allah, in Gardens of delight. A few of those who lived later [after Islam was well established] will be on decorated couches, reclining on them face to face. They will be waited on by immortal young boys with goblets and ewers and a cup of pure wine that gives no headache nor muddles the mind, and with fruits that are most pleasing, and with the flesh of birds that they desire.***

In compensation for their past good deeds, they will have houris with big, dark eyes like pearls peeking from their shells. They will not hear any vain or sinful talk, only the cry, "Peace! Peace!"
56:27 *The people of the right-hand—Oh! How happy the people of the right-hand will be resting on raised couches amid thornless sidrahs [plum trees] and talh trees [banana trees], thick with fruit, and in extended shade and constantly flowing waters, and abundant fruits, neither forbidden nor out of reach. And We have specially made for them houris, companions, chaste and pure virgins, lovers and friends of equal age with them for the people of the right hand, a large number of the people of old, and a large number of the people of the latter generations.*

78:31 *But the Allah-fearing will be fulfilled with enclosed Gardens and vineyards and voluptuous women of equal age [houris] and a full cup [of wine that produces no hangover]. No vain or false talk will be heard there. A reward from your Lord and a fitting gift!*

37:37 *No! He [Mohammed] comes truthfully and confirms the prophets of old. You will surely taste the painful punishment, and you will be punished for what you have done, all except the sincere servants of Allah! They will have a fixed banquet of fruits; and they will be honored in the Garden of delight, facing one another on couches. A cup filled from a gushing spring will be passed among them, crystal clear and delicious to those who drink. It causes neither pain nor intoxication. And with them are companions [houris] with large eyes and modest glances, fair like a sheltered egg. They will ask one another questions. One of them will say, "I had a close friend who said, 'Are you one of those who accept the truth? What? When we have died, and become dust and bones, will we really be judged?'"*

44:51 *The righteous, however, will live in a protected place among gardens and fountains, facing one another and dressed in richly brocaded fine silk. This is how it will be. We will marry them to beautiful virgins with big dark eyes [houris]. There they can call for any kind of fruit in comfort and safety. They have only the first death there, and Allah will save them from the pains of Hell. It is the gracious gift of your Lord! This is the supreme achievement.*

The houris are so fair that they are almost transparent.

[B4,54,468;B4,54,469;B4,54,476;B4,55,544]

Mohammed said, "The first group of people who will enter Paradise will be glittering like the moon when it is full. They will not spit or blow their noses or relieve nature. Their utensils will be of gold and their combs of gold and silver; in their centers the aloe wood will be used, and their sweat will smell like musk. Every one of them will have two wives; the marrow of the bones of the wives' legs will be seen through the flesh of excessive beauty. They will neither have differences nor hatred amongst themselves; their hearts will be as if one heart and they will be glorifying Allah in the morning and in the evening."

HAJJ—PILGRIMAGE

[B1,8,389;B2,26,596;B2,26,690;B2,26,708;B3,28,45;B3,28,46;B3,31,118;B3,31,128]

Following Mohammed's example, it is not permitted for a pilgrim at Mecca to engage in sex with his wife until he has finished certain rituals.

Mohammed himself said, "Whoever performs Hajj for Allah's pleasure, refrains from sexual relations with his wife, and does not commit evil or sins, will return as if he were born anew."

Mohammed has said that those fasting in general should avoid sexual relations with their wives, as well as other pleasures and quarreling. According to Mohammed, "There are two pleasures for the fasting person: one at the time of breaking his fast, and the other at the time when he will meet his Lord; then he will be pleased because of his fasting."

[B1,6,318;B1,6,325;B1,6,326;B2,26,810;B3,31,172]

Menstruating women are allowed to leave in the middle of pilgrimages to Mecca if they have completed the ritual circling of the Kabah. A woman should also not pray or fast during menstruation, and Mohammed said that this is the defect in her religion.

[B2,26,789;B2,26,812;B2,26,813;B2,26,814;B2,26,815;B2,26,823;B7,63,246;B8,73,178]

While on pilgrimage to Mecca, menstruating women were allowed to leave if they had completed the Tawaf-al-Ifada. This occurred with Safiya, and Mohammed allowed her to leave only because she had circumambulated the Kabah.

[B3,29,64]

When asked about the clothing of those in the state of Ihram, Mohammed said, "The Muhrima should not cover her face or wear gloves."

[B2,26,589;B3,29,77;B3,29,79;B3,31,174;B4,51,22;B4,51,23;B9,92,418]

A woman of the tribe of Khatham came to Mohammed and said that the obligation of Hajj had come upon her father, but that he was old and weak. She asked if she could perform the Hajj on his behalf, and Mohammed replied that she could.

A woman of the tribe of Juhaina said that her mother had vowed to perform Hajj, but died before doing so. She asked if she could perform it on her mother's behalf. Mohammed said, "Perform Hajj on her behalf. Had there been a debt on your mother, would you have paid it or not? So, pay Allah's debt as He has more right to be paid."

Mohammed has likewise said that one could fast for another if he died before the fasting could be finished, and that one could give charity on behalf of a dead parent.

FUNERALS

[B1,6,310;B2,23,369;B2,23,370;B2,23,371;B7,63,251;B7,63,252;B7,63,254;B7,63,255;B7,63,257;B7,71,607]

Mohammed decreed, "It is not lawful for a lady who believes in Allah and the Last Day to mourn for any dead person for more than three days except for her husband, for whom she should mourn for four months and ten days."

They were allowed to apply light perfumes at the time of the bath following menses, however.

A woman once asked if her daughter, who was mourning for her husband, could apply kohl to her diseased eyes. Allah said that this was forbidden, and explained how things were worse in the days before Islam: a wife bereft of her husband would live in a small wretched room, put on the worst clothes she had, and refrain from applying any scents or ointments for an entire year. After a year, she would rub her body against an animal, and then throw a globe of dung given to her; after this, she could apply scents.

[B2,23,440]

The funeral prayer should be offered for every child even if he were the son of a prostitute, as he was born with a true faith in Islam. If his parents were Muslims, or even just the father, and a child was born alive, then a funeral prayer must be offered at his death.

[B2,23,370;B2,23,371,B7,63,251]

Narrated Zainab bint Abi Salama :

I went to Um Habiba, the wife of Prophet, who said, "I heard the Prophets saying, 'It is not legal for a woman who believes in Allah and the Last Day to mourn for any dead person for more than three days except for her husband, (for whom she should mourn) for four months and ten days'." Later I went to Zainab bint Jahsh when her brother died; she asked for some scent, and after using it she said, "I am not in need of scent but I heard Allah's Apostle saying, 'It is not legal for a woman who believes in Allah and the Last Day to mourn for more than three days for any dead person except her husband, (for whom she should mourn) for four months and ten days.' "

MISCELLANEOUS

[B1,3,101;2,23,341;B9,92,413]

Some women asked Mohammed to fix a day for them to consult him, as the men were taking all his time. So he promised them one of his days for their religious lessons and commandments. Once during such a lesson Mohammed said, "A woman whose three children die before puberty will be shielded by them from the Hell fire." On that a woman asked, "If only two die?" She repeated her question twice, whereupon Mohammed said, "Even two, even two, even two!"

[B1,12,799;B1,12,809;B1,12,825;B1,12,829]

After Mohammed completed the prayer with Taslim, the women would get up immediately, and he would remain in place. After the women were all gone, Mohammed would get up and the men would do the same.

[B1,8,358;B1,12,778;B2,22,306]

The men used to pray with Mohammed with their izars (waist-cloths) tied around their necks as boys used to. Mohammed told the women not to raise their heads until the men sat straight.

[B2,22,295;B2,22,296]

Mohammed said that, when inviting the attention of the imam during prayer, saying "Subhan Allah" was appropriate for men and clapping hands was appropriate for women.

[B1,12,828]

According to Aisha, Mohammed had forbidden the women of the Jews from going to mosque.

[B1,381;B7,62,158;B7,69,483]

Mohammed said that among the portents of the Hour are (the following): Religious knowledge will be decreased by the deaths of religious learned men; religious ignorance will prevail; there will be a prevalence of open, illegal sexual intercourse; drinking of alcoholic drinks will be very common; women will increase in number and men will decrease in number so much so that fifty women will be looked after by one man.

[B3,31,156;B8,82,811]

A man came to Mohammed in a mosque seeking counsel after having sexual relations with his wife during the month of

Ramadan while fasting. To atone for this, Mohammed told him to give to charity. When the man said that he had nothing to give, Mohammed gave the man his own food and said to give that to charity. The man said that his family had nothing to eat, and so Mohammed allowed him to feed his own family with it.

4:12 *Half of what your wife leaves will be yours if she has no children, but if she has children, then a fourth of what she leaves will be yours, after paying inheritances and debts. And your wives will inherit a fourth of what you leave if you have no children, but if you have children, then they will receive an eighth of what you leave, after paying inheritances and debts. And if a man or a woman does not have either parents or children, and he or she has a sibling, each of them will inherit a sixth. If there are more than two siblings, then they will have a share in a third after payment of inheritances and debts, without incurring losses to anyone. This is a commandment from Allah; Allah is knowing and gracious!*

This is the Sunna of Mohammed

SACRED SLAVERY

THE SLAVE

CHAPTER 11

4:170 People! The Messenger has come to you with truth from your Lord. If you believe, it will be better for you.

- Slavery is part of the natural order of society and pleasing to Allah.
- After the jihad that captures the slaves is over, the slaves are to be treated well.
- Islam has a detailed language and legal code for the treatment of slaves.
- A good slave never tries to escape and honors his master.
- Freeing slaves brings merit to a Muslim.

SLAVERY IS NATURAL

The word slave is a positive one in Islam. Every Muslim is a slave of Allah. Mohammed was involved with every conceivable aspect of slavery. The word Islam means submission and a slave is the ultimate expression of submission.

> 2:23 ***If you doubt what We have revealed to Our slave [Mohammed], then write a sura comparable to it and call your gods other than Allah to help you if what you say is true.***

Bukhari has 42 references to Mohammed as the Slave of Allah.

> [B4,55,654]
> ***Umar heard the Prophet saying, "Do not exaggerate in praising me as the Christians praised the son of Mary, for I am only a slave. So, call me the Slave of Allah and His Apostle."***

Slavery is as natural as breathing in Islam. The word is never used in a negative way in the Koran, Sira or Hadith. Slavery is in the Sunna of Mohammed and part of the Koran.

Slaves are part of the natural order of society.

16:71 ***Allah has given more of His gifts of material things to some rather than others. In the same manner, those who have more do not give an equal share to their slaves so that they would share equally. Would they then deny the favors of Allah?***

DUALITY AND SUBMISSION

Duality is the only way to sustain slavery, and Islam has sustained slavery for 1400 years. Slavery is part of the sacred order. A believer, a Muslim, may not be enslaved. Only the unbelievers, kafirs, can be enslaved. The duality of believer/kafir divides all humanity. The kafirs are fair game and can be attacked, their protectors killed, their wealth taken and the remaining people enslaved. Slavery is Allah's way. If the slave converts to Islam, then freedom is a possibility.

There is one set of rules for Muslims and another set of rules for the kafirs. The only unifying rule in Islam is that every single human being must submit to Islam. Before that submission takes place the Muslim and the kafir have nothing in common.

Slavery is a supreme example of Islam's dualistic ethics and submission. Who submits more than a slave?

To understand this verse, you must remember that a Muslim may not be enslaved. The duality of slavery is clearly stated in the doctrine.

16:75 ***Allah gives you a parable. One man is a slave to another; he has no power. Another man has received many favors from Allah, and he spends from his wealth secretly and openly. Are the two men equal? Praise be to Allah. However, most do not understand.***

39:29 ***Allah sets forth a parable: "There is a slave who belongs to several partners and another slave owned by one man. Are the two in like circumstances?" No, Praise be to Allah. But most of them do not know.***

30:28 ***He gave you a parable that relates to yourselves: Do you equally share your wealth with any slave you own? Would you fear your slave as you would fear a free man? This is how We explain Our signs to those who understand. No, you do not. The wicked, without knowledge, pursue their base desires. But who can guide those whom Allah has allowed to go astray? There will be no one to help them.***

FREEING MUSLIM SLAVES

Freeing slaves has great merit and is approved in both the Koran and the Hadith. However, only slaves who convert are freed. So here we see the great power of Islamic slavery. Kafirs will become Muslims in order to be freed. If they don't convert then their children will.

However, merely converting to Islam after being enslaved does not mean the slave is to be freed. Converting is the first step, but the owner may, or may not, free the converted slave.

In the next verse, Allah gives Islam power over its captives.

> 8:70 ***Messenger! Tell the captives who are under your control, "If Allah finds good in your hearts [if the prisoners convert to Islam], He will give you something better than that which has been taken away from you, and He will show you forgiveness. Truly, Allah is forgiving and merciful." If, however, they plot to betray you, know that they have already betrayed Allah. He has therefore given you power over them. Allah is all-knowing and wise.***

Allah demands the freeing of a Muslim slave for the accidental killing of a Muslim.

> 4:92 ***A believer should never kill a Muslim unless an accident occurs. Whoever kills a fellow Muslim by accident must free one of his believing slaves and pay blood-money to the victim's family unless they give it to charity. If the victim was a believer from a people at war with you, then freeing a believing slave is enough. But if the victim was from a people with whom you have an alliance, then his family should be paid blood-money and a believing slave must be set free. For those who cannot afford to do this, they must fast for two months straight. This is the penance commanded by Allah. Allah is all-knowing and wise!***

Freedom from slavery only comes from submitting to Islam. Slavery changes a kafir into a Muslim. Hence, slavery is a moral good, since the kafir is evil and hated by Allah. Mohammed has total confidence that he can compensate his jihadists for their loss of the value of their captives, in the next jihad battle. Mohammed was always very confident about Islam's power in jihad.

> [B3,46,716;B3,47,778;B4,53,360]
>
> *When the delegates of the tribe of Hawazin came to the Prophet and they requested him to return their properties and captive women and children. The Prophet stood up and said to them, "I have other people with me in this matter (the other jihadists who were due their booty, including the value of the captives as slaves) and the most beloved statement to me is the true one. You may choose either the properties or the prisoners as I have delayed their distribution." The Prophet had waited for them for more than ten days since his arrival from Taif. So, when it became evident to*

them that the Prophet was not going to return them except one of the two, they said, "We choose our wives and children."

The Prophet got up amongst the people and glorified and praised Allah as He deserved and said, "Then after, these brethren (the men of the Hawazin became Muslims) of yours have come to us with repentance, and I see it logical to return them the captives. So, whoever amongst you likes to do that as a favor, then he can do it, and whoever of you likes to stick to his share till we recompense him from the very first war booty which Allah will give us, then he can give up the present captives."

The people unanimously said, "We will return the captives willingly." The Prophet said, "We do not know which of you has agreed to it and which have not, so go back and let your leaders forward us your decision." So, all the people then went back and discussed the matter with their leaders who returned and informed the Prophet that all the people had willingly given their consent to return the captives.

It is a moral good to free a Muslim slave.

B3,46,693

Mohammed said, "If a man frees a Muslim slave, Allah will free him from the fires of Hell in the same way that he freed the slave." Bin Marjana said that, after he related that revelation to Ali, the man freed a slave for whom he had been offered one thousand dinars by Abdullah.

The next story comes from the Sira when Islam first began. A Muslim slave is freed and replaced by a kafir.

I205 One day Abu Bakr passed by while they were thus ill-treating Bilal. He said to Umayya, 'Have you no fear of God that you treat this poor fellow like this? How long is it to go on?' He replied, 'You are the one who corrupted him, so save him from his plight that you see.' 'I will do so,' said Abu Bakr; '***I have got a black slave, tougher and stronger than he, who is a heathen.*** I will exchange him for Bilal.' The transaction was carried out, and Abu Bakr took him and freed him.

[B8,73,226]

Narrated Osama bin Zaid:

[...] When Allah's Apostle had fought the battle of Badr and Allah killed whomever He killed among the chiefs of the infidels, and Allah's Apostle and his companions had returned with victory and booty, bringing with them some of the chiefs of the infidels as captives.

'Abdullah and the idolators who were with him, said, "Islam has now triumphed, so give Allah's Apostle the pledge of allegiance and embrace Islam." Then they became Muslims and were freed.

Again, freedom comes only after submitting to Islam:

I875 During his session there ***some of the slaves besieged in al-Taif came to him and accepted Islam and he freed them.*** Abdullah said that when al-Taif surrendered, some of them talked about these lost slaves, but Mohammed refused to do anything saying that they were Allah's free men.

Another incident:

I878 The apostle asked about Malik and they said that he was in al-Taif. The apostle told them to tell Malik that ***if he came to him as a Muslim he would return his enslaved family and property to him and give him a hundred camels.*** He came out by night, mounted his horse, rode off to join the apostle, overtaking him in Mecca. Mohammed gave him back his family and property and gave him a hundred camels. He became an excellent Muslim.

Islam is very proud of the doctrine of how to treat slaves. Part of the good treatment of their slaves is freeing them.

90:8 ***Have we not given him eyes, and tongue, and lips, and guided him to the two highways?***
90:11 ***But he did not attempt the steep road. Who will teach you what the steep road is? It is to free a slave, or to give food during famine to the orphan of a relative, or to the pauper who lies in the dust. It is also, to be a believer and to urge perseverance and compassion upon one another. These are the people of the right hand.***

2:177 ***Righteousness is not determined by whether you face the east or the west. The one who is righteous believes in Allah, the Last Day, the angels, the Scripture, and the messengers; he gives his wealth for love of Allah to his family, to orphans, to the needy, to the wayfaring traveler, to the beggar, and for the ransom of slaves. The righteous one observes his prayers and pays the poor tax. The righteous one keeps his promises and stands firm in the face of suffering and hardship and war. These are the true believers, the Allah-fearing.***

58:3 ***Those who divorce their wives in this manner [an old Arabic custom of divorce was to say, "Be to me as my mother's back"] and afterwards recant their words, must free one of their slaves as a penalty before they can*** *touch one another again. You are commanded to do this. Allah is aware of all you do. And as for those who do not have a slave to free, they must fast for two consecutive months before they can touch each other. Those who are unable to fast must feed sixty poor people.*

[B3,31,157;B3,31,158;B3,47,772;B7,64,281;B8,73,110;B8,73,185;B8,79,700;B8,79,701;B8,79,702;B8,82,811d]

A man came to Mohammed and said, "I had sexual intercourse with my wife while fasting during Ramadan." Mohammed asked him, "Can you afford to manumit a slave?" He said he could not. Mohammed asked him, "Can you fast for two successive months?" He said no. He asked him, "Can you afford to feed sixty poor persons?" He said he could not.

Abu Huraira added: Then a basket full of dates was brought to the Mohammed and he said to the man, "Feed the poor with this by way of atonement." The man asked, "Should I feed it to people poorer than we? There is no poorer house than ours between Medina's mountains." Mohammed smiled and said, "Then feed your family with it."

[B4,54,514;B8,75,412]

Mohammed said, "If one says one hundred times a day: "None has the right to be worshipped but Allah, He Alone Who has no partners, to Him belongs Dominion and to Him belong all the Praises, and He has power over all things," he will be rewarded as if he had freed ten slaves, one hundred good deeds will be written in his account, one hundred bad deeds will be deducted from his account, and on that day he will be protected from the morning till evening from Satan. Nobody will be superior to him except one who has done more than he has."

BE GOOD TO YOUR SLAVES

It takes a lot of killing to persuade the survivors of a battle to become slaves. Jihad accomplishes this. Part of Islamic duality is the doctrine of how well captive slaves are to be treated after the violent jihad. Slavery is part of the sacred way of Islamic life.

4:36 *Worship Allah and do not acknowledge any as His equal. Be good to your parents, your relatives, to orphans, the poor, to neighbors both new and familiar, to fellow travelers, wayfarers, and the slaves you possess.*

The key to good treatment after capture is to convert to Islam. "If one has a brother under his command" is the operative phrase in this next verse.

[B3,46,721;B1,2,29]

Al-Ma'rur met Abu Dhar, and noticed that he and his slave were wearing similar cloaks. When Al-Ma'rur asked him about that, he replied, "Once I abused a man by calling his mother bad names, so he complained to the Prophet. Mohammed said to me, 'You still show some signs of ignorance. Your slaves are your brothers and Allah has given you authority over them. So, if one has a brother under his command (a Muslim slave), one should feed him what he himself eats and clothe him like himself. Do not ask slaves to do things beyond their abilities and if you do so, then help them.' "

CUSTOM

Islam has the most detailed slave code in the world. [See the last of this chapter to see the vocabulary that has been developed to handle the concepts of the slave culture.] Here are some of the sacred customs in dealing with slaves.

24:58 *Believers, let your slaves and children among you who have not yet come of age ask permission to come into your presence on three occasions: before the morning prayer, when you shed your clothes in the midday heat, and after the evening prayer. These are your three occasions for privacy. There is no blame on them if at other times when they are visiting, they come into your presence without permission.*

5:89 *Allah will not punish you for that which is unintentional in your oaths, but He will punish you in regard to an oath taken seriously. For atonement, feed ten poor persons with such middling food as you feed your own families, or clothe them, or free a slave. If you do not have the means for this, then fast for three days.*

24:31 *And tell the women who are believers that they should lower their eyes and guard their purity, and they should not display their beauty and adornments except that which is normally shown. They should cover their breasts with their veils and only show their adornments to their husband, father-in-law, sons, step-sons, brothers, nephews, or their female servants, eunuch slaves, and children who are innocent and do not notice a woman's nakedness.*

[B7,62,2]

Ursa asked Aisha about the verse:

4:3 If you fear that you will not be able to deal with orphan girls fairly, marry other women of your choice, two, or three, or four; but if you fear that you cannot treat them equally, then marry only one, or any of the slave-girls you have acquired. This will prevent you from being unjust.

Aisha said, "O my nephew! This Verse has been revealed in connection with an orphan girl whose guardian is attracted by her wealth and beauty and intends to marry her with a dowry less than what other women of her standard deserve. So they have been forbidden to marry them unless they do justice to them and give them their full dowry, and they are ordered to marry other women instead of them."

LEGAL

The slave has no means of redress, nor any basis for legal action of any sort. The slaves rights are all based upon the good will of its master.

The only way to gain any rights is to convert to Islam. Then some of the brotherhood rights can be claimed.

The reason for the tax exemption on horses was jihad. Mohammed gave cavalrymen three times the amount he gave foot soldiers from the spoils of war (the wealth of the vanquished) to build a better cavalry.

B2,24,542

Mohammed: "Horses and slaves owned by a Muslim are tax exempt."

Muslims could own shares of a slave, just like any other property.

[B3,44,671;B3,44,672;B3,44,681;B3,44,682;B3,46,697;B3,46,698;B3,46,699;B3,46,701;B3,46,702;B3,46,703;B3,46,704;B3,46,729]

Mohammed said, "Whoever manumits his share of a jointly possessed slave, it is imperative for him to free the slave completely by paying the remainder of the price. If he does not have sufficient money for that, then the price of the slave should be estimated justly, and the slave allowed to work and earn the amount that will free him without overburdening him."

An eye for an eye, a tooth for a tooth is the law of retaliation.

2:178 ***Believers! Retaliation is prescribed for you in the matter of murder: the free man for the free man, a slave for a slave, a female for a female. If the brother of the slain gives a measure of forgiveness, then grant him any sensible request, and compensate him with a generous payment [blood money].***

There are two ambiguities in this next verse. Do not use your slave-girls as prostitutes "if they wish to remain pure." And what if they don't want to remain pure? Also, there is a loophole, "Allah is merciful." Be all that as it may, the use of slaves for sex and prostitution was and is common in Islam.

24:33 *And for those who cannot afford to marry, let them stay pure until Allah fulfills their needs from His bounty. In regard to your slaves who wish to buy their freedom, grant it if you see there is good in them, and give them a part of the wealth that Allah has given you. Do not force your slave-girls into prostitution just to gain the wealth of this world if they wish to remain pure. Yet if they are forced to do so, then truly Allah will be merciful.*

MARRYING SLAVES

A Muslim slave is better in the Islamic hierarchy than a free kafir.

2:221 *You will not marry pagan women unless they accept the faith. A slave girl who believes is better than an idolatress, although the idolatress may please you more. Do not give your daughters away in marriage to kafirs until they believe. A slave who is a believer is better than an idolater, though the idolater may please you more. These lure you to the Fire, but Allah calls you to Paradise and forgiveness by His will. He makes His signs clear to mankind so that they may remember.*

24:32 *And marry those among you who are single, or an honorable male or female slave. And if they are poor, then Allah will give them riches from His own bounty. Allah is bountiful and all-knowing.*

4:25 *If any of you is not wealthy enough to marry a free, believing woman, then allow him to marry a believing slave-girl. Allah knows your faith well, and you come from one another. Marry them with their master's permission, and give them a fair dowry, given that they are chaste, honorable, and have not had lovers. If the slave you marry commits adultery after you are married, then their punishment should be half of that commanded for a free woman. This is a law for those among you who fear sinning, but it will be better for you if you abstain. Allah is forgiving and merciful!*

MOHAMMED AND THE SLAVE CODE

The examples of Mohammed's life form the basis of slave code.

[B3,46,695;B3,46,696;B2,18,163]

Mohammed ordered his followers to free slaves at the time of solar and lunar eclipses.

[B2,24,542;B2,24,543]

Mohammed said, "There is no tax on either a horse or a slave belonging to a Muslim"

[B2,25,579;B2,25,580;B2,25,587;B2,25,587]

Mohammed made it mandatory for every Muslim slave or free male or female – young or old – to pay a small tax, and he ordered that it be paid before the people went out to offer the 'Id prayer. [...]

Wala is the estate of the slave. When the slave dies their estate goes back to the one who freed them

[B3,34,378;B3,46,736;B8,80,749;B8,80,753;B8,80,748]

Mohammed, in forbidding the selling of the wala of slaves or giving it as a present, said: "The wala is for the liberator."

[B6,60,25;B8,80,732;B9,92,420;B9,83,44;B9,83,42;B9,83,42e]

Equality in punishment, called The Law of Retaliation was prescribed for Jews in the Bible, but the payment of blood money, was not ordained for them. Then, according to Mohammed, Allah declared that either blood money or equality in punishment (the free for the free, the slave for the slave, and the female for the female) is prescribed for Muslims in cases of murder.

[...]

[B3,34,362;B3,34,363;B3,46,731;B3,34,435]

Abu Huraira heard Mohammed saying, "If a slave-girl of yours commits illegal sexual intercourse and it is proved, she should be lashed, and after that nobody should blame her. If she commits illegal sexual intercourse the second time, she should be lashed and nobody should blame her after that. If she commits the offense for a third time and it is proved, she should be sold even for a hair rope."

[B9,86,100;B9,86,101]

Mohammed said, "A lady slave should not be given in marriage until she is consulted, and a virgin should not be given in marriage until her permission is granted." The people said, "How will she express her permission?" The Prophet said, "By keeping silent when asked her consent."

[...]

FREED SLAVES

Freed slaves run through the story of Islam. The *hima* is the common pasture of the Islamic state. At this time Umar is the caliph (ruler) and the hima is used for the livestock taken as a tax or taken in jihad. In order for this slave to be free, he had to become a Muslim.

[B4,52,292]

Umar appointed Hunai, his freed slave, to manage the hima. Umar told him, "Allow the shepherds with only a few camels or sheep to graze their animals, but do not allow livestock of the wealth to graze. If their livestock should perish, they have their farms and gardens to support them. But those who own only a few camels and sheep, if their livestock should perish, would bring their dependents to me and appeal for help. I could not ignore them and find it easier to let them have water and grass rather than to give them money from the Muslims' treasury."

The next hadith clearly identifies the freed slave as white. The race of a slave is always given, if the slave is not a Arab. Usually, the identified slave is black. This hadith also shows the moral structure of a Muslim oath. The question is, who determines whether the replacement for the oath is better? Conveniently, it the Muslim oath giver.

[B8,79,712]

Zahdam said: We were sitting with Abu Musa as we had ties of friendship and mutual favors between us. The meal was presented and there was chicken meat in it. Among those present was a white freed slave who did not eat. Abu Musa said to him, "Come along! I have seen Allah's Apostle eat chicken." The man said, "I have seen chickens eating something dirty, so I have taken an oath that I shall not eat them." Abu Musa said, "Listen, I will inform you about your oath:

"Once we went to Mohammed with a group of Ashairiyin, asking him for mounts while he was distributing some camels. Mohammed was in an angry mood at the time, and said 'By Allah! I will not give you mounts, and I have none.' After we had left, some camels of war treasure were brought to Allah's Apostle and he asked for us. We returned and he gave us five very fat good-looking camels. After we mounted them and went away, I said to my companions, Mohammed took an oath that he would not give us mounts, perhaps he forgot his oath. By Allah, we will never be successful, for we have taken advantage of the fact that Allah's Apostle forgot to fulfill his oath. So let us return and remind him.'

We returned and said, 'O Allah's Apostle! You took an oath that you would not give us mounts but later on you gave us mounts, and we thought that you have forgotten your oath.'

Mohammed said, 'Depart, for Allah has given you mounts. By Allah, Allah willing, if I take an oath and then later find another thing better than that, I do what is better, and make expiation for the oath.' "

A freed slave still is not fully free, but still has obligations to the master.

[B4,53,397;B8,80,747;B4,53,404;B3,30,94;B9,92,403]freedslavestillcontrolled

Ali delivered a sermon saying, "We have no book to recite except the Book of Allah and this written paper from the Prophet which contains legal verdicts regarding retaliation for wounds, the ages of the camels paid as tax or blood money, and the fact that Medina is a sanctuary. So, whoever commits heresy in it, or commits a sin or gives shelter to such a heretic in it will incur the Curse of Allah, the angels and all the people, and none of his compulsory or optional good deeds of worship will be accepted. And any freed slave who sides with people other than those masters who freed him, without permission from the latter, will incur the Curse of Allah, the angels and all the people, and his compulsory and optional good deeds of worship will not be accepted." ...

Wala is the estate that the slave accumulates. In short, Aisha, Mohammed's wife, would get whatever the slave had accumulated when the slave died. This is another example of how a freed slave is not as free as if they had never been enslaved. There is also a lesson in how many times a person is identified as a freed slave. It is a permanent attribute.

[B3,34,365:B3,46,737;B3,46,739;B8,79,708;B8,80,743;B7,65,341;B8,80,746;B8,80,750;B2,24,570;B3,47,752;B3,46,713;B3,46,735;B3,50,878;B3,50,889;B3,50,893;B8,80,751;B3,34,377;B3,34,364]

Aisha intended to buy the slave girl Barira in order to free her, but Barira's masters stipulated that after her death her wala would be for them. '

Aisha mentioned that to Mohammed who told her, "Buy her, as the wala is for the one who pays." He then called Barira and gave her the option of either staying with her husband or leaving him. Barira said she preferred her freedom to her husband. ...

[B3,46,707;B3,46,708]

When Abu Huraira and his slave set out intending to embrace Islam they lost each other on the way. Abu Huraira went to Mohammed and pledged allegiance to Islam. As he was sitting with Mohammed, his slave appeared and Mohammed said, "O Abu Huraira! Your slave has come back." Abu Huraira said, "Indeed, I would like you to witness that I free him for Allah's sake." Then he recited a poetic verse:- 'What a long, tedious, tiresome night! Nevertheless, it has delivered us from the land of disbelief.'

Here are two recollections of freed slaves. "Paradise is under the shade of swords" is the most poetic expression of jihad.

[B4,52,210;B4,52,266l]

Salim, Umar's freed slave and his clerk, said that Abdullah once wrote a letter to Umar. The letter said that Mohammed, in one of his military expeditions against the enemy, waited till the sun declined and then he got up amongst the people saying, "O people! Do not wish to meet the enemy, ask Allah for safety, and when you face the enemy, be patient and remember that Paradise is under the shades of swords."

Then he said, "O Allah, the Revealer of the Holy Book, and the Mover of the clouds and the Defeater of the clans, defeat them, and grant us victory over them."

[B8,75,342;B8,77,612]

Warrad, the freed slave of Al-Mughira, said that Muawiya wrote to Mughira. 'Write to me what you heard the Prophet saying at the end of every prayer after the Taslim.' So Al-Mughira dictated to me and said, "I heard the Prophet saying after the prayer, 'None has the right to be worshipped but Allah Alone Who has no partner. O Allah! No one can withhold what You give, and none can give what You withhold, and only good deeds are of value."

A GOOD SLAVE

A good slave is a Muslim and tries in every way to please his Muslim master.

[B3,46,723;B4,52,255:B4,55,655;B7,62,20]

Mohammed said, "Three persons will get a double reward:

A person who has a slave girl, educates her properly, teaches her good manners (without violence), then frees and marries her.

A man who believes in Jesus and then believes in me.

A slave who observes Allah's Rights and Obligations and is sincere to his master."

[B3,46,722;B3,46,726;B3,46,727]

Mohammed said, "If a slave is honest and faithful to his master and worships his Lord (Allah) in a perfect manner, he will get a double reward."

For a slave to flee his Islamic master is a sin against Allah.

> M001,0131
> ***Mohammed: "If a slave flees his master, Allah does not hear his prayer."***

The next story comes from the Sira. Washi is a kafir slave at the time of this battle. Washi was promised his freedom if he would kill Hamza, who had killed the owner's relative at an earlier battle. But after Mohammed had conquered Mecca, Washi had the good sense to submit to Islam. Hamza was Mohammed's uncle and only conversion saved his life.

Notice the reference to the Arabic custom of removing the clitoris of the Arab women.

> I564 The slave Washi. said, 'By God, I was looking at Hamza while he was killing men with his sword, sparing no one, when Siba came up to him before me, and Hamza said, "***Come here, you son of a female circumciser,***" and he struck him a blow so swiftly that it seemed to miss his head. I poised my javelin until I was sure that it would hit the mark, and launched it at him. It pierced the lower part of his body and came out between his legs. He came on towards me, but collapsed and fell. I left him there until he died, when I came and recovered my javelin. Then I went off to the camp, for I had no business with anyone but him.'

EUNUCHS

Before Islam, the Arabs had the custom of castrating slaves. After Islam was established, the castration was done by the slave trader outside of Islam. Muslims paid more for a eunuch since it could be used in the harem.

> 24:31 ***And tell the women who are believers that they should lower their eyes and guard their purity, and they should not display their beauty and adornments except that which is normally shown. They should cover their breasts with their veils and only show their adornments to their husband, father-in-law, sons, step-sons, brothers, nephews, or their female servants, eunuch slaves, and children who are innocent and do not notice a woman's nakedness. And do not let them stamp their feet so as to reveal their hidden adornments [ankle bracelets]. Believers, all of you turn to Allah and repent so that it will go well for you.***

The man in this story was a slave. In all probability, he was black, since African men were castrated, not by removing the testicles, but the penis and testicles.

M037, 6676

Anas reported that a person was charged with fornication with Mohammed's slave-girl. Mohammed said to Ali: Go and strike his neck. Ali came to him and he found him in a well making his body cool. Ali said to him: Come out, and as he took hold of his hand and brought him out, he found that his sexual organ had been cut. Ali refrained from striking his neck. He came to Mohammed and said: Allah's Messenger, he has not even the sexual organ with him.

LANGUAGE

Islam has a very detailed language for a complete and sophisticated system of slavery.

abd, a slave, usually a black slave. Abd is also the word for any African or any black person.

abiq, a fugitive slave.

amah, a female slave.

ghulam, a modern term for a slave.

ghurrah, a slave worth 500 dirhams.

ibaq, the freeing of slaves.

istilad, a legal term signifying that a Muslim master has freed a female slave who has born his child.

istibra, the waiting period for determining whether the slave is pregnant or not.

itaq, freeing a slave.

khaadim, a servant/slave.

kinn, a slave who is not mukatab, nor mudabbar, nor umm walad, nor mubaad, but entirely unfree.

kitaba, a form of a slave buying their freedom.

madhun lahu, a slave who can make business agreements for his master.

mamluk, a slave, usually a white slave.

ma malakat aimanukum, that which your right hand (the sword hand) possesses, a slave taken in jihad. Used in the Koran.

maula, a term used in Islamic law for a slave.

mubaad, a slave with several owners.

mudabbar, a slave who is freed on his master's death.

mukatab, slaves who ransom themselves from their master.

mustabad, slave.

mutaq, a freed slave.

mutiq, the master who frees a slave.

qinn, a slave born from slave parents.

raqabah, the term used for a captured slave.

raqiiq, slave.

surriyah, a non-Muslim woman slave used for sex. She may be bought, taken as a captive, or descended from a slave.

tadbir, a legal term for freeing a slave after the death of the master.

ubudiyah, slavery.

ummu al walad, a legal term for a slave who has borne the master's child.

umm walad, the enslaved mother married to a slave, who gives birth to his child.

wala when freed slaves die, their estate goes to the one who freed them.

zall, a fugitive child slave.

This is the Sunna of Mohammed

SEXUAL SLAVERY

CHAPTER 12

24:54 Say: Obey Allah and the Messenger.

- Having sex with your female slaves is a moral good.
- A married slave can be used for sex.
- The captives of jihad can be used for sex.
- Mohammed always got the pick of the captives to be used for sex.

For a Muslim to have sex with his slaves is in the same moral category as being humble, telling the truth or giving to charity. There is no blame and it is a moral good since it is allowed by the Koran. Allah only allows good. Sex with your slaves is only good for the male Muslim. Of course, for the female Muslim, it is a great sin.

There is a great advantage of having sex with slaves. None of the restrictions of sex apply to the slave, except for sex during the slave's menstrual period. Other than that, anything goes.

> 23:1 ***The successful ones will be the believers who are humble in their prayers who avoid vain conversation, who contribute to the needy, and who abstain from sex, except with their wives or slaves, in which case they are free from blame, but those who exceed these limits are sinners. Those who honor their promises and contracts and who pay strict attention to their prayers will inherit Paradise. They will dwell there forever.***

> 70:22 ***Not the devout, who pray constantly and whose wealth has a fixed portion set aside for beggars and the destitute, and those who believe in the Judgment Day, and those who fear their Lord's punishment—because no one is safe from their Lord's punishment—and who control their sexual desires, except with their wives or slave-girls, with them there is no blame; but whoever indulges their lust beyond this are transgressors), and who keep their trusts and promises, and who tell the truth, and who are attentive to their prayers. These will live with honors in Gardens.***

If the slave is married, then it is still morally good for a Muslim to have sex with her.

4:24 ***Also forbidden to you are married women unless they are your slaves. This is the command of Allah. Other than those mentioned, all other women are lawful to you to court with your wealth and with honorable intentions, not with lust. And give those you have slept with a dowry, as it is your duty. But after you have fulfilled your duty, it is not an offense to make additional agreements among you. Truly Allah is knowing and wise!***

The above verse was given at the time of the jihad at Khaybar. Mohammed attacked the Jews of Khaybar and conquered them. The Jews that survived were doomed to become ***dhimmis.*** A dhimmi is not a Muslim, but one who has agreed to do all things as Islam wishes. In this case the surviving Jews were to work the land and give half of the proceeds to the jihadists. In addition, some women were taken as sex slaves. Mohammed, after taking the most beautiful Jew for his own pleasure, laid out the rules for sex with the captives.

- The marriage of the captive woman is annulled, as per the above Koran verse.
- Don't rape a pregnant slave. Wait until she has delivered.
- Don' have sex with a woman who is having her period.

I758 Dihya had asked Mohammed for Safiya, and when he chose her for himself Mohammed gave Safiya's two cousins to Dihya in exchange. ***The women of Khaybar were distributed among the Muslims.***

I759 A man said, 'Let me tell you what I heard the apostle say on the day of Khaybar. He got up among us and said: "It is not lawful for a Muslim ***to mingle his seed with another man's [meaning to have sex with a pregnant woman among the captives], nor is it lawful for him to take her until he has made sure that she is in a state of cleanness [not having her period].***

Here we see that at first the jihadists were reluctant to have sex with the captive women because of their husbands being nearby. But the Koran established that it was not immoral for them to rape non-Muslim women because they had husbands.

M008, 3432

Mohammed sent an army to Autas and encountered the enemy and fought with them. Having overcome them and taken them captives, the Companions seemed to refrain from having intercourse with captive women because of their husbands being polytheists. Then Allah, Most High, sent down regarding that: "And women already married, except those whom your right

hands possess (iv. 24)" (i. e. they were lawful for them when their menstral period came to an end).

JIHAD AND SEXUAL SLAVERY

The use of women for sex after jihad is a constant in the Hadith and the Sira. Here the men are asking about ***coitus interruptus*** to avoid pregnancy in the sex slaves. If they were pregnant, they had no value on the market as a sex slave. A Muslim is not supposed to have sex with a woman who is carrying another man's child, as per the Koran.

[B3,34,432;B7,62,137;B8,77,600]

Once some of Mohammed's soldiers asked if it was acceptable to use *coitus interruptus* ***to avoid impregnating the female captives they had received as their share of the booty.***

Mohammed asked, "Do you really do that?" He repeated the question three times, then said: "It is better for you not to do it, for there is no soul which Allah has ordained to come into existence but will be created."

[B5,59,459:B3,46,718]

Ibn Muhairiza entered the Mosque and saw Abu Said and sat beside him and asked him about coitus interruptus. Abu Said said, "We went out with Allah's Apostle for jihad. We received captives and we desired women and celibacy became hard on us and we loved to do coitus interruptus. So when we intended to do coitus interruptus, we said, 'How can we do coitus interruptus before asking Allah's Apostle who is present among us?" We asked him about it and he said, 'It is better for you not to do so, for if any soul is predestined to exist, it will exist."

Mohammed instituted a temporary marriage of three days. Later this was canceled. However, the Shia Muslims still honor the temporary marriage.

[B6,60,139;B7,62,9;B7,62,130;]

Those who participated in the holy wars carried on by Mohammed had no wives throughout that time. They asked Mohammed, "Shall we castrate ourselves?" But he forbade them to do that and thereafter allowed them to marry women temporarily by giving them garments, and then he recited:

5:87 Oh, you who believe, do not forbid the good things that Allah allows you, but do not commit excess for Allah does not love those who commit excess.

Notice that Jadd assumes that the Muslims will be raping after they win the battle. That was the normal and expected behavior.

> I894 One day when Mohammed was making his arrangements for the upcoming battle and said to Jadd: 'Would you like to fight the B. Asfar, Jadd?' He replied, 'Will you allow me to stay behind and not tempt me, for everyone knows that I am strongly addicted to women and I am afraid that if I see the Byzantine women I shall not be able to control myself.'

> I689 When Saed reached Mohammed and the Muslims, the apostle told them to get up to greet their leader. Saed asked, 'Do you swear by Allah that you accept the judgment I pronounce on them?' They said 'Yes,' and he said, 'And is it incumbent on the one who is here?' looking in the direction of Mohammed, and Mohammed answered, 'Yes.' Saed said, 'Then I give judgment that the men should be killed, the property divided, and the women and children taken as captives.'

The Jewish women were later wholesaled by Mohammed to buy more horses and weapons for jihad.

If it were not for the cruelty of jihad, this next story has some humor. The female captive might bring a high ransom due to her high status. Mohammed said that he was going to return all of the captives at a price of six camels. Vyayna felt that she was worth more than that. His companions point out that she has no value for sex, she is not a virgin nor a plump matron.

> I878 Vyayna took an old woman of Hawazin as a captive and said as he took her, 'I see that she is a person of standing in the tribe and her ransom may well be high.' When Mohammed returned the captives at a price of six camels each, Vyayna refused to give her back. Zuhayr told him to let her go, for her mouth was cold and her breasts flat; she could not conceive and her husband would not care and her milk was not rich. So he let her go for the six camels when Zuhayr said this. They allege that when Vyayna met al-Aqra later he complained to him about the matter and he said: By God, you didn't take her as a virgin in her prime nor even a plump middle-aged matron!'

Jihad can be ugly:

> I980 When Zayd had raided the Fazara tribe, he and others were injured. Zayd swore he would never have sex until he had avenged his injuries. When he was well, Mohammed sent him against the Fazara.

He was successful and captured some of the women. One of them was an old woman, Umm Qirfa, who husband he had killed. Zayd tied a rope to each leg of Umm Qirfa and tied each rope to a camel and pulled her apart. Her daughter was taken captive and passed around to three different men to use as they would for their pleasure.

MOHAMMED AND SEXUAL SLAVERY

Mohammed was so pure that he would not touch a Muslim woman's hand. But he would have sex with his slaves. This is an excellent example of ethical dualism. There is not one ethical code for all, but two ethical codes—one for the free Muslim and another for the slave.

[B9,89,321]

Mohammed used to take the Pledge of allegiance from the women by words only after reciting this verse: "...that they will not associate anything in worship with Allah." (60.12) And the hand of Allah's Apostle did not touch any woman's hand except the hand of that woman his right hand possessed. (i.e. his captives or his lady slaves).

Here we see that it was expected that the captive women would be used for sex. The jihadist's question about Mohammed is not whether he will have sex with Safiya, but as a wife or slave.

[B7,62,89;B5,59,524;B1,8,367]

[...]

We conquered Khaybar, took captives, and booty was collected.

Dihya asked Mohammed for one of the captive slave girls and was told he could go and take any one he wished. He took Safiya bint Huyai. Later Mohammed was told that Safiya was chief mistress of the tribes of Quraiza and An-Nadir and was suited for none but himself.' So the Prophet called Dihya and Safiya to him and told Dihya that he could take any other slave girl but her. Mohammed then freed Safiya.."

Mohammed stayed for three nights between Khaybar and Medina and was married to Safiya. Anas invited the Muslims to a banquet which included neither meat nor bread, but Mohammed ordered leather mats to be spread, on which dates, dried yogurt and butter were provided. The Muslims wondered whether Safiya would be considered as Mohammed's wife or as a slave. Then they said, "If the Prophet makes her observe the veil, then she will be one of his wives, but if he does not make her observe the veil, then she will be his slave." When Mohammed departed, he made a place for Safiya behind him on his camel and made her observe the veil.

Here is another situation in jihad where Mohammed got a new sexual partner.

[B3,46,717]

Ibn Aun wrote a letter to Nafi. Nafi wrote in reply that the Prophet had suddenly attacked Bani Mustaliq tribe without warning while they were heedless and their cattle were being watered at the places of water. Their fighting men were killed and their women and children were taken as captives; the Prophet got Juwairiya on that day.

The problem here is not that someone had sex with a slave, but that it was not her owner.

[B3,34,421;B4,51,8;B8,80,757;B3,34,269;B9,89,293;B3,46,710;B3,41,603;B8,80,741]

Saed and Abu quarreled over a boy born to the slave girl of Zama. They took the case of their claim of ownership to Mohammed. Saed said, "This (boy) is the son of my brother, Utba, and I promised to be his custodian." Abu bin Zama said, "O Allah's Apostle! This is my brother and was born on my father's bed from his slave-girl." Mohammed looked at the boy and saw a definite resemblance to Utba and then said, "The boy is yours, O Abu bin Zama. The child goes to the owner of the bed and the adulterer gets nothing but stones (despair, i.e. to be stoned to death). Then Mohammed said to his wife Sauda bint Zama, "Screen yourself from this boy," so Sauda never saw him again.

Mohammed's love for one of his slaves, Mary, caused an uproar in his harem. Mohammed was fond of a Coptic (Egyptian Christian) slave named Mary. Hafsa found Mohammed in her room with Mary, a violation of Hafsa's domain. He told a jealous Hafsa that he would stop relations with Mary and then did not. But Hafsa was supposed to be quiet about this matter. But the Koran points out to his wives and Muslims that he can have sex with his slaves as he wishes. Therefore, when he told Hafsa he would quit, he was not bound by that oath.

66:1 *Why, Oh, Messenger, do you forbid yourself that which Allah has made lawful to you? Do you seek to please your wives? Allah is lenient and merciful. Allah has allowed you release from your oaths, and Allah is your master. He is knowing and wise.*

And last, but not least, after life is over, Muslims will still be having sex with slaves.

> Hadith 101, Ibn Arabi, ***Mishkat***
>
> *[...]*
>
> ***Allah says to the Muslims in Paradise: Go to your slave-girls and concubines in the garden of Paradise.***
>
> *[...]*

This is the Sunna of Mohammed

MOHAMMED AND SLAVERY

CHAPTER 13

3:53 "Our Lord! We believe in what Thou hast revealed, and we follow the Apostle; then write us down among those who bear witness."

- Mohammed was surrounded by slaves all of his life.
- Mohammed, the white man, owned many slaves, including black slaves.
- Slaves played a part in every aspect of Mohammed's life, including building his pulpit.
- Mohammed bought and sold slaves in both retail and wholesale lots.
- Sex slaves were part of Mohammed's harem.
- Mohammed gave slaves as gifts and received them as gifts.

Just as Mohammed is the model husband, he is also the model slave owner and slave trader. His Sunna shows the way for Muslims in all aspects of life. There was no aspect of slavery that Mohammed did not practice. Slavery was literally in the very milk he drank as a child.

> [B7,64,285]
>
> ***One of Mohammed's wives, Um Habiba, said to him, "Will you marry my sister? I am not your only wife, and the person I'd like most to share the good with me, is my sister."***
>
> ***Mohammed said, "That is not lawful for me." Um Habiba, "O Allah's Apostle! We have heard that you want to marry the daughter of Um Salama?"***
>
> ***Mohammed said, "She is unlawful for me, for she is my foster niece. The freed slave girl Thuwaiba suckled both me and Abu Salama. You should not present your daughters and sisters to me for marriage."***

His first wife, Khadija, owned a slave who plays a small part in Mohammed's role as a messenger of Allah. This story is one of several in the

Sira which has Jews, Christians and soothsayers predicting the arrival of Mohammed.

> I121 Khadija had a cousin, Waraqa, who was a Christian who had studied the scriptures and was a scholar. She told him what her slave, Maysara, had told her. The slave had been with Mohammed when a monk in Syria had seen two angels shading Mohammed. Waraqa said, 'If this is true, Khadija, verily Mohammed is the prophet of this people. I knew that a prophet of this people was to be expected. His time has come,' or words to that effect.

Mohammed used to sit and talk with a young Christian slave.

> I261 Mohammed used often sat at the booth of a young Christian called Jabr, a slave. The Meccans used to say '***The one who teaches Mohammed most of what he brings is Jabr, the Christian slave.***' Then Allah revealed in reference to their words, "We well know that they say, 'Only a mortal teaches him.' The tongue of him at whom they hint is foreign, and this is a clear Arabic tongue."

SLAVES IN MOHAMMED'S HOME

Here we have a Koranic reference to Mohammed's slaves in his home.

> 33:55 ***There is no blame on the Messenger's wives if they speak unveiled with their fathers, sons, brothers, nephews on either their brother's or sister's side, their women, or their slave-girls. Women! Fear Allah, for Allah witnesses all things.***

> [B9,92,462]
>
> *Aisha said that the Divine Inspiration was delayed after the slanderers gave a false statement against her, so Mohammed called upon Ali and Osama to consult with them about the question of divorcing her. Osama said what he knew about Aisha's innocence, but Ali pointed out Allah had not put restrictions on Mohammed and that there were many women other than her. He suggested asking the slave girl because she would tell the truth."*
>
> *So Mohammed asked Aisha's slave girl, Barira, if she had seen anything that aroused her suspicion. ...*

Barira was the slave girl of Aisha, Mohammed's wife.

> [B7,63,204;B7,63,205]
>
> *Ibn Abbas: said that Barira's husband was Mughith – the black slave of Bani so-and-so—and used to walk behind her along the streets of Medina.*

It is intriguing how the race of a slave is frequently given. Mohammed had more than one black slave.

[B7,72,734:]

[...]

He said, 'Greater than that! Allah's Apostle has divorced his wives! I went to them and found all of them weeping in their dwellings, and the Prophet had ascended to an upper room of his. At the door of the room there was his black slave to whom I went and said, 'Ask the permission for me to enter.' He admitted me and I entered to see the Prophet lying on a mat.

[...]

[B8,73,182;B8,73,221]

Once Um Sulaym was on a journey with Mohammed and Mohammed's black slave Anjasha, who was driving the camels very fast. The women in charge of the luggage were riding on those camels, and Mohammed said: "May Allah be merciful to you, O Anjasha! Drive the camels with the glass vessels (women) slowly!"

[B2,24,569]

Mohammed saw a dead sheep which had been given in charity to a freed slave-girl of Maimuna, the wife of Mohammed. Mohammed said, "Why don't you get the benefit of its hide?" They said, "It is dead." He replied, "Only to eat its meat is illegal."

Mohammed allows Aisha to watch some black slaves in the Mosque:

B2,15,103

During the days of Mina, Abu Bakr visited Aisha. While Mohammed was lying down, two young slave girls were beating a tambourine. Abu Bakr yelled at them to stop their noise. Mohammed uncovered his face and told Abu Bakr, "Leave them alone. It is a festival day."

Aisha also said, "One time Mohammed was hiding me from public view so that I might watch some black slaves in the Mosque display their skill with weapons.

Umar scolded them for exhibiting themselves in the presence of a Muslim woman, but Mohammed said, "Leave them alone. You Negroes may continue; you have my protection."

When men kill a slave shepherd of Mohammed's, they reap a terrible death.

I999 *Mohammed captured a slave called Yasar*, and he put him in charge of his milch-camels. Some men of Qays came to the apostle suffering with an illness, and the apostle told them that if they went to the milch-camels and drank their milk and urine they would recover. When they recovered their health, they fell upon the apostle's shepherd Yasar and killed him and stuck thorns in his eyes and drove away his camels. Mohammed sent Kurz in pursuit and he overtook them and brought them to the apostle as he returned from a jihad raid. Mohammed cut off their hands and feet and gouged out their eyes. They were left to die of thirst lying on sharp rocks. [Their wounds were cauterized so they did not bleed to death, but died of thirst.]

A Muslim accumulates merit by freeing slaves. Aisha was Mohammed's wife and she gets some easy merit here.

I983 The apostle sent him to raid them, and he killed some and captured others. Asim told me that Aisha said to ***Mohammed that she must free a slave***, and he said, 'The captives are coming now. We will give you one whom you can set free.'

Mohammed also freed slaves.

I763 Abdullah told me from one of his family from Abu Rafi, *freed slave of Mohammed*: We went with Ali, Mohammed's nephew, when the apostle sent him into battle. When he got near the fort, the garrison came out and he fought them. A Jew struck him so that his shield fell from his hand, so Ali laid hold of a door by the fort and used it as a shield. He kept it in his hand as he fought until Allah gave victory, throwing it away when all was over.

Fatima was Mohammed's daughter.

[B5,57,55]

Fatima complained of the suffering caused to her by the hand mill. Some female slaves were brought to Mohammed, she came to him but did not find him at home. Aisha was there to whom Fatima told of her desire for a slave. When Mohammed came, Aisha informed him about Fatima's visit.

Slaves were part of Mohammed's funeral.

I1020 When the preparations for burial had been completed on the Tuesday, he was laid upon his bed in his house. Abu Bakr said, 'I heard the apostle say, "No prophet dies but he is buried where he died."' The bed on which he died was taken up and they made a grave beneath it. Then the people came to visit the apostle praying over him by companies: first came the men, then the women, then the children, ***then the slaves.***

MOHAMMED AND THE TRADES

The pulpit that Mohammed spoke from was built by a slave.

> [B1,8,374;B1,8,440;B2,13,40;B3,34,307;B3,34,308;B3,47,743]
> *Sahl bin Saed was asked about Mohammed's pulpit. He said Mohammed had sent for an Ansari woman who had a slave carpenter and asked to have a place built for him to sit when addressing the people. The slave gathered wood from the tamarisk and built the pulpit. Then Mohammed prayed on it, stepped down and prostrated himself on the ground at its foot, then ascended again and finished praying. Then Mohammed said: "I have done this so that you may follow me and learn the way I pray."*

Mohammed had a slave tailor.

> [B7,65,346;B7,65,344]
> *Anas said that when he was a young boy he once went walking with Mohammed. Mohammed entered the house of his slave tailor and was offered a dish of food covered with pieces of gourd, which he started eating. Anas said that he has loved to eat gourd since he saw Mohammed eating it.*

Mohammed was medically treated by a slave. Cupping is an old medical treatment for bleeding, which supposedly had beneficial benefits.

> [B3,34,412;B3,36,481;B3,34,315]
> *Mohammed sent for a slave who had the profession of cupping, and he cupped him. Mohammed ordered that the slave be paid a small amount and appealed to the slave's masters to reduce his taxes.*

Mohammed ate food prepared by a slave.

> [B3,43,636:B3,34,295;B7,65,345;B7,65,371]
> *An Ansari man called Abu Shuaib said to his slave butcher, "Prepare a meal sufficient for five persons so that I might invite Mohammed and four other persons." Abu Shuaib had seen signs of hunger on Mohammed's face. Another man, who was not invited, followed Mohammed, who said to Abu Shuaib, "This man has followed us. Do you allow him to share the meal?" Abu Shuaib said, "Yes, he is welcome." ...*

MOHAMMED AND THE SALE OF SLAVES

[B3,34,351;B9,89,296;B3,34,351;B8,79,707;B9,85,80]achristianslave

Mohammed found out one of his companions had promised to free his slave after his death. Later on the man was in need of money, but he had no property other than that slave, so Mohammed took the slave and said, "Who will buy this slave from me?" Noaim bin Abdullah bought the slave and Mohammed took its price and gave it to the owner.

Here Mohammed wholesales female slaves to fund jihad.

I693 Then Mohammed sent Saed with some of the captive Jewish women of B. Qurayza to Najd and he sold them for horses and weapons.

Mohammed was very parsimonious about all household expenses.

[B4,53,344;B7,64,274]

Fatima went to Mohammed to complain about the bad effect on her hand of grinding with the stone hand-mill. She heard that he had received the booty of a few slave girls and went to request one for a maidservant. Mohammed was not home, so she mentioned her problem to Aisha. When Mohammed returned, Aisha informed him about that. Later Ali said, "So the Prophet came to us when we had gone to bed. We wanted to get up but he said, 'Stay where you are.' Then he came and sat between me and Fatima, and I felt the coldness of his feet on my abdomen. He said, 'Shall I direct you to something better than what you have requested? When you go to bed say ' Glorified be Allah' thirty-three times, All the Praises are for Allah' thirty three times, and Allah is Great' thirty four times, for that is better for you than a servant.'"

MOHAMMED, SLAVES AND SEX

Mohammed got this sex slave from the Jews after he killed all of the adult males.

I693 Mohammed had chosen one of their women for himself, Ayhama, one of the women of Qurayza Jews, and she remained with him until she died, in his power. The apostle had proposed to marry her and put the veil on her, but she said: 'No, Leave me in your power, for that will be easier for me and for you.' So he left her. She had shown repugnance towards Islam when she was captured and clung to Judaism.

Here we have Koranic references to Mohammed's sex life and how it included sex slaves.

> 33:50 *Messenger! We allow you your wives whose dowries you have paid, and the slave-girls Allah has granted you as spoils of war, and the daughters of your paternal and maternal uncles and aunts who fled with you to Medina, and any believing woman who gives herself to the Messenger, if the Messenger wishes to marry her. This is a privilege for you only, not for any other believer. We know what We have commanded the believers concerning wives and slave-girls. We give you this privilege so you will be free from blame. Allah is forgiving and merciful!*
> 33:51 *You may turn away any of them that you please, and take to your bed whomever you please, and you will not be blamed for desiring one you had previously set aside for a time. Therefore, it will be easier for you to comfort them and prevent their grief and to be content with what you give each of them. Allah knows what is in your hearts, and Allah is all-knowing and gracious.*
> 33:52 *It will be unlawful for you to marry more wives after this or to exchange them for other wives, even though you are attracted by their beauty, except slave-girls you own. [Mohammed had nine wives and several slave-girls.] And Allah watches over all things.*

Here Mohammed gets a gift of four Christian slaves.

> T1561,I972 Then Mohammed divided his companions and sent Salit to the ruler.. He handed over to him the apostle's letter and the ruler gave Mohammed four slave girls, one of whom was Mary, mother of Ibrahim the apostle's son.

Mohammed would not touch a female Muslim, but he would touch his female slaves.

> [B9,89,321]
>
> *Narrated Aisha:*
>
> *The Prophet used to take the Pledge of allegiance from the women by words only after reciting this Holy Verse:*
>
> 60:12 Oh, Messenger, when believing women come to you and pledge an oath of allegiance to you and ascribe no other gods as partners to Allah
>
> *And the hand of Allah's Apostle did not touch any woman's hand except the hand of that woman his right hand possessed. (i.e. his captives or his lady slaves).*

Mohammed killed Safiya's husband, father and cousin, as well as many members of her Jewish tribe. She choose to be his wife rather that his slave.

[B5,59,524]

Mohammed stayed for three nights between Khaybar and Medina and was married to Safiya. He invited the Muslims to his marriage banquet and there was neither meat nor bread in that banquet. Mohammed ordered Bilal to spread the leather mats on which dates, dried yogurt and butter were put.

The Muslims said amongst themselves, "Will Safiya be one of the wives of the Prophet or just a slave-girl?" Some of them said, "If the Prophet makes her observe the veil, then she will be one of the Prophet's wives, and if he does not make her observe the veil, then she will be his slave-girl." So when he departed, he made a place for her behind him on his camel and made her observe the veil.

Mohammed made the same deal with Juwairiya.

[B3,46,717]

Ibn Aun wrote a letter to Nafi and Nafi wrote in reply to my letter that Mohammed had suddenly attacked the Bani Mustaliq without warning while they were heedless and their cattle were being watered at the places of water. Their fighting men were killed and their women and children were taken as slaves; the Prophet got Juwairiya on that day.

THE BEATING OF SLAVES

Mohammed stood by and prayed while his men beat and tortured two slaves. He then took part in their interrogation.

I436 Then the apostle returned to his companions; and when night fell he sent Ali, al-Zubayr and Saed, with a number of his companions to the well at Badr in quest of news of both parties. They fell in with some water-camels of the Quraysh, among whom were two slaves, and they brought them along and questioned them while the apostle was standing praying. They said, 'We are the water carriers of the Quraysh; they sent us to get them water. 'The people were displeased, at their report, for they had hoped that they would belong to Abu Sufyan, so *they beat the slaves, and when they had beaten them until they were weak*, the two slaves said, 'We belong to Abu Sufyan,' so they let them go.

> I436 The apostle bowed and prostrated himself twice, and said, 'When they told you the truth you beat them; and when they lied you let them alone. They told the truth; they do belong to the Quraysh.

Mohammed stood by while one of his men beats a slave. This slave lived in his house and was his favorite wife's slave.

> I735 As for Ali he said: "Women are plentiful, and you can easily change one for another. ***Ask the slave girl***, for she will tell you the truth." So Mohammed called Burayra to ask her, and Ali got up and ***gave her a violent beating, saying***, "Tell the apostle the truth," to which she replied, "I know only good of her. The only fault I have to find with Aisha is that when I am kneading dough and tell her to watch it she neglects it and falls asleep and her pet lamb comes and eats it!"

SLAVES AS A GIFT

Here Mohammed gives one of his men a fine home and a sex slave.

> I739 Then they came to Mohammed and told him of the affair and he summoned Hassan and Safwan. The latter said, 'He insulted me and I became so angry I hit him.' Mohammed said to Hassan, 'Do you look with an evil eye on my people because Allah has guided them to Islam?' He added, 'Be charitable about what has befallen you.' Hassan said, 'It is yours'.
>
> I739 To compensate him, Mohammed gave him a castle in Medina. ***He also gave him Sirin, a Coptic (Egyptian Christian) slave girl, and she bore him a boy.*** "

Mohammed was a generous man. Here he gives his foster sister two slaves:

> I857 Yazid told me that when she was brought to the apostle she claimed to be his foster-sister, and when he asked for proof she said, 'The bite you gave me in my back when I carried you at my hip.' The apostle acknowledged the proof and stretched out his robe for her to sit on and treated her kindly. He gave her the choice of living with him in affection and honor or going back to her people with presents, and she chose the latter. The B. Saed allege that ***Mohammed gave her a slave called Makhul and a slave girl***; the one married the other and their progeny still exist.

Here Mohammed receives a slave as a gift.

> I963 Rifa'a came to the apostle during the armistice of al-Hudaybiya before Khaybar. ***He gave the apostle a slave and he became a good Muslim.*** The apostle gave him a letter to his people.

Mohammed gave sex slaves to his chief lieutenants. Umar, in turn, gave his sex slave to his son.

> I878 Mohammed gave Ali a girl called Rayta and he gave Uthman a girl called Zaynab and he gave Umar a girl, whom Umar gave to his son Abdullah.

MOHAMMED'S WHITENESS

There is an odd item about race that must be mentioned. In America the descendents of slavery are told that Christianity is the white man's religion. Islam is the natural religion of the black man.

It is a fact that Islam is based upon the Sunna of Mohammed. The Sunna is exceedingly clear about race and Mohammed. The Hadith goes out of its way to say that Mohammed was white. So a white man who owned black slaves started the natural religion of the black man.

These are a few of the hadiths that report Mohammed's whiteness.

> B4,56,765
>
> *When Mohammed prostrated himself to pray, he would spread his arms so wide apart, that we could see his armpits. Ibn Bukair described it as "the whiteness of his armpits."*

> B3,47,769
>
> *Mohammed delegated a man from the Al-Azd tribe to be a tax collector. When the man returned he said to Mohammed, "This is the money that I have collected for you and this money was given to me as a present."*
>
> *Mohammed said, "If this man wanted presents, why didn't he stay at home with his parents? By Allah, if someone takes something from the tax collection, they will carry that weight around their neck on Judgment Day. If it is a camel, it will be grunting when he is judged; if it is a cow, it will be mooing; if it is a sheep it will be bleating."*
>
> *Mohammed then raised his hands up high, exposing his white armpits, and said, "Allah, haven't I told the people your instructions?"*

[B4,52,90;B490,769]

At the battle of Al-Ahzab I saw Mohammed carrying dirt which covered his white belly. He was saying, "Without your help Allah, we would have no guidance, we would neither pray nor give charitably. Give us peace and courage when we battle our enemies. Our enemies have rejected you and Mohammed, but we will never give up if they try to attack us."

B2,17,122

Abdullah Bin Dinar once heard Ibn Umar recite some of Abu Talib's poetic verse: "And a white man (Mohammed) who is asked to pray for rain and who is the protector of orphans and the guardian of widows."

B1,3,63

We were sitting with Mohammed in the Mosque one day when a man rode up on a camel. He asked, "Which one of you is Mohammed?" We answered, "That white man leaning on his arm…"

B1,8,367

Just before the battle of Khaybar, we and Mohammed gave the Fajr prayer before sunup. I [Anas] was riding behind Abu Talha and next to Mohammed. We were so close, that as we rode down the main street of Khaybar, my knee touched Mohammed's leg. His garment moved and exposed the whiteness of his thigh.

M004,1208

'Amir b. Sa'd reported: I saw the Messenger of Allah pronouncing taslim on his right and on his left till I saw the whiteness of his cheek.

M030,5778:

Abu Tufail reported: I saw Allah's Messenger and there is one amongst the people of the earth who are living at the present time and had seen him except me. I said to him: How did you find him? He said: He had an elegant white color, and he was of an average height.

OTHER REMARKS ABOUT RACE

Mohammed's Night Journey is known by every Muslim. The house he stayed in that night had a black slave.

I267 Um Hani said: 'The apostle went on no night journey except while he was in my house. He slept that night in my house. He prayed the final night prayer, then he slept and we slept. A little before dawn the apostle woke us, and when we had prayed the dawn prayer he said, "Umm Hani', I prayed with you the last evening prayer in this valley as you saw. Then I went to Jerusalem and prayed there. Then I have just prayed the morning prayer with you as you see." He got up to go out and I took hold of his robe. I said, "O prophet of Allah, don't talk to the people about it for they will give you the lie and insult you." He said, "By Allah, I certainly will tell them." ***I said to a Negress, a slave of mine***, "Follow the apostle and listen to what he says to the people, and what they say to him."

I357 Mohammed said, 'Whoever wants to see Satan should look at Nabtal!' He was a black man with long flowing hair, inflamed eyes, and dark ruddy cheeks.... Allah sent down concerning him:

9:61 ***To those who annoy the Prophet there is a painful doom.***

I357 Gabriel came to Mohammed and said, 'If a black man comes to you, his heart is more gross than a donkey's.'

B9,89,256

Mohammed said, 'You should listen to and obey your ruler even if he is a black slave whose head looks like a raisin.'

I614 Thabit said, "It is your folly to fight the Apostle, for Allah's army is bound to disgrace you. We brought them to the pit. Hell was their meeting place. We collected them there, black slaves, men of no descent."

I562 The black troops and slaves of the Meccans cried out and the Muslims replied, 'Allah destroy your sight, you impious rascals.'

B4,52,137

Mohammed said, 'Let the black slave of Dinar perish. And if he is pierced with a thorn, let him not find anyone to take it out for him.... If the black slave asks for anything it shall not be granted, and if he needs intercession to get into paradise, his intercession will be denied.'

This is the Sunna of Mohammed

THE HISTORY OF ISLAMIC SLAVERY

CHAPTER 14

If you live in America, you know the modern historical theory of slavery. Evil white men brought Africans to the Western hemisphere, where they were sold for profit and put to work as slaves. The modern theory is true as far as it goes, but it does not go nearly far enough. Slavery goes far beyond the 300-year period when whites bought slaves from the Muslim wholesalers on the West coast of Africa.

Every culture has had some form of slavery in its past. Slavery is an answer to how to get hard, rough work done. We feel ethically superior to our ancestors because we don't have slaves. But the reason that slavery was finally ended was a combination of ethics and the discovery of a better slave—the machine.

WHITE SLAVES

For 1400 years—until the slave market was officially closed in the early 1960s—the highest priced slave in Mecca was the white woman. The price of a white slave girl was from three to ten times that of a black girl. When Islam invaded Spain, the first thing exported back to Islamic North Africa were a thousand blond-haired girls.

Our word for slave comes from the Slavs of eastern Europe. So many of them were taken by the Muslims of the Ottoman Empire that the very term ***Slav*** came to mean slave. Black slaves were so numerous that the term ***abd*** came to mean black or African. Muslims called the white slaves ***mamluk.***

Not only were there words for slaves to differentiate them but the uses of the slaves were different. The white woman was favored for sex. That is why she brought the best price. White slaves were not used for rough labor but were used for higher positions in domestic and administrative work. Both white and black men were used as eunuchs in the harem.

Also both white and black male slaves were used in the armies of Islam; however, whites could become officers, governors, and rulers. Advancement happened only rarely for blacks. Only one black slave rose to the rank of ruler, Abu I Misk Kafur who was a eunuch and became a governor of Egypt.

In Eastern Europe, the Islamic rulers taxed the Christian families at the rate of one fifth; one child in five was taken for slavery. These children were forcibly converted to Islam and trained to form the core of the ***janissaries***, the military troops used by the Turkish sultan. The sultan reserved younger children for the palace, where they were trained by the eunuchs for positions in the administration of the Islamic empire. This theft took place annually among the Greeks, Serbs, Bulgarians, Albanians, and Armenians. At a fixed date, each father had to appear in the town square for the sultan's man to come pick the best of his children for Islam.

The strategy ensured that the population of Muslims increased and the population of Christians decreased.

When the Serbs revolted against Islamic oppression and were crushed in 1813, eighteen hundred women and children were sold in one day to Muslims in Belgrade.[1] During the Greek revolt against Islamic rule, the Islamic ruler sent four to five thousand rebels to be sold in Constantinople and thirty-four hundred women to be sold as slaves.[2]

In the seventeenth century, Jean de Chardin wrote:

> Shah Abbas I transported settlements of twenty or thirty thousand souls at a time, two or three hundred leagues from their native land. Almost all of them were Georgian and Armenian Christians [...] It was in this way that the kings of Persia rose to that point of absolute power which I will show, and which they sustain [...] because as almost all the Georgians and Iberians [from South Caucasus region] who are given the status to govern are slaves by origin, and genuine outsiders in the government, they have no contacts either in the kingdom or with one another. As most of them know neither from where nor from whom they come, it happens that they are not driven by any desire for freedom on the one hand and are incapable of forming leagues or conspiracies on the other. Men who have no relationship among themselves do not rise in rebellion on behalf of each other, either to save their lives or to ascend the throne.
>
> This name of ***coular*** means slave, not that these men are not as free as other Persians, but because they are natives of countries such as Georgia, Circassia, Iberia, and of Moscow, from where slaves are drawn. Thus they are of Christian origin. Some were sent to the king as gifts, being still young; others are descended from the peoples of these countries, who

1. Castellan, ***Histoire des Balkans***, 254.
2. Broughton, ***Travels,*** letter written May 11, 1825 by Jean-Bafriel Eynard.

> have become accustomed to Persia. As almost all of them embrace the Islamic religion, they are all renegades or the children of renegades.[3]

BLACK SLAVES

In theory, the races are equal in Islam, but they have not been so in practice. Long before Islam, the Arabs had enslaved blacks. After Islamic expansion, the Islamic empire needed more slaves, so they came from the traditional source, sub-Saharan Africa. Massive importation of illiterate people performing hard labor did not enhance the Muslim view of blacks, no matter how vital they had been in Mohammed's day. Here is one caliph's opinion of the black slave he received as a gift:

> Had you been able to find a smaller number than one and a worse color than black you would have sent that as a gift.[4]

And another opinion:

> Therefore, the Negro nations are, as a rule, submissive to slavery because Negroes have little that is essentially human and have attributes that are quite similar to those of dumb animals, as we have stated.[5]

The major exploitation of black slaves took place outside the cities. Since Islam is primarily an urban culture, it is the urban culture recorded in its writings. Therefore, we don't know much about the lives of the rural slaves. The picture we have of Islamic slavery is that of the palace, the army, and domestic workers.

Large gangs of slaves were used for heavy construction, agriculture, mining, and dredging operations. Large landowners would employ thousands of black slaves for agricultural work. Urban slaves performing administrative and domestic work had relatively light duty, but those performing manual labor led a brutal life. The slaves, mainly men, who worked the Saharan salt mines lasted an average of five years before death. Slave women were used as prostitutes, although the practice was forbidden by the Koran. The Koran also says that if they are prostituted, Allah is forgiving.

Over time, there has been a great deal of discussion about the enslavement of Muslim blacks. Islamic law about this is exceedingly clear; any non-Muslim could be enslaved after jihad, but no Muslim, black or any

---

3. Jean de Chardin, ***Voyages du Chevalier de Chardin En Perse***, Paris, 1811, 5226-28, 306-8.

4. Jahsihari, ***Kitab Al-Wuzara wa l-Kuttab*** (Cairo, 1938), p. 81.

5. Translated by F. Rosenthal, Ibn Khaldun, ***The Muqaddimah***, vol. 1 (New York, 1958), p. 301.

other, was to be enslaved. To resolve the matter, one simply disputed the devoutness of the slave's faith and concluded he or she was "not really a Muslim."

The Muslims of North Africa captured so many of their black brothers that there was a body of legal rulings, *fatwas*, on the subject. The fatwas concluded that the benefit of the doubt went to the owner, not the slave.[6] There was an immediate outcry from black Muslim rulers, decrying the jihad launched against their subjects, and their black jurists protested the enslavement of Muslims, but the practice continued.[7]

Enslavement went hand in hand with death. Not only were family members killed protecting their loved ones, but many others died on the relentless march from their villages of capture. Only the best humans were taken; thus, villages were left under-populated with the young, weak, sick, and very old. Starvation, disease, and heartbreak destroyed those who remained. One author of the nineteenth century estimated that, for every slave on the auction block, nine others died.[8]

Here is a quote from David Livingstone about the aftermath of slave trading in Africa:

> Now as the exploring party ascended the river the desolation was heart-breaking. Corpses floated past them in such numbers that the paddle-wheels had to be cleared from them every morning. Wherever we took a walk, human skeletons were seen in every direction, and it was painfully interesting to observe the different postures in which the poor wretches had breathed their last. Many had ended their misery under shady trees, others under projecting crags in the hills, while others lay in their huts with closed doors, which when opened disclosed the moldering corpse with the poor rags around the loins, the skull fallen off the pillow, the little skeleton of the child, that had perished first, rolled up in a mat between two large skeletons. The sight of this desert, but eighteen months ago a well peopled valley, now literally strewn with human bones, forced the conviction upon us that the destruction of human life in the middle passage, however great, constitutes but a small portion of the waste, and made us feel that unless the slave-trade—that

---

6. Amad Al-Wansharisi, ***Kitab Al-Miyar Al-mughrib***, vol. 9 (1895-96), 71-72

7. EII, s.v. "Abd" (by r. Brunschvig), p.32a; Rotter, ***Die Stellung des Negers***, 44, 49ff.

8. Hourst, ***Mission hydorgraphique du Niger,*** 1896.

monster inequity, which has so long brooded over Africa—is put down, awful commerce cannot be established.[9]

And why did the killing and slaving take place?

> We had a long discussion about the slave trade. The Arabs have told the chief that "our object in capturing slaves is to get them into our own possession and make them of our own religion."[10]

And what was the emotional impact on the survivors?

> The strangest disease I have seen in this country seems really to be broken-heartedness, and it attacks non-Muslim men who have been captured and made slaves. Speaking with many who died from it, they ascribed their only pain to the heart, and placed the hand correctly on the spot, though many think that the organ stands high up under the breast-bone. Some slavers expressed surprise to me that they should die, seeing they had plenty to eat and no work. It seems to be really broken hearts of which they die.[11]

Islamic slavery was the basis of all the slavery in the West. When the white slaver arrived in his boat on the coast of Africa, he went to see a Muslim trader. The New World was a new market for the ancient Islamic slave trade. The only change was the boat and the direction it sailed. Three hundred years went by before the Atlantic slave trade was stopped. But it never has stopped in Islam.

AFRICAN DEATHS DUE TO SLAVERY

Thomas Sowell estimates that 11 million slaves were shipped across the Atlantic and 14 million were sent to the Islamic nations of North Africa and the Middle East[12]. For every slave captured many others died. Estimates of this collateral damage vary. The renowned missionary David Livingstone estimated that for every slave who reached the plantation five others died by being killed in the raid or died on the forced march from illness and privation[13]. Those who were left behind were the very young, the weak, the sick and the old. These soon died since the main

9. Mrs. J. H. Worcester, Jr., ***Life of David Livingstone*** (Chicago: Women's Presbyterian Board of Missions of the Northwest, 1888), 59-60.

10. Ibid. 62.

11. Ibid.

12. Thomas Sowell, ***Race and Culture***, BasicBooks, 1994, p. 188.

13. Woman's Presbyterian Board of Missions, ***David Livingstone,*** p. 62, 1888.

providers had been killed or enslaved. So, for 25 million slaves delivered to the market, we have the death of about 120 million people due to the Islamic wholesale slave trade in Africa over the centuries.

SEX SLAVES

The great Islamic geographer, Al-Idris, was of the opinion that Nubian women made the best slaves of pleasure.

> Their women are of surpassing beauty. They are circumcised and fragrant-smelling...their lips are thin, their mouths small and their hair flowing. Of all black women, they are the best for the pleasures of the bed...It is on account of these qualities of theirs that the rulers of Egypt were so desirous of them and outbid others to purchase them, afterwards fathering children from them.[14]
>
> By the early nineteenth century the taste in slaves for sex (concubines) had changed to Ethiopian women, at least in Mecca.
>
> There are few families at Mecca, in moderate circumstances, that do not keep slaves...the concubines are always Abyssinian slaves. Wealthy Meccans do not prefer domestic peace over the gratification of their passions; they keep mistresses in common with their lawful wives...Many Meccans have no other than Abyssinian wives, finding the Arabians more expensive, and less disposed to yield to the will of the husband...The same practice is adopted by many foreigners, who reside in the Hijaz for a short time. Upon their arrival, they buy a female companion, with the design of selling her at their departure; but sometimes their stay is protracted; the slave bears a child; they marry her, and become stationary in the town. There are very few unmarried men, or those without a slave.[15]

When wealthy Muslims had enough money, they preferred white sex slaves. A white female slave was about three times more expensive than an Ethiopian woman.

> The white female slaves are mostly in the possession of wealthy Turks. The concubine slaves in the houses of Egyptians of the higher and middle classes are, generally, what are termed "Habasheeyehs," that is, Abyssinians.[16]

---

14. J. O. Hunwick, "Black Africans in the Islamic World: An Understudied, Dimension of the Black Diaspora," ***Tarikh 5*** (1978), no. 4:27.

15. John Lewis Burckhardt, ***Travels in Arabia, vol. 1*** (London:1829), 340-42.

16. E. W. Lane, ***An Account of the Manners and Customs of the Modern Egyptians,*** 5th ed., vol. 1 (London: 1871), 168-169, 233-34.

There is one more aspect of sexual slavery involving mutilation: the eunuchs. The removal of a man's sex organs made him socially available to all women, even in the harem. Since Islamic prohibitions would not allow Muslims to castrate slaves, they chose to pay a higher price for slaves castrated in ***dar al harb***, [outside of Islamic territory] not ***dar al Islam.***

There is a fascinating aspect of Islamic castration: white male slaves had only their testicles removed. Blacks lost both testicles and penis. Black eunuchs were traditionally used for the attendants of the Mosque of the Prophet in Medina.

HINDU SLAVERY

If you study the history of slavery there is no mention of the existence of massive slavery in India. As always, the slavery was the result of jihad.

Koenard Elst in ***Negationism in India***[17] gives an estimate of 80 million Hindus killed in the total jihad against India. The country of India today is only half the size of ancient India, due to jihad. The mountains near India are called the Hindu Kush, meaning the "funeral pyre of the Hindus".

Here is just one small part of the killing of 80,000,000 Hindus and the taking of slaves:

> When Mahmud Ghaznavi attacked Waihind in 1001-02, he took 500,000 persons of both sexes as captives. This figure of Abu Nasr Muhammad Utbi, the secretary and chronicler of Mahmud, is so mind-boggling that Elliot reduces it to 5000. The point to note is that taking of slaves was a matter of routine in every expedition. Only when the numbers were exceptionally large did they receive the notice of the chroniclers. So that in Mahmud's attack on Ninduna in the Punjab (1014), Utbi says that "slaves were so plentiful that they became very cheap; and men of respectability in their native land (India) were degraded by becoming slaves of common shop-keepers (in Ghazni)". His statement finds confirmation in later chronicles including Nizamuddin Ahmad's Tabqat-i-Akbari which states that Mahmud "obtained great spoils and a large number of slaves". Next year from Thanesar, according to Farishtah, "the Muhammadan army brought to Ghaznin 200,000 captives so that the capital appeared like an Indian city, for every soldier of the army had several slaves and slave girls". Thereafter slaves were taken in Baran, Mahaban, Mathura, Kanauj, Asni etc. When Mahmud returned to Ghazni in 1019, the booty was found to consist of (besides huge wealth) 53,000 captives. Utbi says that "the number of prisoners may be conceived from the fact that, each was sold for

17. Koenard Elst, ***Negationism in India***, Voice of India, New Delhi, 2002, pg. 34.

> from two to ten dirhams. These were afterwards taken to Ghazna, and the merchants came from different cities to purchase them, so that the countries of Mawarau-un-Nahr, Iraq and Khurasan (Persia) were filled with them". The Tarikh-i-Alfi adds that the fifth share due to the Saiyyads was 150,000 slaves, therefore the total number of captives comes to 750,000.[18]

What can be said? The great tragedy is that they all died in vain. There is no room for the story of the victims in the modern study of slavery.

SLAVERY TODAY

The practice of Islamic slavery is alive and well today. In 1983 the Sudan became an Islamic state with Sharia law. The Muslims have brutalized the Christians and other religious followers. Even the UN has documented the slavery in the Sudan. Islam in the Sudan has shown a creative approach to genocide. The government is slowly starving the population. The army attacks villages, kill the old and young, then captures the healthy kafirs for slaves:

> Thousands of men, women and children are captured when their villages are surrounded, or are snatched while tending their crops, herding their animals, or collecting water. Many people run to hide in caves to escape government attacks, but they are driven even from these refuges by hunger and thirst, or by attacks using tear gas. Captives are taken to garrisons, forced to carry their own looted possessions, or drive their own stolen animals in front of them. These captives—or 'returnees,' as the government calls them—usually never see their families or villages again. Many are tortured. Women are raped and forced to work, often in special labour camps. All but the youngest children are separated for 'schooling'—i.e. conversion to Islam [Facing Genocide: The Nuba of Sudan, published by African Rights on 21 July 1995].

The government uses food as a means for luring Sudanese Christians into its "peace camps" located in the desert. Food distribution is carried out by Islamic organizations. They use the promise of food as a means of converting Christians and animists to Islam. The technique is very simple: if one does not bear an Islamic name, one is denied food. Without any means of alternative support the choice is Islam or death (Sabit A. Alley's paper delivered at the 19th Annual Holocaust and Genocide Program, Institute for Holocaust and Genocide Studies, March 17, 2001).

---

18. K.S. Lal, ***Muslim Slave System in Medieval India***, Voice of Dharma, 1994.

In Mauritania, slavery is openly practiced. Arab-Mauritanians hold an estimated half million slaves. Female slaves have their clitorises removed. No child can be in school without a Muslim name.

THE DHIMMITUDE OF THE KAFIR

Historically, Muslims are superior to every other demographic group. No one is lower than a slave. No one is higher than the slave's master. For 1400 years Islam has enslaved African, Asians, Christians, Hindus, Buddhists, Europeans and even Americans. On the other hand, no one enslaves Muslims, unless the African slaver runs out of non-Muslims. But even then, it is a Muslim who enslaves the Muslim.

The absolute superiority of the Muslim is shown by the fact that no one blames them or holds them responsible for slavery. Islam not only enslaves the bodies of the kafirs, but enslaves the minds of the kafir intellectuals. One of the most forbidden topics to be discussed is the role of Islam in slavery, both today and throughout the last 1400 years.

As a cruel example of how the kafir mind submits to Islam regarding slavery, go to an event where freed slaves from Africa or the "Lost Boys" of the Sudan are featured. Money is raised, sympathy is given and not one word about Islam is ever mentioned. Slavery just happens. We get to see an effect without a cause, an impossibility, but a pseudo-reality, nevertheless.

This mental submission of the kafir to Islam is called dhimmitude. There are three ways to submit to the duality of Islam. The first is to be a Muslim. The second is to be a slave. But Mohammed invented a third way of submission—the dhimmi. The dhimmi was invented when Mohammed conquered the Jews of Khaybar. They could still be Jews in the privacy of their homes, but all public space became Islamic. The government, taxes, and laws were Islamic.

When the kafir lets Islam have its way in public affairs, the kafir becomes a dhimmi. When kafirs teach about slavery and don't teach about Islam and slavery, the kafir is a dhimmi. When the university curriculum about "gender studies" does not include the servitude of the Islamic woman, the mind set of the curriculum is dhimmitude. When the rabbi or the minister says that they worship the same god as the Muslim, but have never read the Trilogy, the rabbi and the ministers are dhimmis. When the media reports or talks about Islam and has no knowledge about the doctrine or history of political Islam, they are dhimmis.

IN THE BEGINNING

CHAPTER 16

8:13 This [Allah cast terror into the kafir's heart] was because they opposed Allah and His messenger. Ones who oppose Allah and His messenger will be severely punished by Allah.

Up to this point, the Hadith and the Koran have furnished the doctrine of women and slaves. But this is not the whole story. Mohammed did not create the doctrine out of thin air or as a philosophical exercise. Each verse and hadith is a response to events in Mohammed's life. In short, there is a context and that context comes from the Sira, Mohammed's biography.

In the Hadith we see the small details, but no big picture. The Koran has almost no story and very little reference to any history. The Sira provides a compelling vision of Mohammed and the explosion of Islam. Only the Sira gives an explanation of how Islam and the doctrine of women and slaves are a historical development. In the condensed version of the Sira that follows, all the references to women and slaves are included.

Mohammed went from being a preacher to a politician and warrior. As a preacher he garnered only 150 followers in 13 years. Then he changed Islam's strategy into a political form. After 10 years of jihad—holy war—Mohammed became the first ruler of all of Arabia and he did not have a single opponent left alive in Arabia. He was completely and totally politically triumphant.

The process required 9 years of effort with a violent event every 7 weeks. The Islamic doctrine of women evolved over the the 23-year career of Mohammed, but the doctrine of slavery developed over the last 9 years of his life.

The Sira is primarily about jihad. Over 75% of the text is about a political struggle, raids, battles and theft. It is jihad that produces slavery and the political basis for the legal subjugation of women.

The Sira gives a context to Islam. Without the Sira and the Hadith, there is no Islam. Without the story of Mohammed, the Koran is incomprehensible and meaningless.

The paragraphs of the Sira that relate to women have this symbol in the margin. ♀

If the paragraph is about slaves there is this symbol in the margin. §

And if it relates to a female slave or women and slavery, there is a double symbol. ♀ §

CHILDHOOD

Mohammed's father was called Abdullah, meaning slave of Allah. Allah was a high god of the many gods worshiped in the town of Mecca. His father died while his mother was pregnant. When he was five years old, his mother died and his grandfather took over his upbringing. Then Mohammed was orphaned for the third time when his grandfather died and his raising was assumed by his uncle, Abu Talib. All were of the Quraysh tribe. These brief facts are the history known about his early childhood.

I115[1] When Mohammed was eight years old, his grandfather died. He was then taken in by Abu Talib, his uncle. His uncle took him on a trading trip to Syria, which was a very different place from Mecca. Syria was a sophisticated Christian country very much a part of the cosmopolitan culture of the Mediterranean. It was Syrian Christians who gave the Arabs their alphabet. When Mohammed was a child, there had never been a book written in Arabic. Only poems and business correspondence were written in Arabic.

MARRIAGE

I120 When Mohammed was grown, he was hired by the wealthy widow, Khadija, a distant cousin, to act as her agent in trading with Syria. Mohammed had a reputation of good character and good business sense. Trading between Mecca and Syria was risky business because it took skill to manage a caravan and to make the best deal in Syria. ♀

I120 On one trip Mohammed took one of Khadija's slaves along. When they returned, the slave related a story that a Christian had said Mohammed was destined to be a man of power. On the same trip Mohammed managed to double Khadija's investment. She proposed marriage to him. ♀ §

1. The number is a reference to Ishaq's *Sira Rasul Allah*, the Sira.

They married and had six children, two sons who died in childhood, and four daughters who lived to adulthood.

MECCA AS A RELIGIOUS CENTER

In Mecca there was a stone building in the shape of a cube called the Kabah. The Kabah was a religious site that contained many images of several tribal gods. We know of at least six other square stone houses called Kabahs that were in other towns in Arabia. However, Islam holds that the Kabah in Mecca was built by Abraham, the patriarch of the Jews.

The Kabah was the focus of religious rituals and was also a community center. One of Mohammed's ancestors, Qusayy, was a pagan religious leader. Rituals established by Qusayy included prostrations, ritual prayers, and circling the Kabah while praying and drinking from the well called Zam Zam. Other rituals included throwing stones at pillars which symbolized the devil. Most of Islam's rituals come from the aboriginal Arabic religions.

Stones played an important part in the religions of Arabia. The Kabah was made of stone and had an important stone, the Black Stone, built into one corner. It was probably a meteorite and was a composite of several stones. It is small in size, roughly seven inches in diameter. This stone was touched only with the right hand and kissed by pilgrims. All of these native rituals were incorporated into Islam.

The god, Allah, seems to have been a male god of the moon and was probably the god of the Quraysh, Mohammed's tribe. Each tribe had its gods. There was not much organization of the gods, unlike those of the Greeks or Romans.

MAP OF
ARABIA
600 A.D.
MEDITERRANEAN SEA
SYRIA
MESOPOTAMIA
(IRAQ)
MUTA
TABUK
FADAK
KHAYBAR
ARABIA
MEDINA
BADR
RED SEA
MECCA
HUDABIYA
HUNAIN
EGYPT
YEMEN
N
ABYSSINIA
(ETHIOPIA)

MECCA

BEGINNING TEACHINGS

CHAPTER 17

4:13 These are the limits set up by Allah. Those who obey Allah and His Messenger will be led into the Gardens watered by flowing rivers to live forever. This is the ultimate reward!

I150 Mohammed would take month-long retreats to be alone and practice the Quraysh religion. After the retreat he would go and circumambulate (circle and pray) the Kabah.

I152 At the age of forty Mohammed began to have visions and hear voices. His visions were first shown to him as bright as daybreak during his sleep in the month of Ramadan. Mohammed said that the angel, Gabriel, came to him with a brocade with writing on it and commanded him to read. "What shall I read?" The angel pressed him and said, "Read." Mohammed said again, "What shall I read?" The angel pressed him again tightly and again commanded, "Read!" Again the reply, "What shall I read?"

The angel said:

> 96:1 ***Recite: In the name of your Lord, Who created man from clots of blood.***
> 96:3 ***Recite: Your Lord is the most generous, Who taught the use of the pen and taught man what he did not know.***

T1150 Khadija, his wife, sent men looking for him and brought him back to the house. He told her that he was afraid that he had gone insane or become an ecstatic poet and that he hated both things. She sent him to her cousin who was a Christian. The cousin told Mohammed that he was a prophet. ♀

I154 Khadija told Mohammed to let her know the next time that Gabriel arrived. When he told her that Gabriel had come, she had Mohammed sit next to her on her right side. She asked, "Can you see Gabriel?" Mohammed said, "Yes," he said. Then she asked him to sit next to her on her right side and asked if he could see Gabriel and Mohammed said that he could. Then she told Mohammed to sit in her lap and asked if Gabriel was still there. Yes. Then she took off her clothes and asked if Gabriel was still there. Mohammed said, "No." Khadija said, "Rejoice, he is an angel, not a devil." ♀

THE FIRST CONVERT

♀ I156 Mohammed's wife was the first convert. From the beginning, she had encouraged and believed him. She knew that he was of good character and did not think him to be deceived or crazy.

Soon he stopped hearing voices or seeing visions, became depressed and felt abandoned. Then his visions started again.

PRAYER

I157 Mohammed began to pray with a new understanding. At first he performed two prostrations with each prayer. Later he understood that he should use four prostrations per prayer and use two prostrations when he was traveling.

I158 Then, when he was on a mountain, he saw a vision in which Gabriel showed him how to use ritual ablutions as a purification before prayer. He went home and showed his wife, Khadija, that he now understood how the prayer rituals were done and she copied him.

♀ T1162 Mohammed, his wife and nephew, Ali, started praying at the Kabah incorporating these new rituals of ablutions and prayer with prostrations. A visitor asked about this new ritual and was told that it was a new religion with Mohammed as its prophet.

EARLY ISLAM

The idea of having an Arabian prophet was new. The sources of the native religions were unknown, but the new religion of Islam had a self-declared prophet. The Jews had prophets, and now the Arabs had their own prophet in Mohammed. The religion was called Islam, meaning submission. Those who joined Islam were called Muslims, meaning those who submitted.

I161 A new element was added to the religion. Any person who rejected the revelations of Mohammed would be eternally punished. Only Islam was acceptable.

I166 The Muslims went to the edge of Mecca to pray in order to be alone. One day a group of the Quraysh came upon them and began to mock them and a fight started. Saed, a Muslim, picked up the jaw bone of a camel and struck one of the Quraysh with it and bloodied him. This violence was the first blood to be shed in Islam.

I167 When Mohammed first spoke about his new religion, it did not cause any concern among the Meccans. Then Mohammed began to condemn the ancient religions.

I168 Some of the Quraysh went to Abu Talib, Mohammed's uncle and tribal protector, and said to him, "Your nephew has cursed our gods, insulted our religion, mocked our way of life, criticized our civilization, attacked our virtues, and said that our forefathers were ignorant and in error. You must stop him, or you must let us stop him. We will rid you of him." Abu Talib gave them a soft reply and sent them away.

I169 The Quraysh realized that Abu Talib was not going to help. Mohammed continued to preach Islam and attack them and their lives. Mecca was a small town, everyone knew everyone else. Islam had split the town of Mecca and divided the ruling and priestly tribe.

I170 Things worsened. Soon there was open hostility in Mecca. Quarrels increased, arguments became very heated. Complete disharmony dominated the town. The tribe started to abuse the recently converted Muslims, but Mohammed's uncle Abu Talib was a respected elder and was able to protect them from real harm.

The Koran gives such precise details and direct quotes of their arguments that if you were a Meccan of that day, you would easily know recognize the person.

> 111:1 ***Let the hands of Abu Lahab [Mohammed's uncle and an opponent] die and let him die! His wealth and attainments will not help him. He will be burned in Hell, and his wife will carry the firewood, with a palm fiber rope around her neck.***

I178 Fortunately for Mohammed, the Arabs of Medina were attracted to Islam's message. Since half of their town consisted of Jews, the Arabs of Medina were used to the concept of only one god.

This is the Sunna of Mohammed

PUBLIC TEACHING

CHAPTER 18

3:32 Say: Obey Allah and His messenger, but if they reject it, then truly, Allah does not love those who reject the faith.

At first Mohammed only told close friends and relatives about his message. Then he began to preach more publicly. The Koran condemns those who argue with Mohammed, since to argue against Islam is to be an enemy of Allah. The Koran gives an exact accounting of the arguments of the opponents of Mohammed.

The Meccans reasoned that if the all-knowing god of the universe was the author of the Koran, then why did he not deliver the entire Koran at once, instead of delivering it a piece at a time.

Mohammed continued to preach about Judgment Day, Paradise and Hell:

> 43:68 ***My servants, there is no fear for you that day, nor will you grieve, because you have believed in Our signs and surrendered your will to Allah. You and your wives shall enter the Garden rejoicing. Trays and goblets of gold will be passed around to them, and they will have everything they desire. They will dwell there forever. This is the Garden that will be given you because of your good deeds in life. There is an abundance of fruit there for you to enjoy.***
>
> 43:74 ***The guilty, however, will dwell forever in the torment of Hell. The punishment will not be lightened for them, and they will be overwhelmed with despair. We were not unjust toward them. It was they who were unjust. They will cry, "Malik [an angel who is a keeper of Hell], let your Lord put us out of our misery." He will respond, "No! You will remain here." Surely, We have brought the truth to you, but most of you hate the truth.***
>
> 43:79 ***Do they make plots against you? We also make plots. Do they think that We do not hear their secrets and their private conversations? We do, and Our messengers are there to record them.***

I183 Mohammed continued to preach the glory of Allah and condemn the Quraysh religion. He told them their way of life was wrong and their ancestors would burn in Hell. He cursed their gods, disparaged their religion and divided the community, setting one tribesman against another. The Quraysh felt that this was unbearable. Tolerance had always been their way. There were many clans, many gods, many religions. Another religion was fine, why did Mohammed demean the other religions?

MORE ARGUMENTS WITH THE MECCANS

I188, 189 Another group of Meccans sent for Mohammed to see if they could settle this painful division of the tribes. They went over old ground, and again Mohammed refused the money and power that was offered. He said they needed to decide whether or not they wanted to suffer in the next world and he had the only solution. If they rejected him and his message, Allah would tend to them. One of the Quraysh said, "Well, if you speak for and represent the only true god, then perhaps his Allah could do something for them."

"This land is dry. Let his Allah send them a river next to Mecca."

"They were cramped being next to the mountains. Let his Allah open up some space by moving the mountains back."

"Our best members are dead. Let your Allah renew them to life and in particular send back the best leader of our tribe, Qusayy. We will ask Qusayy whether or not you speak truly."

I189 Mohammed said that he was sent as a messenger, not to do such work. They could either accept his message or reject it and be subject to the loss. Then one of them said, "If you won't use your Allah to help us, then let your Allah help you. Send an angel to confirm you and prove to us that we are wrong. As long as the angel is present, let him make you a garden and fine home and present you with all the gold and silver you need. If you do this, we will know that you represent Allah and we are wrong." The Quraysh wanted miracles as a proof.

I189 Mohammed did not perform miracles, because such things were not what Allah had appointed him to do.

I189 Then one of the Quraysh said, "Then let the heavens be dropped on us in pieces as you say your Lord could do. If you do not we will not believe." Mohammed said that Allah could do that if Allah wished or he might not if he wished.

I189 They then said, "Did not your Lord know that we would ask you these questions? Then your Lord could have prepared you with better answers. And your Lord could have told you what to tell us if we don't believe. We hear that you are getting this Koran from a man named Al Rahman from another town. We don't believe in Al Rahman. Our conscience is clear. We must either destroy you or you must destroy us. Bring your angels and we will believe them."

I191 Mohammed would go to the Kabah and tell the Meccans what terrible punishments Allah had delivered to others in history who had not believed their prophets. This was now one of his constant themes. Allah destroyed others like them who did not listen to men like Mohammed.

I206 Some of the first Muslims were slaves and the Meccans prosecuted them when they could. Abu Bakr was a wealthy man and bought and freed six Muslim slaves to stop their persecution.

This is the Sunna of Mohammed

STRUGGLES

CHAPTER 19

8:20 Believers! Be obedient to Allah and His messenger, and do not turn your backs now that you know the truth. Do not be like the ones who say, "We hear," but do not obey.

I226 Umar's sister and husband submitted to Islam, but Umar, at this time, hated it. He strapped on his sword and went out looking for Mohammed. One of his friends saw him and told him that he should deal with his own family first. Did Umar not know that his sister and her husband had submitted to Islam? He went to their house, and when he got there, he could hear a verse from the Koran being recited. Umar stormed in and demanded to know more about the "garbage" he had just heard. He accused his sister of being a Muslim and hit her. When she cried, his heart softened. Umar read the Koran verses and became convinced that Mohammed was right and he went to Mohammed and submitted to Islam. ♀

I231 With Umar's conversion, Islam became stronger and the Meccans decided to try a boycott as a non-violent way to pressure Mohammed. So the Quraysh posted a notice in the Kabah that no Meccan should marry any Muslim woman or sell them food. ♀

I239 Some Meccans approached Mohammed and said, "Let us worship what you worship. Then you worship what we worship. If what you worship is better than what we worship, then we will take a share of your worship. And if what we worship is better, then you can take a share of that."

THE SATANIC VERSES

T11921 Mohammed was always thinking of ways to persuade all the Meccans to accept Islam. It came to him that the three gods of the Quraysh could intercede with Allah. Mohammed said, "These are the exalted high flying cranes whose intercession is approved." The Meccans were delighted and happy. When Mohammed led prayers at the Kabah, all the Meccans, Muslim and non-Muslim, took part. The Quraysh hung about after the

1. The T references are to Al Tabari's ***History of Prophets and Kings.***

combined service and remarked how happy they were. The tribe had been unified in worship, as before Islam.

Then Mohammed said that he had been deceived by Satan. There was no bridge between Islam and the religion of the Meccans. The retraction by Mohammed made the relations between Islam and the Meccans far worse than it had ever been.

THE POET'S SUBMISSION

I252 Al Dausi was a poet of some standing in Arabia. When he visited Mecca, Al Dausi went to the mosque and heard Mohammed preaching. He liked what he heard and followed Mohammed home. They spoke for some time and Al Dausi decided to submit to Islam.

I253 He then entered his home and told his wife, "Leave me, I want nothing to do with you." She cried, "Why?" Al Dausi said, "Islam has divided us and I now follow Mohammed." She replied, "Then your religion is my religion." He then instructed her in Islam.

The Koran is constant in its admonitions about with whom a Muslim should be friends.

> 4:144 ***Believers! Do not take kafirs as friends over fellow believers. Would you give Allah a clear reason to punish you?***

I260 There was one Christian in Mecca in whom Mohammed took an interest. He was a Christian slave who ran a booth in the market. Mohammed would go and speak with him at length. This led to the Quraysh claiming that what Mohammed said in the Koran, came from the Christian slave.

THE NIGHT JOURNEY

I264 One night as he lay sleeping, Mohammed said that the angel nudged him with his foot. Mohammed awoke. They went out the door and found a white animal, half mule and half donkey. Its feet had wings and could move to the horizon at one step. Gabriel put Mohammed on the white animal and off they went to Jerusalem to the site of the Temple.

I264 There at the temple were Jesus, Abraham, Moses, and other prophets. Mohammed led them in prayer. Gabriel brought Mohammed two bowls. One was filled with wine and the other was filled with milk. Mohammed took the one with milk and drank it. That was the right choice.

I265 Aisha, Mohammed's favorite wife, said that Mohammed never left the bed that night, however, his spirit soared. When Mohammed went out into Mecca to tell the story of his Night Journey, the owner of the home that Mohammed in which Mohammed had slept in sent her black, female slave to follow Mohammed and see how the Meccans reacted to his story.

I266 Mohammed reported that Abraham looked exactly like himself. Moses was a ruddy faced man, tall, thin, and with curly hair. Jesus was light skinned with reddish complexion and freckles and lank hair.

I269 Then he saw women hanging from their breasts. These women had given birth to bastards on their husbands. Mohammed said that Allah hates women who birth bastards. They deprive the true sons of their portion and learn the secrets of the harem. ♀

I270 Abraham took Mohammed into Paradise and there was a beautiful woman with red lips. Mohammed asked who she belonged to, for she was very attractive to him. She belong to Zaid. When he got back, Mohammed told Zaid of this. ♀

I272 Mohammed continued to preach Islam and condemn the old Arabic religions. There were those of the Quraysh who defended their culture and religion and argued with him. Mohammed called them mockers and cursed one of them, "Oh Allah, blind him and kill his son."

The Koran records the actual quotes of Mohammed's opponents.

> 41:26 ***The kafirs say, "Do not listen to this Koran. Instead speak during its reading so that you might gain the upper hand." But We will certainly give the kafirs a taste of a terrible punishment, and We will repay them for their evil deeds. The reward of Allah's enemies is the Fire. The Fire will be their immortal home, a fitting reward for rejecting Our signs.***

I272 One day Mohammed stood with the angel, Gabriel, as the Quraysh performed the rituals of their religion. Among them were the leaders who defended their native culture and religion and opposed Mohammed. When the first leader passed by Gabriel, Gabriel threw a leaf in his face and blinded him. Gabriel then caused the second one to get dropsy which killed him. Gabriel caused the third man to develop an infection which killed him. The fourth man was caused later to step on a thorn which killed him. Gabriel killed the last man who dared to not worship Allah with a brain disease.

MOHAMMED'S PROTECTOR AND WIFE BOTH DIE

I278 Mohammed's protector was his uncle, Abu Talib. When Abu Talib fell ill, some of the leaders of the Quraysh came to his bedside. They said to him, " Please work out a compromise between Mohammed and us."

I278 So Abu Talib called Mohammed to his side. "Nephew, these men have come so that you can give them something and they can give you something." Mohammed said, "If they will give me one word, they can rule the Persians and the Arabs. And they must accept Allah as their Lord and renounce their gods."

I278 Mohammed turned his attention to his dying uncle. He asked him to become a Muslim and then Mohammed could intercede for him on judgment day. His uncle died as a kafir.

Abu Talib had taken the orphan Mohammed into his home and raised him. He took Mohammed on caravan trading missions to Syria and taught him how to be a businessman. Abu Talib was the clan chief who protected Mohammed's life when the rest of Mecca wanted to harm him. Abu Talib was Mohammed's life and security, but he was damned to Hell.

After Abu Talib's death, the pressure on Mohammed was greater. It reached the point where one of the Quraysh threw dust at Mohammed. This was the worst that happened.

♀ The death of his wife, Khadija, had no political effect, but it was a blow to Mohammed. His wife was his chief confidant, and she consoled him.

MARRIAGE

♀ M113[1] About three months after the death of Khadija Mohammed married Sauda, a widow and a Muslim.

♀ M113 Abu Bakr had a daughter, Aisha, who was six years old. Soon after marrying Sauda, Mohammed was betrothed to Aisha, who was to become his favorite wife. The consummation of the marriage would not take place until she turned nine.

> M031, 5977[2] ***Aisha reported Mohammed having said: I saw you in a dream for three nights when an angel brought you to me in a silk cloth and he said: Here is your wife, and when I removed (the cloth) from your face, lo, it was yourself, so I said: If this is from Allah, let Him carry it out.***

I279 With Abu Talib's death, Mohammed needed political allies. Mohammed went to the city of Taif, about fifty miles away, with one servant. In Taif he met with three brothers who were politically powerful. Mohammed called them to Islam and asked them to help him in his struggles with those who would defend their native religions.

His trip was a failure and he returned to Mecca.

---

1 The M refers to the page of Sir William Muir's ***The Life of Muhammad.***

2 An M reference with a comma is Muslim's Hadith, ***Sahih Muslim.***

THE BEGINNING OF POWER AND JIHAD IN MEDINA

Medina was about a ten-day journey from Mecca, but since ancient times the Medinans had come to Mecca for the fairs. Medina was half Jewish and half Arabian, and there was an ongoing tension between the two. The Jews worked as farmers and craftsmen and were literate. They were the wealthy class, but their power was slowly waning. In times past the Arabs had raided and stolen from the Jews who retaliated by saying that one day a prophet would come and lead them to victory over the Arabs. In spite of the tensions, the Arab tribe of Khazraj were allied with them.

I294 At the next fair in Mecca, many of the new Muslims from Medina showed up. During the early part of the night about seventy of them left the caravan to meet with Mohammed. He recited the Koran and said, "I invite your allegiance on the basis that you protect me as you would your children." The Medinans gave their oath. After the oath, one of them asked about their now-severed ties to the Jews of Medina. If they helped Mohammed with arms and they were successful would he go back to Mecca? Mohammed smiled and said, "No, blood is blood, and blood not to be paid for is blood not to be paid for." Blood revenge and its obligation were common to them. "I will war against them who war against you and be at peace with those at peace with you."

I312 One of the two women who gave their oath of allegiance was named Nusayba. She took part in the battle of Yamama and was wounded twelve times. ♀

I299 One of the Medinans said to those who made the pledge, "Do you realize to what you are committing yourselves in pledging your support to this man? It is war against all. If you think that if you lose your property and your best are killed, and then you would give him up, then quit now. But if you think that you will be loyal to your oath if you lose your property and your best are killed, then take him, for it will profit you now and in Paradise." They asked what they would receive for their oath, Mohammed promised them Paradise. They all shook hands on the deal.

BACK IN MEDINA

I304 Back in Medina the Muslims now practiced their new religion openly. But most of the Arabs still practiced their ancient tribal religions. The Muslims would desecrate the old shrines and ritual objects. They would even break into houses and steal ritual objects and throw them into the latrines. On one occasion they killed a dog and tied the dog's body to a ritual object and thew it into the latrine.

IMMIGRATION

I314 The Muslim Medinans had pledged to support Mohammed in war and to help the Muslims from Mecca. The Muslims in Mecca left and went to Medina. The Muslims from both Mecca and Medina were about to be tested.

This is the Sunna of Mohammed

MEDINA

THE BATTLE THAT CHANGED THE WORLD

CHAPTER 20

64:12 So obey Allah and His messenger. But if you turn your backs to them, Our messenger is not to blame, for his duty is only to deliver Our warning clearly. Allah! There is no god but Him! Let the faithful put their trust in Allah.

Mohammed was one of the last to leave Mecca for Medina. In Medina Mohammed built the first mosque. There were now two types of Muslims in Medina. The native Medinan Muslims were called the Helpers, and the new arrivals were called the Immigrants.

♀ I335 Ali left for Medina three days after Mohammed. Ali spent two nights in a town on the way to Medina. He noticed that every night a man came to the door of an unmarried Muslim woman. Ali questioned her about this. She told Ali that the man was bringing stolen non-Muslim ritual objects to her and that she would burn them.

THE COVENANT

Mohammed drew up a political charter that included the basis of war. The Jews were included in the charter as allies of the Muslims. Mohammed was to be the arbitrator in disputes.

MARRIAGE

♀ M177 About seven months after arriving in Medina, Mohammed, aged fifty-three, consummated his marriage with Aisha, now age nine. She moved out of her father's house into what was to become a compound of apartments adjoining the mosque. She was allowed to bring her dolls into the harem due to her age.

THE JEWS

In Mecca, Mohammed had divided the community into Muslims and those practicing the native Arabic religions. In Mecca he adopted all the classical Jewish stories to prove his prophecies and spoke well of the Jews. However, there were almost no Jews living in Mecca, and therefore, no one to differ with him.

In Medina, half of the population were Jews who let Mohammed know they disagreed with him. So in Medina, Mohammed argued with Jews as well as the non-Muslim Arabs. Even though there were very few in the town who were Christian, Mohammed argued against them as well. All non-Muslims were verbally attacked in Medina.

I415 Thirteen years after he started preaching and one year after going to Medina, Mohammed began to prepare for war as commanded by Allah. He would fight his enemies: the kafirs.

THE FIRST RAIDS

I416-423 Mohammed sent his fighters out on seven armed raids to find a trade caravan headed to Mecca.

On the eighth try the jihadists found the caravan. They killed one man and captured the rest. The booty and captives were taken back to Medina. There was a small problem. They had raided and killed someone in a sacred month of peace. This violated Arabic tribal custom.

But the Koran said that killing the kafirs in the sacred months was a moral act. For the Meccans to resist Islam was an offence against Allah, so the killing was justified.

FIGHTING IN ALLAH'S CAUSE—BADR

The next Meccan caravan was large. When the Meccans got wind that the Muslims were going to attack, they sent out a small army to protect it. Mohammed sent out his men to either attack the caravan or do battle with the protecting army.

I433 Mohammed and his men headed out of Medina for what would prove to be one of the most important battles in all of history, a battle that would change the world forever.

I435 Mohammed was cheered. He said, "I see the enemy dead on the ground." They headed towards Badr and camped near there for the night. He sent several scouts to the well at Badr and the scouts found two slaves with water camels. They felt sure they were from the caravan and brought back them back to Mohammed. Two of Mohammed's men questioned them as Mohammed was nearby praying. Mohammed wanted to know which group they were facing—the Quraysh caravan or the army under Abu Sufyan. The men replied that they were from the Quraysh. While

Mohammed prayed, his men began to beat them and torture the captured slaves.

I436 Mohammed told his men that the slaves told them the truth until they started to beat and torture them. Then the slaves had lied but it had been the lie that the Muslims wanted to hear. Mohammed asked the slaves how many of the Meccan army there were and who were the leaders? When they told him, he was delighted and told his warriors that Mecca had sent their best men to be slaughtered.

I440-444 The Meccans marched forth at daybreak. The battle began.

I445 Some arrows flew and one Muslim was killed. Mohammed addressed his army. "By Allah, every man who is slain this day by fighting with courage and advancing, not retreating, will enter Paradise." One of his men had been eating dates said, "You mean that there is nothing between me and Paradise except being killed by the Quraysh?" He flung the dates to the side, picked up his sword and set out to fight. He got his wish and was killed later.

I452 The battle went well for the outnumbered Muslims. After the battle a jihadist brought Mohammed the head of his enemy, Abu Jahl. He said, "Here is the head of the enemy of Allah" and threw it at Mohammed's feet. The Prophet said, "Praise be to Allah."

I455 As the bodies were dragged to a well, one of the Muslims saw the body of his father thrown in. He said, "My father was a virtuous, wise, kind, and cultured man. I had hoped he would become a Muslim. He died a kafir. His abode is hellfire forever."

Before Islam the killing of kin and tribal brothers had been forbidden since the dawn of time. After Islam, brother would kill brother and sons would kill their fathers, fighting in Allah's cause—jihad.

I454 The bodies of the Quraysh were thrown into a well. The Apostle of Allah leaned over the well and shouted at the bodies, "Oh people of the well, have you found what Allah promised to be true?" The Muslims were puzzled by his question. Mohammed explained that the dead could hear him.

I459 They set off for Medina with the spoils of war and the prisoners to be ransomed, except for one who had spoken against Mohammed. He was brought in front of the Prophet to be killed, but before the sword struck, he asked, "Who will care for my family?"

M230 The Prophet replied, "Hell!" After he fell dead, Mohammed said, "Unbeliever in Allah and his Prophet and his Book! I give thanks to Allah Who has killed you and made my eyes satisfied."

I481 After war and victory there were the spoils of war to divide. One fifth went to the Apostle, Allah's prophet.

THE AFFAIR OF MOHAMMED'S DAUGHTER

I465 Among the prisoners was Mohammed's son-in-law, Abul-As, who was also the nephew of Khadija, Mohammed's wife. As a matter of fact, Khadija had asked Mohammed to look for a wife for her nephew, and it had been Mohammed who suggested marriage to their daughter, Zaynab. This was before Mohammed became a prophet and he never opposed Khadija at that time. When Mohammed went to Medina, the Meccans had tried to get Abul-As to divorce Mohammed's daughter, but he refused, even though Abul-As had never become a Muslim himself. Mohammed was fond of him. ♀

I465 But there was a second Meccan, Utba, who had married Mohammed's second daughter. When the Meccans approached him to divorce Mohammed's daughter, Utba agreed on the condition he could have his pick of two women. They agreed and Utba divorced Mohammed's daughter. ♀

I466 Abul-As was captured at Badr. His wife sent the money for his ransom and included with it a necklace that Khadija, Mohammed's wife, had given her on her wedding day. When Mohammed saw the necklace, he softened and asked the captors to forgo the ransom and return Abul-As to his daughter. The captors agreed. ♀

I467 Mohammed set a condition that his daughter, Zaynab, be allowed to come and see him. So when Abul-As returned to Mecca, he told Zaynab to go to Medina to see Mohammed. She prepared and left on a camel with her brother-in-law. The Meccans decided to chase after them and caught her on the road. One of the Meccans approached with his spear and threatened her. The story is vague, but she may have been pregnant and the panic caused her to abort. Her brother-in-law drew his bow and threatened to kill all of the Meccans. ♀

I467 The leader of the Meccans asked him to unstring his bow and talk. He said, "Look, we have just been humiliated by Mohammed, and now you are taking his daughter to him very publicly. Come back to Mecca and wait until the anger has died down and then leave quietly." And that is what they did. Later he took her away in the middle of the night. ♀

I469 Later when Mohammed sent out raiders, he told them that if they found one of the two men who threatened his daughter, they were to burn them to death. Later, he told them not to burn them because that was Allah's punishment. They should just kill them, instead. ♀

♀ I470 Zaynab continued to live in Medina, while Abul-As lived in Mecca. Abul-As headed a trading expedition to Syria. Mohammed warriors attacked the caravan and captured all of the goods, while Abul-As escaped to Medina where he hid out with Zaynab. Mohammed agreed that he was not to be harmed, but that he and Zaynab could not have sex since she was a Muslim.

♀ I470 Mohammed then went to the warriors who had taken Abul-As's property and asked them to return it and they did. Abul-As then submitted to Islam. He and Zaynab were then considered to be married again.

THE RAID ON THE TRIBE OF B. SULAYM

I540-543, T1365 Seven days after Mohammed returned from Badr, there were four more armed raids, but no contact with the enemy, the kafirs.

Mohammed had become a political force unlike any ever seen before in history. The fusion of religion and politics with a universal mandate created a permanent historic force. Muslims believer will be no peace until all the world is Islam. The spoils of war will provide the wealth of Islam. The awe of Mohammed is the fear of Allah.

> *B1,7,331 The Prophet said, "I have been given five things which were not given to anyone else before me.*
> *1. Allah made me victorious by awe, by His frightening my enemies for a distance of one month's journey.*
> *2. The earth has been made for me and for my followers a place for praying and to perform my rituals, therefore anyone of my followers can pray wherever the time of a prayer is due.*
> *3. The spoils of war has been made Halal (lawful) for me yet it was not lawful for anyone else before me.*
> *[...]*

Mohammed left Mecca as a preacher and prophet. He entered Medina with about 150 Muslim converts. After a year in Medina there were about 250-300 Muslims and most of them were very poor. After the battle of Badr, a new Islam emerged. Mohammed rode out of Medina as a politician and general. Islam became an armed political force with a religious motivation, jihad.

This is the Sunna of Mohammed

THE JEWS

CHAPTER 21

9:63 Do they not know that whoever opposes Allah and His Messenger will abide in the Fire of Hell, where they will remain forever? This is the great shame.

When Mohammed arrived in Medina about half the town were Jews. There were three tribes of Jews and two tribes of Arabs. Almost none of the Jews had Hebrew names. They were Arabs to some degree. At the same time many of the Arabs' religious practices contained elements of Judaism. The Jews were farmers and tradesmen and lived in their own fortified quarters. In general, they were better educated and more prosperous than the Arabs.

Before Mohammed arrived, there had been bad blood and killing among the tribes. The last battle had been fought between the two Arab tribes, but each of the Jewish tribes had joined the battle with their particular Arab allies. In addition to that tension between the two Arab tribes, there was a tension between the Jews and the Arabs. The division of the Jews and fighting on different sides was condemned by Mohammed. The Torah preached that the Jews should be unified, and they failed in this.

All of these quarrelsome tribal relationships were one reason that Mohammed was invited to Medina, but the result was further polarization, not unity. The new split was between Islam and those Arabs and their Jewish partners who resisted Islam.

I351 About this time, the leaders of the Jews spoke out against Mohammed. The rabbis began to ask him difficult questions. Doubts and questions arose about his doctrine. But for Mohammed, doubts about Allah were evil. However, two of the Jewish Arabs joined with Mohammed as Muslims. They believed him when he said that he was the Jewish prophet that came to fulfill the Torah.

THE REAL TORAH IS IN THE KORAN

Mohammed said repeatedly that the Jews and Christians corrupted their sacred texts in order to conceal the fact that he was prophesied in their scriptures. The stories in the Koran are similar to those of the Jew's scriptures, but they make different points. In the Koran, all of the stories found in Jewish scripture indicated that Allah destroyed those cultures that did not listen to their messengers. According to Mohammed, the scriptures of the Jews had been changed to hide the fact that Islam is the true religion and that he was the last prophet of the Jews.

I369 The Jews' sins are so great that Allah has changed them into apes. Still they will not learn and refuse to admit that Mohammed is their prophet. They know full well the truth and hide and confuse others. Even when they say to Mohammed they believe, they conceal their resistance.

> 2:63 ***And remember, Children of Israel, when We made a covenant with you and raised Mount Sinai before you saying, "Hold tightly to what We have revealed to you and keep it in mind so that you may guard against evil." But then you turned away, and if it had not been for Allah's grace and mercy, you surely would have been among the lost. And you know those among you who sinned on the Sabbath. We said to them, "You will be transformed into despised apes." So we used them as a warning to their people and to the following generations, as well as a lesson for the Allah-fearing.***

I370 The Jews have understood the truth of Mohammed and then changed their scriptures to avoid admitting that Mohammed is right.

MOHAMMED TRULY FOLLOWS THE RELIGION OF ABRAHAM

♀ I375 A group of rabbis came to Mohammed and asked him, "Why does a boy resemble his mother if the sperm comes from the father?" Mohammed replied that a man's fluid is thick and white and a woman's fluid is yellow and thin. The child resembles the mother or the father depending upon whose fluid was on top.

♀ I394 The Jews asked Mohammed to deliver judgment against a married man and a married woman who had committed adultery. Mohammed delivered the full judgment found in the Torah, which was stoning. The Jews had stopped using capital punishment. So the couple was brought to the mosque and they were stoned to death. When the man felt the first stone, he crouched over the woman until they were both dead.

> [B3,41,596;B4,51,9;B7,63,216;B9,83,15;B9,83,16;B9,83,18;B9,83,23;]
>
> ***During the lifetime of Mohammed, a Jew attacked a girl and took some silver ornaments she was wearing and crushed her head between two stones. Her relatives brought her to Mohammed while she was taking her last breaths and was unable to speak. He asked her who had killed her, and mentioned different names. She shook her head with each name, until Mohammed finally mentioned the name of the criminal, and she nodded. So the***

Jew was questioned until he confessed. Then Mohammed ordered that the head of that Jew be crushed between two stones.

AN OMINOUS CHANGE

I381 In Mecca, Mohammed spoke well of the Jews, who were very few. In Medina there were many Jews and his relations with them were tense. Up to now Mohammed had led prayer facing in the direction of Jerusalem. Now the ***kiblah***, direction of prayer, was changed to the Kabah in Mecca. Some of the Jews came to him and asked why he had changed the direction of prayer. After all, he said that he followed the religion of Abraham.

Since Islam is the successor to Judaism, Allah was the successor to Jehovah. It was actually Allah who had been the deity of the Jews and the Jews had deliberately hidden this fact by corrupting the scriptures. For this, Muslims believe, the Jews have been cursed.

THE AFFAIR OF THE JEWS OF QAYNUQA

I545 There were three tribes of Jews in Medina. The Beni Qaynuqa were goldsmiths and lived in a stronghold in their quarters. It is said by Mohammed that they broke the treaty that had been signed when Mohammed came to Medina. How they did this is unclear.

I545 Mohammed assembled the Jews in their market and said: "Oh Jews, be careful that Allah does not bring vengeance upon you like what happened to the Quraysh. Become Muslims. You know that I am the prophet that was sent you. You will find that in your scriptures."

I545 They replied: "Oh, Mohammed, you seem to think that we are your people. Don't fool yourself. You may have killed and beaten a few merchants of the Quraysh, but we are men of war and real men."

I546 Some time later Mohammed besieged the Beni Qaynuqa Jews in their quarters. Neither of the other two Jewish tribes came to their support. Finally the Jews surrendered, expecting to be slaughtered after their capture.

But one of the Jews' old allies persuaded Mohammed not to kill them. Mohammed exiled the Jews and took all of their wealth and goods.

THE RAID TO AL QARADA

I547 Mohammed's victory at Badr and ongoing jihad caused the Quraysh to choose a different route to Syria. They hired a new guide to take them over the new route. Mohammed had received intelligence about their route and sent a party to raid them. They were carrying a great deal of silver when the caravan stopped at a watering hole. The Muslims surprised them and the Quraysh managed to escape but Mohammed's men were able to steal all the caravan's goods, including the silver. The stolen goods were delivered to Mohammed in Medina.

THE ASSASSINATION OF AL ASHRAF, THE JEW

I548 When Al Ashraf, a Jew of Medina, heard that two of his friends had been killed at Badr, he said that it was better to be in the grave than on earth with Mohammed. So the "enemy of Allah" composed some poems bewailing the loss of his friends and attacking Islam.

♀ T1369 Then Al Ashraf wrote a sexual poem about a Muslim woman.

I551 When Mohammed heard of Al Ashraf's critical poetry about his politics, he said, "Who will rid me of Al Ashraf?" A Muslim said, "I will kill him for you." Days later, Mohammed found out that his assassin was not doing anything, including eating or drinking. Mohammed summoned him and asked what was going on. The man replied that he had taken on a task that was too difficult for him to do. Mohammed said that it was a duty which he should try to do. The assassin said, "Oh Apostle of Allah, I will have to tell a lie." The Prophet said, "Say what you like, you are free in the matter."

I552 Through the use of lies three Muslims were able to kill Al Ashraf. When they returned to Mohammed, he was praying. They told him that they had killed the enemy of Allah. Their attack terrorized all the Jews. There was no Jew in Medina who was not afraid.

KILL ANY JEW THAT FALLS INTO YOUR POWER

I554 The Apostle of Allah said, "Kill any Jew who falls into your power." Hearing this Muhayyisa fell upon a Jewish merchant who was a business associate and killed him. Muhayyisa's brother was not a Muslim and asked him how he could kill a man who had been his friend and partner in many business deals. The Muslim said that if Mohammed had asked him to kill his brother he would have done it immediately. His brother said, "You mean that if Mohammed said to cut off my head you would do it?" "Yes," was the reply. The older brother then said, "By Allah, any religion which brings you to this is marvelous." And he decided then and there to become a Muslim.

This is the Sunna of Mohammed

THE CHRISTIANS

CHAPTER 22

24:52 It is such as obey Allah and His Apostle, and fear Allah and do right, that will win.

1404 While some Christians were in Medina, they argued religion with Mohammed. They held forth with the doctrine of the Trinity and the divinity of Christ. Mohammed later laid out the Islamic version of the Christian doctrine. The Koran tells in detail the true story of Jesus, who is just another of Allah's prophets, and that the Trinity of the Christians is Allah, Jesus and Mary.

1406 No one has power except through Allah. Allah gave the prophet Jesus the power of raising the dead, healing the sick, making birds of clay and having them fly away. Allah gave Jesus these signs as a mark of his being a prophet. But Allah did not give the powers of appointing kings, or the ability to change night to day. This lack of power show that Jesus was a man, not part of the Trinity. If he were part of God, then all powers would have been in his command. Then he would not have to have been under the dominion of kings.

MARY, THE MOTHER OF JESUS

1407 Imran was the father of Moses, Aaron and Mary, the mother of Jesus[1].

> 19:16 ***And mention Mary in the Scripture, when she withdrew from her family to a place in the East. She took a veil to screen herself from them. Then We sent Our spirit [Gabriel] to her in the form of a perfect man. She said, "I seek protection from you with Merciful Allah. If you fear Him, then do not come near me."***
>
> 19:19 ***He said, "I am merely your Lord's messenger. I come to announce to you the gift of a holy son."***
>
> 19:20 ***She said, "How can I have a son when no man has touched me, and I am chaste?"***
>
> 19:21 ***He said, "Even so, it will happen. Your Lord says, 'That is easy for Me.' We will make him a sign for all men and a mercy from Us. It is something***

1. This version of history is at variance with Christian doctrine. Jesus was born 1600 years after Moses.

that is decreed." And she conceived him, and she withdrew with him to a remote place. When the pain of childbirth drove her to the trunk of a palm-tree, she said, "If only I had died before this."
19:24 *But a voice from below her said, "Do not grieve; your Lord has provided a stream beneath you. Shake the trunk of the palm-tree towards yourself; it will drop fresh ripe dates upon you. So eat and drink and dry your eyes. And if you should see any man, say, 'I have promised a fast to Allah. I will speak to no one today.'"*

I407-8 Christ spoke in the cradle and then spoke to men as a grown man. Speaking from the cradle is a sign of his being a prophet. Christ's prophethood was confirmed by making clay birds fly. By Allah's power, Christ healed the blind, the lepers, and raised the dead.

19:27 *Later, she brought the baby to her people, carrying him in her arms. They said, "Mary, you have come with an amazing thing. Sister of Aaron, your father was not a wicked man, and your mother was not unchaste." But she merely pointed to the baby. They said, "How can we speak with an infant in a cradle?" The child said, "Surely, I am the servant of Allah. He has given me the Book and has made me a prophet. He has made me blessed wherever I am; and has urged me to pray and give alms, as long as I live; and to be dutiful to my mother; and He has not made me arrogant or miserable. The peace of Allah was on me the day I was born, and will be on me the day that I die; and on the day I will be resurrected."*
19:34 *This was Jesus, the son of Mary; this is a statement of truth about which they [Christians] dispute. It does not befit the majesty of Allah to father a son. Glory be to Him! When He decrees something, He only needs to say, "Be," and it is. Surely, Allah is my Lord and your Lord, so serve Him. That is the right path.*

I408 Christ only comes through Allah. Christ's signs of being a prophet come only from Allah. Jesus enjoins others to worship Allah, not him. But when the people refused to hear him, the Disciples came forth to help him with his mission. The Disciples were servants of Allah and were Muslims just like Christ.

I409 Christ was not crucified. When the Jews plotted against Christ, they found Allah to be the best plotter. Allah took Jesus up directly to him and will refute those who say he was crucified and was resurrected. On the final day, the Day of Resurrection, those who follow Christ but do not believe in his divinity will be blessed. Those who insist that Christ is God, part of the Trinity, and reject true faith will be punished in Hell.

This is the Sunna of Mohammed

JIHAD, A SETBACK

CHAPTER 23

4:14 But those who disobey Allah and His Messenger and go beyond His limits, will be led into the Fire to live forever, and it will be a humiliating torment!

THE BATTLE OF UHUD

The Meccans had lost at the battle of Badr, but they raised an army and returned to fight the Muslims at Uhud, near Medina.

I560 When they saw the Meccans, Mohammed said, "Let there be no fighting until I give the word." Mohammed placed 50 archers to protect his rear and flank. They must not move but hold that ground.

I562 The morrow came and the battle was to begin. Now the Meccans had brought their women for the sole purpose urging on the men. Men do not want to be cowards in front of women. The women began to beat their tambourines and chant poetry:

If you advance we will hug you
And place soft rugs beneath you
If you retreat we will leave you
Leave and no more love you.

I557 Hind, a Meccan woman, had a black slave called Washi, who was an expert with the javelin. She told Washi that if he could kill Hamza [Hamza had killed Hind's uncle at Badr.] he would give him his freedom. On the way to the battle, whenever Hind saw Washi, she would say, "Come on, you father of blackness, satisfy your vengeance and ours."

I557 During the battle Washi hung near the edge of the fighting and looked for Hamza. Hamza fought like a lion as Washi watched. As Hamza fought one of the Meccans, he said, "Come here, you son of a clitoris cutter. " Hamza then killed the man whose mother performed the female circumcision [removed the girl's clitoris, common surgery in Arabia.] Then Washi threw his javelin and killed Hamza. Washi was now free and left the field.

The Muslims lost because the archers did not hold their position, and instead they ran to the Meccan camp to steal their goods.

The Meccans won, but they did not press their advantage and let Mohammed escape.

♀ I578 Hind and other women went through the battlefield and mutilated the corpses. Hind cut off their ears and noses to make them into bracelets. Hind removed Hamza's liver and chewed it raw.

> ***We have rewarded you for Badr***
> ***Continued war is violent***
> ***I was broken by the loss of my father and brother***
> ***I have fulfilled my vengeance***
> ***Washi has slacked the burning in my breast***
> ***Thank you Washi. —Hind***

♀ I586 The dead Muslims were buried in the battlefield. Mohammed said, "I testify that all who are wounded in jihad will be raised by Allah with his bleeding wounds smelling like the finest perfume." Mohammed heard the women weeping for their dead, but he wanted wailing for his uncle Hamza as well. So the women wailed for Hamza and Mohammed felt better.

The Muslims had lost because they did not obey Mohammed's orders. So the Koran said that from now on Muslims must obey Mohammed in all things. They were not to lose courage, as there would be opportunity in the future to get more war booty.

I606 The Koran said that the success that the kafirs experienced was temporary. They would grow in their evil and be punished. Allah would not leave the believers in this state. But this trial would separate the weak from the strong. Those who have wealth should spend it on jihad.

ASSASSINATION AS JIHAD

M276 After Uhud, several tribes allied themselves under the leadership of Sufyan Ibn Khalid. Mohammed dispatched an assassin to kill him, for without his leadership the coalition would fall apart. So the assassin, Abdullah, joined Sufyan's forces and waited until he was alone with him. He killed Sufyan and cut off his head and went back to Medina.

M276 Abdullah then went straight to Mohammed. Mohammed welcomed him and asked him how it went. Abdullah presented Mohammed with the head of his enemy. Mohammed was gratified and presented him with his walking stick. He said, "This is a token between you and me on the day of resurrection. Very few will have such to lean on in that day." Abdullah attached it to his sword scabbard.

THE RAID ON THE MUSTALIQ TRIBE

I725 When Mohammed heard that the Arab tribe, the Mustaliq, were opposed to him and were gathering against him, he set out with his army to attack. He found them at a watering hole and combat started. Islam was victorious and the Mustaliq and their women, children, and goods were taken as spoils of war and distributed to the fighters. ♀

I729 The captives of the tribe of Mustaliq were parceled out as spoils. There was a ransom price set upon their heads. If the ransom were not paid then the people were treated as spoils and slaves. Now, one was a beautiful woman with a high price on her. She came to Mohammed and asked him to see if the price could be reduced. Mohammed had a better idea. He paid the ransom and the beautiful woman became wife number seven. ♀

I729 This marriage had a side effect. The captives were now related to Mohammed's wife. They were all released without ransom.

THE DEATH OF A POETESS

I996 There was a poetess who wrote a poem against Islam. Mohammed said, "Who will rid me of Marwan's daughter?" One of his followers, a blind man, heard him and on that very night he went to the woman's home to kill her. ♀

M239 The blind assassin was able to do the work in the dark as the woman slept. Her other children lay in the room, but her babe lay on her breast. The stealthy assassin removed the child and drove the knife into her with such force that he pinned her to the bed. ♀

I996 In the morning he went to Mohammed and told him. Mohammed said, "You have helped Allah and his Apostle."

M239 Mohammed turned to the people in the mosque, he said, "If you wish to see a man who has assisted Allah and his Prophet, look here." Omar cried, "What, the blind Omeir!" "No," said Mohammed, "call him Omeir the Seeing."

I996 The poetess had five sons and the assassin went to them and taunted them saying, "I killed Bint Marwan, Oh sons. Withstand me if you can; don't keep me waiting." Islam became powerful that day and many became Muslims when they saw the power of Islam. ♀

This is the Sunna of Mohammed

JIHAD, THE JEWS SUBMIT

CHAPTER 24

58:20 Those who oppose Allah and His Messenger will be laid low. Allah has declared, "Surely I will be victorious, along with My messengers." Truly Allah is strong and mighty.

CLEANSING

Mohammed attacked the second of the two Jewish tribes in Medina. The Jews would not admit that he was a real prophet and for this they would pay. Mohammed put the Jews under siege and burned their date palm plantations. The other Jews would not help them. They cut a deal and got to leave alive with all they could carry.

Since there was no actual fighting and the jihadists did no work, Mohammed got all of the booty.

The burning of the date palms violated Arabic tribal customs. But the Koran said that it was a moral act against the kafir Jews.

THE BATTLE OF THE TRENCH

The Meccans came back to Medina to fight against Islam. But Mohammed had spies in Mecca, so he knew they were coming. At the suggestion of a Muslim who had been to Persia, the Muslims built a defensive trench.

I677-683 Mohammed was able to use his agents to sow discord among those allied against him. The trench defense frustrated the Meccans. The weather was bad, and the allies were distrustful of each other. In terms of actual combat only a handful of men were killed over the twenty-day siege. The Meccans broke camp and went back home. It was a victory for Mohammed.

♀ I680 While the armies were facing each other, Hassan was back at a fort. A Jew was seen going around the fort and Hassan was afraid that he would find a way in. Hassan's wife said that Hassan should go down and kill the Jew. But Hassan was a poet who wrote satire for Mohammed and he was not about to take up arms and told his wife so. The wife took a club and went outside and beat the Jew to death. She went back to the fort and told Hassan to go and strip the body. [The killing was an act of jihad and the killer got to take the goods as booty.] But Hassan refused to do even that much.

THE SOLUTION FOR THE JEWS

I684 That same day the angel Gabriel came to Mohammed at noon. He asked if Mohammed were through fighting. Gabriel and the angels were going to attack the last Jewish tribe in Medina. Gabriel said, "Allah commands you to go to the Jews. I am headed there now to shake their stronghold."

Mohammed put the Jews under siege. They surrendered and submitted to the judgment of Saed, an old ally.

I688 The Jews decided to let a Muslim they thought was their friend, Saed, deliver judgment if they surrendered to Mohammed. Saed's judgment was simple. Kill all the men. Take their property and take the women and children as captives. Mohammed said, "You have given the judgment of Allah." ♀ $

I690 The captives were taken into Medina. They dug trenches in the market place of Medina. It was a long day, but 800 Jews were beheaded that day. Mohammed and his twelve-year-old wife, Aisha, sat and watched the slaughter the entire day and into the night. The Apostle of Allah had every male Jew killed. ♀

> [B5,59,362]
>
> ***The Bani An-Nadir and Bani Quraiza violated their peace treaty with Mohammed. He exiled the former and treated the latter with lenience, allowing them to remain in their lands in Medina. When the Bani Quraiza fought Mohammed again, he killed their men and distributed their women and children as slaves among the Muslims. Those who came to Mohammed and embraced Islam were granted safety. He exiled all Jews from Medina.***

I691 Only one of the female Jews was killed. She sat with Aisha the entire time the males were being beheaded and laughed and talked. Then a voice called the Jew's name and Aisha asked why she was being called. The Jew said that she had done something. She was taken away and beheaded. ♀

I693 Mohammed took the property, wives and children of the Jews, and divided it up amongst the Muslims. Mohammed took his one-fifth of the slaves and sent a Muslim with the female Jewish slaves to a nearby city where the women were sold for pleasure. Mohammed invested the money from the sale of the female slaves for horses and weapons. ♀ $

♀ I693 There was one last share of the spoils for Mohammed. The most beautiful Jewess became his slave for pleasure.

I696-7 In the battle of the Trench it was Allah who had won the day. Allah gives the Muslim his strength and will. No matter what the kafirs do Allah will triumph. Allah totally approves of the killing of the Jews, enslaving the women and children. It was good to give the Jew's property to the Muslim warriors. After all, Allah wanted it done and helped to do it.

> 33:25 ***And Allah drove back the kafirs in their wrath, and they gained nothing by it. Allah aided the believers in the war, for Allah is strong and mighty. He brought down some of the People of the Book [the Jews] out of their fortresses to aid the confederates and to strike terror into their hearts. Some you killed, and others you took captive. He made you heirs of their land, their homes, and their possessions, and even gave you another land on which you had never before set foot. Allah has power over everything. [800 male Jews were executed, their property taken, and women and children enslaved.]***

THE KILLING OF THE JEW, SALLAM

I714-6 A Jew named Sallam helped to plan and organize the confederation of the tribes that attacked Mohammed in the Battle of the Trench. Mohammed sent five Muslim men to assassinate Sallam. When the men had done their work, they returned to Mohammed and fell to arguing as to who actually killed Sallam. Mohammed demanded to see their swords. He examined them one by one and then pointed to the sword that had been the killing weapon. It had food on it still from the thrust to the victim's stomach.

This is the Sunna of Mohammed

JIHAD, THE FIRST DHIMMIS

CHAPTER 25

4:80 Those who obey the Messenger, obey Allah. As for those who turn away from you, We have not sent you to watch over them.

TREATY OF AL HUDAYBIYA

Mohammed decided it was time for the Muslims to make a pilgrimage to Mecca and the Kabah. But the Meccans would not let the Muslims enter, even though they were unarmed and in pilgrimage clothing. So Mohammed parlayed with the Meccans.

I747 They drew up a treaty to the effect that there would be no war for ten years, there would be no hostilities, and no one could convert to Islam without their guardians' permission. In turn the Muslims could come next year and stay for three days in Mecca, but they could not enter this year.

I748 Many of the Muslims were depressed. Mohammed had promised that they could enter Mecca. Now they could not. Before they left they sacrificed the camels and shaved their heads, doing as many of the rituals as they could without getting into Mecca.

I749 On the way back to Medina, Mohammed added to the Koran, the sura called Victory, about this treaty. Those who held back [the desert Arabs, Bedouins] and did not come on the pilgrimage would not profit by receiving any spoils of war. And there was more war to come in the future.

I750 This was a victory for Islam. The government of Mecca dealt with Mohammed as an independent political power. Because of this power many more Arabs were attracted to Islam.

I755 The treaty declared that Mohammed was to return the women of Medina who migrated from Mecca. But Mohammed decided to return the dowries of those women who had come from Mecca to become Muslims without permission of their guardians. Normally, he would have kept the women and the dowries. He also asked the Meccans to return the dowries of those kafir women who had left Medina to live in Mecca. ♀

KHAYBAR

I756 After the treaty of Al Hudaybiya, Mohammed stayed in Medina for about two months before he collected his army and marched to the forts of Khaybar, a community of wealthy Jewish farmers who lived in a village of separate forts about 100 miles from Medina.

I758 Mohammed seized the forts one at a time. Among the captives was a beautiful Jewess named Safiya. Mohammed took her for his sexual pleasure. One of his men had first chosen her for his own slave of pleasure, but Mohammed traded him two of her cousins for Safiya. Mohammed always got first choice of the spoils of war and the women.

I759 On the occasion of Khaybar, Mohammed put forth new orders about sex with captive women. If the woman was pregnant, she was not to be used for sex until after the birth of the child. Nor were any women to be used for sex who were unclean with regards to the Muslim laws about menstruation.

I764 Mohammed knew that there was a large treasure hidden somewhere in Khaybar, so he brought forth the Jew who he thought knew the most about it and questioned him. The Jew denied any knowledge. Mohammed told one of his men, "Torture the Jew until you extract what he has." So the Jew was staked on the ground, and a small fire built on his chest to get him to talk. When the man was nearly dead and still would not talk, Mohammed had him released and taken to one of his men whose brother had been killed in the fight. This Muslim got the pleasure of cutting off the tortured Jew's head.

I763 Mohammed had his freed slave, Bilal, to go and get the two best looking women and bring them to him. Bilal brought the women past the dead Jews. One of them began to shriek and pour dust on her head. Mohammed said, "Take this she-devil away from me." Then he threw his mantle over Safiya so that the men would know that she was his. Mohammed then told Bilal, "Do you not have any compassion, bringing these two women past their dead husbands?"

[B2,14,68;B3,34,431;B3,34,437;B4,52,143;B5,59,512;B5,59,513;B5,59,522;B5,59,523]

After conquering Khaybar, Mohammed was told of the beauty of Safiya, whose husband had been killed. She was a captive, but he freed her as a marriage gift, and so chose her for his bride. He brought her with the army until they reached Sidd-as-Sahba, and he married her after she became clean of her menstrual cycle.

I764 At Khaybar Mohammed instituted the first dhimmis. After the best of the goods were taken from the Jews, Mohammed left them to work the land. Since his men knew nothing about farming, and the Jews were skilled at it, they worked the land and gave Mohammed half of their profits.

I765 After Mohammed rested, the wife of Sallam prepared a meal for him. She asked which piece of meat he preferred and gave it to him. He chewed a bite and spit it out and declared it to be poisoned. He asked the Jewess about this and she agreed it was poisoned. She said that after what he had done to other Jews, she wanted to rid herself of him if he were only a king. If he were a prophet, he would know not to eat it. The Muslim at the table with Mohammed did not spit his meat out and he died. ♀

I767 It was time for Safiya's wedding, so she was 'beautified' by a Muslim for her wedding night with Mohammed. When Mohammed awoke in the morning he found a young Muslim walking around his tent with a drawn sword. He asked what he was doing. He said, "I was afraid for you. You killed her husband, tortured her father to death, and destroyed her people." Mohammed asked Allah to preserve the fighter as well as he preserved Mohammed. ♀

I768 Mohammed gave the women a small share of the booty. He gave a portion of Khaybar to his wives as well. ♀

FADAK

I777 The Jews of Fadak panicked when they saw what Mohammed did at Khaybar. They would be next, so they surrendered to Mohammed without a fight. Since there was no battle Mohammed got all of their goods and they worked the land and gave half to Mohammed each year. They became dhimmis like those of Khaybar.

This is the Sunna of Mohammed

MOHAMMED'S FINAL JIHAD

CHAPTER 26

3:53 "Our Lord! We believe in what Thou hast revealed, and we follow the Apostle; then write us down among those who bear witness."

MECCA CONQUERED

The treaty of Hudaybiya was broken by a fight between allies of Mohammed and allies of Mecca. Mohammed took advantage of this and attacked Mecca.

♀ I810 A Muslim of Medina, Hatib, wrote a letter to the Meccans saying that Mohammed was coming to Mecca. He then paid a woman to take the letter to Mecca. She concealed the letter in her hair. Mohammed received information that she was carrying the letter and sent two men after her. They caught up with her, searched her and found nothing. Ali ordered her to produce the letter or they would strip her naked. She gave them the letter.

I810 When they returned to Medina, Mohammed called for Hatib and demanded an answer. He said that he was not a man of importance and he was just trying to take care of family left in Mecca. Umar wanted to behead him, but Mohammed pointed out that Hatib had fought at Badr and could do as he pleased.

I811 As a result of the fighting between a tribe allied with the Meccans and a tribe allied with Mohammed, he marched on Mecca with 10,000 men to punish them.

The Meccans decided to yield without a fight. The Meccan leader submitted to Islam. The leader went ahead and announced to the citizens that Mohammed's army was coming. They were not to resist but to go into their houses, his house or the Kabah and that they would be safe.

I819 Mohammed had told his commanders only to kill those who resisted. Otherwise they were to bother no one except for those who had spoken against Mohammed. The list of those to be killed:

- One of Mohammed's secretaries, who had said that when he was recording Mohammed's Koranic revelations sometimes Mohammed let the secretary insert better speech. This caused him to lose faith and he became an apostate (left Islam).

- Two singing girls who had sung satires against Mohammed.
- A Muslim tax collector who had become an apostate.
- A man who had insulted Mohammed.

T1642 Hind was the Meccan woman who had mutilated Hamza at the battle of Uhud. When she came before Mohammed to become a Muslim, he told her that her duties included not killing children. She replied that she had raised them and not killed them. But when they were grown Mohammed had killed both of her sons at Badr. ♀

I821 Mohammed went to the Kabah, prayed and then destroyed all of the religious art in Mecca.

Mohammed announced the end of all feuds, all revenge killings, and payment of blood money. Veneration of the ancestors was over.

KHALID'S EXPEDITIONS

I834 Mohammed sent Khalid out to the tribes around the Meccan countryside.

I837 Khalid attacked one tribe, bound and beheaded many of them. One of those who was tied asked to be taken over to a girl. The man said, "Good bye, though life is at an end." He then quoted a love poem to her: ♀

Was I not a worthy lover?
Did I not undertake journeys day and night for you?
Reward me with love before tragedy
Reward me with love before the distance is too great
Even when our tribe's troubles took my attention
Even then my love was there.

I838 She replied, "May your life be lengthened for years." He was taken away and beheaded. ♀

I840 Mohammed sent Khalid to an ancient temple near Mecca that was used by several tribes for worship. When Khalid got there, he destroyed it completely.

THE BATTLE OF HUNAIN

I840 When Mohammed took Mecca, the surrounding Arab tribes saw that if he were not opposed, he would become King of Arabia. The Hawazin Arabs decided to oppose him under the leadership of Malik.

I842 Mohammed sent a spy to gather intelligence about the Arabs. When he received the information, he began preparing for jihad. He first borrowed armor and lances from a wealthy Meccan and then marched out with 12,000 men.

1845 The army descended into a broad area and they found the enemy prepared and hiding, waiting to attack. The Muslim troops broke and ran. Mohammed stood in his stirrups and called out, "Where are you going? Come to me, the Apostle of Allah." Most of the men continued to retreat except his battle-hardened core troops who regrouped around him. A group of about 100 led the charge to turn the tide. They were steadfast. Mohammed looked at the carnage and said, "Now the oven is hot!"

♀ 1847 One of the Muslim women was near Mohammed and said about those who were retreating, "Kill those who flee just as you kill those who are attacking us."

Once again, Islam defeated the kafirs.

BATTLE OF TAIF

1872 Mohammed attacked al Taif, a walled town. The Muslims pitched their tents near the walls and settled down for a siege. Mohammed had brought two wives and put them into two tents. The battle did not go well and the town was successful in resisting jihad. Mohammed had the fighters destroy all of their vineyards.

♀ 1873 One of the Muslim women asked Mohammed if she could have the jewelry of two of the richest women in Taif. Mohammed said she could but he doubted that they were going to succeed. Shortly after that he called off the attack. On the way back, one of the Muslims said that he did not mind losing the battle, but he did regret not getting a woman from Taif for a slave. The people of Taif were noted for their intelligence and he wanted to breed the slave to have smart children from her.

THE HAWAZIN

1877 The Hawazin had been beaten by the Muslims. As Mohammed came back from Taif, he stopped to deal with them. They had submitted to Islam and wanted relief from their loss. Their leaders pointed out to Mohammed that some of his prisoners were members of his foster family. Mohammed gave the leaders a choice. They could have their cattle and goods back or their wives and sons back. They choose their families.

♀ 1877 Mohammed asked the various tribal leaders of his army if they would turn the Hawazin loose. Most of them did, but two tribes said no, so Mohammed offered them six camels for each person they freed. The debt would be paid from the next battle. They then freed all of the captives, but one. One of the captors had a old woman that he did want to free for six camels. He thought that she was rich and worth more. His friend said, "Let her go. Her breasts are flat. She can't conceive and her mouth is cold. It is not like she is a virgin in her prime or even a plump middle-aged matron." He let her go for six camels.

I878 Mohammed gave three of his companions a slave girl for each to use for sex. Uthman took his sex slave and gave her to his son. ♀ ⚤

THE RAID ON TABUK

I894 Mohammed decided to raid the Byzantines. Normally he never let his men actually know where he was headed. He would announce a destination, but after they were on the way, he would announce the actual target. This raid was far away and the weather was very hot, so greater preparations had to be made. The men began to prepare, but with no enthusiasm because of the heat. It was time for the harvest to begin, and they remembered the last combat with the Byzantines where they lost badly.

I894 When Mohammed asked one of his best men if he wanted to go, the man replied, "Would you allow me to stay? You know how much I love women and when I see the Byzantine women, I don't know if I will be able to control myself." So Mohammed told him to stay. ♀

I896 So Mohammed set off, but there were many Muslims who were slow to leave or they came with misgivings. After the first camp some of the Muslims left and returned to Medina. These were called hypocrites.

I902 When they got to Tabuk, the people there paid the poll tax, ***jizya***. By paying the poll tax, a per-person tax, they would not be attacked, killed or robbed by the Muslims. Those who paid the jizya were under the protection of Islam

I903 Mohammed sent Khalid to the fort of a Christian chief. When the chief and his brother rode out of their fort to inspect the cattle, Khalid killed the chief's brother and captured the ruler. The chief agreed to pay the poll tax to Islam. Mohammed returned to Medina.

ETERNAL JIHAD

M448 After all the victories, some Muslims said that the days of fighting were over and even began to sell their arms. But Mohammed forbid this, saying, "There shall not cease from the midst of my people a party engaged in fighting for the truth, until the Antichrist appears." Jihad was recognized as the normal state of affairs.

ABU BAKR LEADS THE PILGRIMAGE

1919-20 Abu Bakr led the pilgrimage from Medina to Mecca. While they were in Mecca, major changes were made to the treaty of Hudaybiya, which are recorded in the Koran. The treaty was only to be good for four more months, then jihad would be declared if the kafirs didn't submit to Islam.

1922 After this time, those who practiced the old native religions of Arabia would no longer be able to go to Mecca for pilgrimage.

1924 Because the kafirs are considered unclean, they could not approach the Kabah. The money lost from their pilgrimages would be taken care of by Allah. Jihad would bring in the lost money.

1933 When Mohammed had taken Mecca and Tabuk, deputations began to come from the Arabs. The Arabs were waiting to see what would happen between the Quraysh and Mohammed. When Mohammed was victorious, the Arabs came in groups and joined with him.

1956 The kings of Himyar wrote to Mohammed that they had submitted to Islam. Mohammed wrote them back, "... I received your message and am informed of your conversion to Islam and your killing kafirs. Allah has guided you. ... send the one-fifth of the spoils of war and tax the believers... Christians and Jews who do not convert must pay the poll tax..."

♀ 1957 Mohammed sent Muadh to Yemen to proselytize. While he was there a woman asked what rights a husband has over his wife. He replied to the woman who asked, "If you went home and found your husband's nose running with pus and blood and you sucked it until it was cleaned, you still would not have fulfilled your husband's rights."

1965 Mohammed sent out tax collectors to every part of Islam to collect the tax.

This is the Sunna of Mohammed

MOHAMMED'S LAST YEAR

CHAPTER 27

24:51 But when Allah and His Messenger call the true believers to judge between them, their response is, "We have heard, and we obey."

THE FAREWELL PILGRIMAGE

I966 Mohammed took Aisha with him on the pilgrimage to Mecca. However, Aisha's menstrual period had started and she was unclean. So she started to cry, but Mohammed said that she could observe all of the rituals except for going around the Kabah.

I968 Ten years after entering Medina, Mohammed made what was to be his last pilgrimage to Mecca. There he made his farewell address:

I969 The men have rights over their wives and the wives have rights over the men. The wives must never commit adultery nor act in a sexual manner towards others. If they do, put them in separate rooms and beat them lightly. If they refrain from these things, they have the right to food and clothing. Lay injunctions on women lightly for they are prisoners of the men and have no control over their persons.

M473 Feed and clothe your slaves well.

THE FINAL STATE OF CHRISTIANS AND JEWS

M453 When Mohammed first started preaching in Mecca, his religion was Arabian. Then Allah became identified with Jehovah and Jewish elements were introduced. When Mohammed moved to Medina, he argued with the Jews when they denied his status as a prophet in the Judaic line. He then annihilated the Jews.

M453 In his last statement, Jews and Christians became perpetual second class political citizens, dhimmis. Only those Christians and Jews who submit to Islam are protected. The real Christians are those who deny the Trinity and accept Mohammed as the final prophet. The real Jews are those who accept Mohammed as the final prophet of their god, Jehovah. Both Christians and Jews must accept that the Koran is the true Scripture and that the Old Testament and New Testament are corrupt and in error. All other Jews and Christians are false and kafirs.

> 9:29 ***Make war on those who have received the Scriptures [Jews and Christians] but do not believe in Allah or in the Last Day. They do not forbid what Allah and His Messenger have forbidden. The Christians and Jews do not follow the religion of truth until they submit and pay the poll tax [jizya], and they are humiliated.***

The Christians have hidden their prophesies that Mohammed would come to fulfill the work of Christ. To believe in the divinity of Christ is to refuse to submit to Islam. Like the Jews, only those Christians who submit to Islam, honor Mohammed as their last prophet, become dhimmis and are ruled by the Sharia (Islamic law) are actual Christians. Islam defines all religions. All religions must submit to Islam.

SUMMARY OF MOHAMMED'S ARMED EVENTS

I973 In a nine year period Mohammed personally took part in twenty-seven raids. There were thirty-eight other battles and expeditions. This is a total of sixty-five armed events, not including assassinations and executions, for an average of one armed event every seven weeks.

MOHAMMED'S DEATH

♀ I1000 When Mohammed spoke to Aisha, his favorite wife, she complained of a headache. Mohammed said, "No, Aisha, Oh my head. Would it distress you if you were to die before me so that I might wrap you in your shroud and pray over you?" Aisha said, "I think that if you did that, that after you returned to the house you would simply spend the night with one of your other wives." But the pain became worse and he took his final illness in the house of Aisha.

♀ I1006 Mohammed weakened and was in a great deal of pain. Later he died with his head in Aisha's lap. His final words were the perfect summation of Islam, political action based upon religion.

> B4,52,288 ***Mohammed said, "There should be no other religions besides Islam in Arabia" and that money should continue to be paid to influence the foreign, kafir ambassadors.***

T1831 Mohammed was buried beneath his bed. The bed was removed and a grave was dug where it had stood.

This is the Sunna of Mohammed

THE TEARS OF JIHAD

CHAPTER 28

These figures are a rough estimate of the death of kafirs by the political act of jihad.

AFRICA

Thomas Sowell estimates that 11 million slaves were shipped across the Atlantic and 14 million were sent to the Islamic nations of North Africa and the Middle East[1]. For every slave captured many others died. Estimates of this collateral damage vary. The renowned missionary David Livingstone estimated that for every slave who reached the plantation five others died by being killed in the raid or died on the forced march from illness and privation[2]. Those who were left behind were the very young, the weak, the sick and the old. These soon died since the main providers had been killed or enslaved. So, for 25 million slaves delivered to the market, we have the death of about 120 million people. Islam ran the wholesale slave trade in Africa.

120 million Africans

CHRISTIANS

The number of Christians martyred by Islam is 9 million[3]. A rough estimate by Raphael Moore in ***History of Asia Minor*** is that another 50 million died in wars by jihad. So to account for the 1 million African Christians killed in the 20th century we have:

60 million Christians

---

1. Thomas Sowell, ***Race and Culture***, BasicBooks, 1994, p. 188.
2. Woman's Presbyterian Board of Missions, ***David Livingstone,*** p. 62, 1888.
3. David B. Barrett, Todd M. Johnson, ***World Christian Trends AD 30-AD 2200***, William Carey Library, 2001, p. 230, table 4-10.

HINDUS

Koenard Elst in ***Negationism in India***[4] gives an estimate of 80 million Hindus killed in the total jihad against India. The country of India today is only half the size of ancient India, due to jihad. The mountains near India are called the Hindu Kush, meaning the "funeral pyre of the Hindus".

80 million Hindus

BUDDHISTS

Buddhists do not keep up with the history of war. Keep in mind that in jihad only Christians and Jews were allowed to survive as dhimmis (servants to Islam); everyone else had to convert or die. Jihad annihilated the Buddhists in Turkey, Afghanistan, along the Silk Route, and in India. The total is roughly 10 million[5].

10 million Buddhists

JEWS

Oddly enough there were not enough Jews killed in jihad to significantly affect the totals of the Great Annihilation. The jihad in Arabia was 100% but the numbers were in the thousands, not millions. After that the Jews submitted and became the dhimmis (servants and second class citizens) of Islam and did not have geographic political power.

TOTAL

This gives a rough estimate of **270 million** killed by jihad.

4. Koenard Elst, ***Negationism in India***, Voice of India, New Delhi, 2002, pg. 34.
5. David B. Barrett, Todd M. Johnson, ***World Christian Trends AD 30-AD 2200***, William Carey Library, 2001, p. 230, table 4-1.

ETHICS

CHAPTER 29

4:42 On that day, the kafirs and those who disobeyed the Messenger will wish they could sink into the earth for they cannot hide a single thing from Allah.

Ethics is at the root of every human action and underlies our motivation. Ethics determine our point-of-view. For 1400 years Islam has taken slaves and waged jihad. In order to justify this, Islam's ethical system supports slavery and jihad.

Fundamentally, there are only two ethical systems. The first is based upon the ideal of:

Treat others as you would be treated.

This idea is called the Golden Rule and is found in most cultures. This ethic is based upon the idea that others are fundamentally the same as ourselves. [This does not mean we are equal in abilities. Any teacher or coach knows that.] It is a unitary ethical system, since it sees humanity as one spirit and one ethical body.

Everyone wants to be treated as a human being. In particular, we all want to be equal under the law and be treated as social equals. On the basis of the Golden Rule—the equality of human beings—we have created democracy, ended slavery and treat women and men as political equals. So the Golden Rule is a unitary ethic. All people are to be treated the same. All religions have some version of the Golden Rule except Islam.

Now mind you, kafirs have frequently failed at applying the Golden Rule, but they can be judged and condemned on its basis. They may fall short, but it is the ideal.

DUALISTIC ETHICS

But there is another basis for ethics—dualism. In dualistic thought there is no such thing as a unified humanity, but a division into two parts, them and us. Much of the Trilogy is devoted to establishing the division between Islam and the kafir.

At a political level, the duality manifests as:

dar al Islam, land of submission
dar al harb, land of war against the kafirs.

Duality is the very basis of Islam's ethics. It could not be any other way. Islam's ethics are based upon on the Koran and the Sunna of Mohammed. Over half of the Koran deals with the division between Islam and the kafir. The Koran is based upon duality.

There is no such thing as a universal statement of ethics in Islam. Muslims are to be treated one way and kafirs another way. The closest Islam comes to a universal statement of ethics is that the entire world must submit to Islam. After Mohammed became a prophet, he never treated a kafir the same as a Muslim. Islam denies the truth of the Golden Rule.

The term "human being" has no meaning inside of Islam. There is no such thing as humanity, only the duality of the believer and kafir. In the ethical statements found in the Hadith, a Muslim should not lie, cheat, kill or steal from other Muslims. But a Muslim may lie, deceive or kill a kafir if it advances Islam.

Every action and word of Mohammed was based upon whether he was dealing with a Muslim or a kafir. Mohammed's every action and word as recorded in the Sira and Hadith, define Islamic ethics. It is impossible for an action or word of Mohammed to be unethical.

Mohammed's ethics were dualistic. Therefore, Islam's ethics are dualistic.

Islam's ethics are supremely powerful and effective in politics. Dualism is the foundation of jihad, dhimmitude and slavery.

There is not one sentence in the Trilogy that has the slightest sympathy for the suffering of the kafir. Mohammed never once expressed any regret at the torture, killing, enslavement, rape and humiliation of the kafir. The suffering of the kafir is defined as good. The Koran is ecstatic at the suffering of the kafir. Indeed, the finest and most poetic imagery is reserved for the torture and suffering of the kafir. The kafir is pure "other" and Islam cannot be too deceptive or too cruel to the kafir.

Mohammed's response to the heads of the kafirs thrown at his feet was pure joy.

KAFIR

Kafir defines the dualism of Islam at a personal level. No one can be more "other" than a kafir.

A Muslim can not be the friend of the kafir (this is repeated 14 times in the Koran). A Muslim may be friendly to a kafir if it advances Islam. A Muslim is superior in every way to a kafir. Muslims are the only real humans. The only good in a kafir is how the kafir can serve or enrich Islam.

Every unbeliever, non-Muslim, is a kafir. That is the decree of Allah and the Sunna of Mohammed. When a Muslim uses the name kafir, it is a sacred word.

To call someone a kafir is an ethical statement. The difference between a kafir and a Muslim is as great as the difference between heaven and hell.

JIHAD

The political system of jihad is based upon ethical dualism. Jihad is defined in the Trilogy. In the Sira, jihad is war against the kafir. There is a second kind of jihad found in the Hadith called the greater jihad, which is inner, spiritual struggle. However, by actual count, only 3% of the jihad hadiths in Bukhari are about inner, spiritual struggle. 97% of the hadith refer to war against the kafir. In the Koran, jihad is called "struggle in the cause of Allah." And 100% of the "struggle in the cause of Allah" is devoted to killing, enslaving and berating the kafir until the kafir submits to Islam.

Jihad is a political method with political goals. The goal of jihad is to make the kafir submit to Islam. The only reason that Mohammed ever attacked anyone was purely based upon the fact that they had not submitted to his god, Allah.

Muslims kill other Muslims, but that is never jihad. Jihad is reserved for the kafir. The subtext of kafir is that the kafir has offended Allah by rejecting Him. Hence, all jihad is defensive. Jihad is always caused by the offense of unbelief. Jihad is pure political dualism.

SLAVERY

Slavery, like jihad, is the logical conclusion to dualistic ethics. Slavery was used by Mohammed for very simple reasons. He had known slavery from his first breath. There was never a Mohammed without slavery. Slaves were as common as camels in Arabia. Slaves were a free source of energy, power and money. And the slaves eventually became Muslims.

So for Mohammed, slavery was totally positive. Allah said so. Just treat the slaves well. Rape was part of the good treatment of slaves. Rape as sex is pure dualism. When Muslims were raping the women of the conquered tribes after killing their men, we find no empathy or compassion, only the triumph of dualism. A Muslim's ghira, maleness, power and prestige is increased with the rape of the inferior kafir woman. Dualism transforms rape into a sacred good.

Slavery is good. All Muslims are slaves of Allah. So the enslavement of others enriches Islam and helps to Islamicize the kafir world.

The ethics of dualistic slavery can be seen in Islam's attitude about the history of slavery. Islam never acknowledges its role in the history of the suffering of slavery. Islam has no regrets or guilt about slavery.

THE ETHICS OF KILLING AND DECEPTION

Kafir, jihad, dualism and slavery are the results of a very detailed system of ethics. Islamic ethics determine what is truth, honesty, how to treat Muslims and how to treat the kafir. All of these underlie the ability of Islam to carry out jihad, slavery and making the kafir submit. Everything in Islam is directed towards submission and is based upon a dualistic system of thought.

Dualistic ethics that define brotherhood, honesty, truth and the legal system make it possible to kill, enslave, deceive, cheat and rape the kafir.

BROTHERHOOD

Brotherhood is the opposite of slavery. The brother of a Muslim is another Muslim.

B1,2,12

Mohammed: "True faith comes when a man's personal desires mirror his wishes for other Muslims."

B8,73,99

Mohammed: "Worshipers of Allah, do not allow hatred or jealousy to divide you. Live as brothers. It is sacrilege for one Muslim to desert his brother or to refuse to speak with him for three successive nights."

B9,85,83

Mohammed: "A Muslim is a brother to other Muslims. He should never oppress them nor should he facilitate their oppression. Allah will satisfy the needs of those who satisfy the needs of their brothers."

B3,34,366

Jarir gave an oath to Mohammed that he would always proclaim that there is no god but Allah and Mohammed is His prophet. He also promised to follow all prayer rituals, pay his

taxes, hear and obey Allah's and Mohammed's commands, and never give bad advice to another Muslim.

HONESTY

A Muslim should always be honest in dealing with other Muslims.

B3,34,301

A man selling wares in the market place swore by Allah that he had been offered a certain price for his goods when, in fact, no such offer existed. He lied about the offer to drive up the price for his goods and thus cheat a fellow Muslim. Consequently, this verse in the Koran was revealed to Mohammed:

3:77 Those who sell their covenant with Allah and their oaths for a meager price will have no part in the world to come. Allah will not find them worthy to speak to or even glance in their direction on the Day of Resurrection, nor will He forgive them. They will have a painful end.

B1,2,54

Jirir promised Mohammed that he would strictly follow prayer ritual, pay his taxes to help the needy, and be faithful and truthful to all Muslims.

TRUTH

In Islam something that is not true is not always a lie.

B3,49,857

Mohammed: "A man who brings peace to the people by making up good words or by saying nice things, though untrue, does not lie."

A Muslim's oath is flexible.

B8,78,618

Abu Bakr faithfully kept his oaths until Allah revealed to Mohammed the atonement for breaking them. Afterwards he said, "If I make a pledge and later discover a more worthy pledge, then I will take the better action and make amends for my earlier promise."

When deception advances Islam, the deception is not a sin. To deceive the kafir about slavery is not a sin.

B5,59,369

Mohammed asked, "Who will kill Ka'b, the enemy of Allah and Mohammed?"

Bin Maslama rose and responded, "O Mohammed! Would it please you if I killed him?"

Mohammed answered, "Yes."

Bin Maslama then said, "Give me permission to deceive him with lies so that my plot will succeed."

Mohammed replied, "You may speak falsely to him."

Ali was raised by Mohammed from the age of ten and became the fourth caliph. Ali pronounced the following on lies and deception.

B9,84,64

When I relate to you the words of Mohammed, by Allah, I would rather die than bear false witness to his teachings. However, if I should say something unrelated to the prophet, then it might very well be a lie so that I might deceive my enemy. Without question, I heard Mohammed say, "In the final days before Redemption there will emerge groups of foolish youths who will say all the right things but their faith will go no further than their mouths and will flee from their religion like an arrow. So, kill the apostates wherever you find them, because whoever does so will be rewarded on Judgment Day."

Deceit is part of Islamic war against the kafir. So a Muslim can and will deceive the kafir about slavery.

B4,52,267

Mohammed: "The king of Persia will be destroyed, and no one shall assume his throne. Caesar will certainly be destroyed and no Caesar will follow him; his coffers will be spent in Allah's cause." Mohammed cried out, "Jihad is deceit."

Deceit is permissible in jihad:

M032,6303

According to Mohammed, someone who strives to promote harmony amongst the faithful and says or conveys good things is not a liar. Ibn Shihab said that he had heard only three exceptions to the rules governing false statements: lies are permissible in war, to reconcile differences between the faithful, and to reconcile a husband and wife through the manipulation or twisting of words.

The name for deception that advances Islam is *taqiyya* (safeguard, concealment, piety). But a Muslim must never lie to another Muslim. A lie should never be told unless there is no other way to accomplish the task Al

Tabarani, in Al Awsat, said, "Lies are sins except when they are told for the welfare of a Muslim or for saving him from a disaster." [1]

An example of sacred deceit, *taqiyya*:

I224 A member of the Abyssinian royalty, called the Negus, became convinced of the truth of Islam. He was accused by the Christians of leaving his religion. The Negus wrote on a piece of paper, "There is no god but Allah and Mohammed is his prophet. Jesus was a Muslim, born of Mary, conceived without a father." He the then pinned the statement under his shirt over his heart. [These are classical Islamic statements.] When the other Abyssinians accused the Negus of leaving Christianity and they said, "Jesus was the Son of God." The Negus placed his hand over his heart (and the paper with the statement) and told the Christians, "I testify that Jesus was no more than this." The Christians took him at his word and left him. When Mohammed heard this, he prayed for the Negus when he died.

LAW

The hadiths are the basis of the Sharia, Islamic law. Here is a hadith about capital crimes. Killing a non-Muslim is not a capital crime.

B1,3,111

I [Abu] asked Ali, "Do you know of any sources of law that were revealed to Mohammed other than the Koran?" Ali responded, "None except for Allah's law, or the ability of reason given by Allah to a Muslim, or these written precepts I possess." I said, "What are these written rules?" Ali answered, "They concern the blood money paid by a killer to a victim's relatives, the method of ransoming a captive's release from the enemy, and the law that a Muslim must never be killed as punishment for killing a non-Muslim."

If a father converts to Islam and his child or wife does not, then he or she cannot be an heir.

B8,80,756

Mohammed: "A Muslim cannot be the heir of a non-Muslim and a Muslim cannot have a non-Muslim as an heir."

---

1. Bat Ye'or, *The Dhimmi* (Cranbury, N.J.: Associated University Presses, 2003), 392.

TREATMENT OF FELLOW MUSLIMS

Do not harm another Muslim.

B1,2,9

Mohammed: "The difference between a Muslim and an Immigrant[1] is that a Muslim avoids harming other Muslims with words or deeds, while an Immigrant merely abandons everything that Allah forbids."

Weapons in the mosque are acceptable. The mosque is a political center as well as a community center and a place of worship.

B1,8,443

Mohammed: "Arrows should be held by their heads when carried through mosques or markets so that they do not harm a Muslim."

B9,88,193

Mohammed: "You should not aim your weapons at other Muslims; you never know, Satan might tempt you to harm them, and your sin would send you to Hell."

Killing a Muslim is a crime.

B5,58,194

I asked Ibn Abbas about these two verses from the Koran:

25:68 They do not call upon other gods along with Allah and do not kill those whom Allah has forbidden to be killed [other Muslims] except for just cause.

4:93 For those who intentionally kill another Muslim, Hell will be their punishment, where they will live forever. The wrath of Allah will be upon them, He will curse them, and they will receive terrible torture.

He said, "When the verse from sura 25 was revealed to Mohammed, the pagans in Mecca wondered about their chances at salvation and said, 'We have taken lives that Allah has declared sacred. We have worshiped other gods alongside Allah, and we are guilty of fornication.' Allah then revealed to Mohammed:

25:70 Allah is forgiving and merciful, and whoever repents and does good has truly turned to Allah with an acceptable and true conversion.

---

1. Mohammed emigrated from Mecca to Medina. The Immigrant is a sacred figure in Islam.

This verse then dealt with the pagans from Mecca.

4:93 For those who intentionally kill another Muslim, Hell will be their punishment, where they will live forever. The wrath of Allah will be upon them, He will curse them, and they will receive terrible torture.

This verse means that if a man murders another, despite a full understanding of Islam and its laws and requirements, then he shall be punished by burning in Hell forever.

I then mentioned this to Mujahid who elaborated by saying, 'The man who regrets his crime is excepted.'"

In business, a Muslim should never cheat a Muslim.

B9,86,109

Mohammed said, "A neighbor has a greater expectation of help from his neighbor[2] than anyone else." Some said, "If a man wants to buy a house there is no harm done if he uses trickery to prevent another from buying it." Abu Abdullah said, "So that man says that some people are allowed to play tricks on other Muslims though Mohammed said, 'When doing business with other Muslims do not sell them sick animals or defective or stolen goods.' "

B8,73,70

Mohammed: "Harming a Muslim is an evil act; killing a Muslim means rejecting Allah."

A Muslim can swear a false oath by any other god and not be accountable.

B8,73,73

Mohammed: "A Muslim who swears a false oath by the god of another religion is not obligated to fulfill that promise because he cannot be bound by a faith he does not hold."

POSITION TOWARD OTHER RELIGIONS

Well before Mohammed, since the most ancient days, Mecca had been a center of religious tolerance. Many religions used Mecca as a pilgrimage site. The Kabah was a temple of every known religion, including Christianity. This Sunna occurred after Mohammed conquered Mecca.

---

2. Other hadiths show that neighbor meant other Muslims who lived in their own neighborhoods.

B1,8,365

On the Day of Nahr, Abu Bakr dispatched Ali and others to Mecca to make a public declaration: "After this year no kafirs may make a pilgrimage to Mecca to worship, and the ancient rituals performed around the Kabah are now forbidden."

Mohammed's deathbed wishes were to create religious apartheid in Arabia and to use money to influence nonbelievers for Islam.

B4,52,288

Ibn Abbas said, "Thursday, what a momentous thing happened on Thursday!" He then wept until his tears muddied the earth. Then he said, "On Thursday, Mohammed's condition worsened and he [Mohammed] said, 'Bring me a scribe with his tools so that I may leave you instructions that will keep you from going astray.' Those present disagreed with one another, something one should not do in the presence of a prophet. They said, 'Mohammed is gravely ill.' Mohammed said, 'Leave me alone; my condition now is better than what you wish for me.'

"On his deathbed Mohammed gave three final orders saying, 'First, drive the non-Muslims from Arabia. *Second, give gifts and show respect to foreign officials as I have done.' I forgot the third command."*

THEFT

Taking the wealth of the kafir is sanctioned by the Koran as the legalization of booty.

B1,7,331

Mohammed said, "I have been given five things which were not given to any one else before me.

1. Allah made me victorious by awe, by His frightening my enemies for a distance of one month's journey.

2. The earth has been made for me and for my followers a place for praying and a place for our rituals.

3. The booty of war has been made lawful for me yet it was not lawful for anyone else before me.

4. I have been given the right of intercession on the Day of Resurrection.

5. Every Prophet used to be sent to his nation only but I have been sent to all mankind.

ETHICS OF KILLING WOMEN AND CHILDREN IN JIHAD

Killing children in jihad is acceptable. But in other hadiths we find they should not be killed. Both moral positions are Sunna; so both positions are available to Muslims.

M019,4322

When Mohammed was told that Muslims had killed the children of their enemies during raids, Mohammed said that it was permissible because "they are from them."

But here we find that only certain children should be killed.

M019,4457

Yazid B. Hurmus said that Mohammed disapproved of killing children and believed that Muslims should not kill them unless they could tell the difference between a prospective Muslim and a prospective non-Muslim. In which case, it was permissible to kill the prospective non-Muslim child and allow the potential Muslim child to live.

Here are two examples that determine the rules of jihad. They contradict each other, so the resolution is that either can be used as needed.

M019,4319

In one of Mohammed's battles, it was discovered that a woman had been killed by the Muslims; however, he did not approve of killing women and children.

M019,4321

Mohammed said, "They are from them," when told of the killing of women and children by Muslims during a raid.

A CONCLUSION

There is no hadith that ever refers to humanity as one body. Every hadith that refers to humanity is dualistic—divided into Muslims and kafirs. Islamic ethics are completely dualistic.

Islamic ethics have no place for integrity. Indeed, integrity is not possible within any dualistic system. Integrity cannot be logically defined within a dualistic system. If deceit is a virtue, then integrity is not a possibility.

No one who adheres to Islamic ethics can have integrity. They cannot tell the kafir the whole truth, and nothing but the truth, about Islam.

This is the Sunna of Mohammed

EPILOGUE

CHAPTER 30

SUBMISSION

The doctrine concerning slavery and women is based upon duality and submission. Islam is a civilization of duality and submission. The subjugation of women shows its internal politics of dualism and slavery shows its external politics of dualism.

Submission is always about the master/slave relationship. Allah is the master of the Muslim slaves. The Muslim is the master of the dhimmi slaves. The Muslim male is the master of the Muslim female. And the Muslim is the slave master of all slaves, in particular, the African slaves today. In submission, there is always a master and a slave.

DUALISM

Any reading of the Koran shows that it is filled with contradictory statements. The Koran itself refers to saying one thing at one time and another at a later time. One verse can contradict another, so how can the Koran be true or perfect? Muslims do not use the same logic to determine truth and perfection as the kafir does.

In the unitary logic used by all kafirs, if one thing contradicts another, then at least one of the things is false. If someone told you it was raining outside and you looked and saw that the ground was dry, you would not believe that it had been raining. There is a contradiction between dry and rain.

The formal way that Islam deals with the contradiction is called "abrogation." The later verse cancels or abrogates the earlier verse. But that is not the way it really works. Any verse in the Koran is used when it is needed.

The peaceful verses are used when needed and the war verses are used when they are needed. So both sides of the contradiction are true. Besides, since all of the verses are the product of a perfect god, then each is true. How could a verse from god be false?

This is dualistic logic. Both sides of a contradiction can be true. This dual system is the basis of all Islamic doctrine.

THE IMPORTANCE OF CONTRADICTIONS

Understanding that Islam uses dualistic logic is critical. It is just as critical to know how Islam's dualistic logic differs from a unitary civilization's unitary logic.

All of science and math are based upon unitary logic. If the answers from an experiment differ from theory, then either the theory is wrong or the data is wrong (wrong data means that the measurements were taken incorrectly). In short, a contradiction means that something is wrong.

So to eliminate the contradictions, you need a better theory or a better way to gather data. Either way, eliminating the contradictions is how we improve our understanding or advance our technology.

We build a better society by eliminating the ethical contradictions. Slavery was eliminated because of the contradiction between unitary ethics and the actual state of slavery. No one wants to be a slave. So if the Golden Rule is to treat someone else as they want to be treated, then you cannot treat them like a slave.

A unitary civilization is built upon the Golden Rule and eliminating contradictions.

THE DUALISM AND SUBMISSION OF WOMEN

The Islamic Trilogy defines the roles of a man and a woman and how they relate to each other and the world.

The submission of the woman can be measured easily. Each hadith, and verse dictates what the status and place of a woman in the world and in relation to a man. We can go through and categorize each verse and hadith into one of four categories—superior, equal, neutral and inferior. All of these are in reference to the woman. Superior means that the woman is held in high regard. Equal is equal power. Neutral is a mention of women that does not imply any power relationship. Inferior means that the woman is controlled by the man, under his power and below him. The data is shown in the table:

	Superior	Equal	Inferior	Neutral
Number of verses and hadiths	7	8	157	47
Percentage based on superior, equal and inferior	**4%**	**5%**	**91%**	Not included in calculations

Equality of Sexes in Hadith and Koran

The only way that a Muslim woman is superior to a man is by being a mother. The equality issue is interesting. Woman are equal to men only in that both sexes will be judged equally on Judgment Day. But there is a catch. All will be judged upon the basis of how well they have followed the laws and rules of Islam. Since most of these rules include submitting to men, the woman's equality is based on how well she submitted to men.

The results are clear. An Islamic woman must submit to a Muslim man in all things—family, business, religion, work, war, sex, law, her behavior during her menstrual cycle, travel, relationships, and marriage. Submission is Islam. Submission is Sunna. Submission is the way of Allah.

For someone from the civilization of unitary ethics, these results seem misogynistic or anti-female. Unitary ethics strives for equality of the sexes, not submission. Submission is not negative, but a summation of the right order of the Islamic world. Allah made the woman subordinate to the man in most things.

But there is also a bright light for the Islamic woman. Islam uses a dualistic logic, so that one thing does not cancel out the other, as it would if you took an average of the results. Each category stands on its own and can be used when needed. A summary statement cannot be made about a dualistic system. Only statistics can be used. It is not true that a woman is inferior to a man in Islam. This denies the truth of the fact that she is superior 4% of the time. But it can be said that she is inferior to the male 91% of the time.

So a Muslim woman proudly points to the verses that make her an equal and is elated that the mother is superior to all men. That is enough for the contentment of the Muslim female.

Dualism means that both sides of the paradox are correct. Things that are contradictory are both true. Dualistic logic is totally different from unitary logic.

The Muslim woman may submit to the men in all things, but she is totally equal to the Muslim man. This is dualistic Islamic logic. Also, the Muslim woman has full knowledge that she is superior to the kafir male. Kafir males, like kafir females, must one day submit to the Islamic woman. So the women of Islam are happy in their position in life. In a civilization of submission, submission is good.

It is simply a question of who is submitting to whom. The Muslim male has submitted to rules of all the Hadith and is a slave of Allah. Islam is one vast slave plantation with a precise hierarchy. Allah is at the top, with the kafir slaves at the bottom, and the Muslim slaves are in the middle.

The submission of women produces peace and tranquillity. A common Arabic term for a woman is ***fitna***, sedition, disorder or chaos. And if the woman were equal, it would produce fitna. Equality is not possible in a civilization of duality and submission. Attempts at equality produce chaos. The peace of Islam comes through submission. When the woman submits, there is peace and order in society.

AL GHAZALI

One of Islam's greatest scholars was Al Ghazali, a Sufi mystic called the "proof of Islam". He summarized the state of women[1].

> As for the distinctive characteristics with which God on High has punished women, the matter is as follows:
>
> When Eve disobeyed Almighty God and ate fruit which He had forbidden to her from the tree in Paradise, the Lord, be He praised, punished women with eighteen things:
> (i) menstruation;
> (ii) childbirth;
> (iii) separation from mother and father and marriage to a stranger;
> (iv) pregnancy through him;
> (v) having no control over her own person;
> (vi) having a lesser share in inheritance;
> (vii) her liability for being divorced and her inability to divorce;
> (viii) it is lawful for men to have four wives, but for a woman to have only one husband;
> (ix) the fact that she must stay secluded in the house;
> (x) the fact that she must keep her head covered inside the house;
> (xi) (the fact that) two women's testimonies have to be set against the testimony of one man;
> (xii) the fact that she must not go out of the house unless accompanied by a near relative;
> (xiii) the fact that men take part in Friday and Feast Day prayers and funerals while women do not;
> (xiv) disqualification for rulership and judgeship;
> (xv) the fact that merit has one thousand components, only one of which is attributable to women, while nine hundred and ninety nine are attributable to men;

1. Al-Ghazali, ***Counsel for Kings***, translated F. R. C. Bagley (Oxford University Press, 1964) 164-65.

(xvi) the fact that if women are profligate, they will be given only half as much torment as the rest of the Muslim community at the Resurrection Day;
(xvii) the fact that if their husbands die, they must observe a waiting period of four months and ten days before remarrying;
(xviii) the fact that if their husbands divorce them, they must observe a waiting period of three months or three menstruation periods before remarrying.

SUBMISSION AND DUALITY—SLAVERY

It is obvious to the casual observer that slavery rests upon ethical duality and submission. The object of slavery must be less than human, a kafir.

Slavery is the fruit of Islamic duality. Mohammed, the master of dualism and submission, used slavery because it worked and it was as Arabic as sand. Mohammed's life was infused with slavery. His pulpit was build by a slave, a slave gave him a son, a slave cooked his food, cut his hair, and made his clothes. The money from slavery gave Mohammed more material for war, so he could get more slaves. Slaves were the lifeblood of Islam. And Mohammed, the white man, owned both male and female black slaves.

Mohammed's attitude was pure dualism. He preached freeing slaves after they converted to Islam, while he killed others to make more slaves. He preached being good to slaves while he organized rapes of the new slaves. Mohammed never expressed the slightest doubt about the ethics of enslavement of others.

SUBMISSION AND DUALITY—ALLAH

Allah is the perfect god of submission and duality. There are over 300 references in the Koran to Allah and fear; there are 49 references to love. Of these 49 references, 39 are negative such as the 14 negative references to love of money, power, other gods and status.

Only 3 verses command humanity to love Allah and 2 are verses about how Allah loves a believer. There are 25 verses about how Allah does not love kafirs.

This leaves 5 verses about love. Of these 5, 3 are about loving kin or a Muslim brother. One verse commands a Muslim to give charity to Muslims for the love of Allah. This leaves only one quasi-universal verse about love: give what you love to charity and even this is contaminated by dualism since Muslim charity only goes to other Muslims.

There is not a verse about either compassion or love of a kafir, but there are 14 verses that teach that a Muslim is not a friend of the kafir. There are 99 names for Allah and not one of them is love.

Allah does not love humanity. Love is about equality. Fear is about separation and submission. Even a Muslim is a slave to Allah and fears Allah. Islam is a fear-based civilization of submission and duality.

SUBMISSION AND DUALITY—MOHAMMED

Before Mohammed became a messenger of Allah, he was fair to all and a healer in the community. He helped to bring people together. After he became a Muslim, he brought about division, hatred, fights, killings, arguments and threats. He brought duality and demanded that everyone submit and do everything exactly as he said. How he treated someone depended only on one thing—were you or were you not a believer in his god, Allah?

SUBMISSION AND DUALITY ETHICS

There is no Golden Rule in Islam. In fact, Islam denies the truth of the Golden Rule. Muslims are treated as a brother. Kafirs are to be treated in whatever way advances Islam. Will friendliness and honesty advance Islam? Then be friendly and honest. Will deceit advance Islam? Then lie to the kafir about Islam.

Mohammed deceived the kafirs and his words and deeds, Sunna, are the model behavior for all Muslims.

SUBMISSION AND DUALITY—THE SHARIA

The Sharia is nothing more than a condensation of the Trilogy with respect to legalities. Once you have read the Trilogy, the Sharia is obvious. Any Muslim who does not want Sharia to rule over their community is a hypocrite or a secret apostate. The Sharia is pure Islam and Muslims believe that it is the fate of the world to have all man-made constitutions replaced by the Sharia.

In Europe, Sharia law is being demanded for Islamic family law. Europe is yielding on this issue. Soon there will be separate forms of law, until the day Islam is supreme and the Sharia rules the European kafirs.

The Sharia fully implements the legal doctrine of duality and submission for women and kafirs.

SUBMISSION

Islam has made dhimmis out of the kafirs. Dhimmis were forbidden to study the Koran, and as kafirs, we have have made ignorance about the doctrine our official policy. Consider our submission by ignorance:

- Almost none of our diplomats and "experts" have ever read any of the Trilogy, nor were they taught the doctrine of political Islam in college.
- Jews and Christians do not know about the Arabian Annihilation (the elimination of all Jews and Christians from Arabia).
- People don't know that white women were the slaves of choice among Muslims for 1,400 years.
- Blacks do not recognize and teach the Islamic origins of their slavery.
- Our media and intellectuals do not acknowledge rape of the kafir as a weapon of war.
- Christians don't realize that they lost half their territory and 60 million people to Islam in Turkey, Syria, and North Africa.
- Political Islam destroyed half of Hindu culture.
- Political Islam annihilated most of Central Asian Buddhist culture.
- Islam destroyed all of the native religious culture of Africa in Islamic areas.
- The theory and history of jihad are not taught in any military academy, foreign service school, or law enforcement school
- No Christian or Jewish school of religion teaches about the political doctrine and history of Islam.
- No school teaches the Islamic annihilation of the 270,000,000 victims of jihad over the last 1400 years.

What is significant about the kafir response to Islam is: we have done nothing; we know nothing. It is this "nothing" that must be explained.

THE ACCEPTANCE OF IGNORANCE

We know more about Mars than we do political Islam. Muslims have been killing, enslaving, and raping for 1,400 years and we ignore it. Why don't we even know we are ignorant? Denial. Profound denial.

We accept violence and fear from Islam. Any author who writes a book critical of Islam can share Salman Rushdie's fate—a death sentence handed down by Islamic clerics. We don't protest. We show no outrage. How can we have come to this? Have we no sense of decency left? No honor? No shame? No common sense?

MOLESTATION OF THE MIND

The kafirs accept violence and threats from Islam without protest. This acceptance of violence is the sign of a profoundly molested psyche. The kafirs are like the battered wife and molested child of Islam.

Violent molestation can cause denial.

Islam's explosive jihad destroyed half of Christianity, Hinduism, and Buddhism. Now let's look at what manifests after violent molestation. The ***YWCA Rape Crisis Counselor Training Manual*** shows the following reactions are common among victims of rape and child molestation:

Disbelief: the victim has an incredibly hard time believing that the attacks took place.

The media reports very little of the jihad around the world and never connects the dots between the violent events.

Fear: fear is the tool that the abuser uses to control the victim.

Islam has used fear against the kafirs since its beginning. The first person Mohammed had assassinated was a poetess who mocked him. Any public critic of Islam lives in fear. The kafir society will not protect their critic out of dhimmitude.

Fear the attacker will return.

When will the next attack occur?

Guilt: the victim finds a way to blame himself/herself.

It is our fault. We have not treated Islam in the right way.

Branded: the victim does not want others to find out about the crime.

We do not teach the history of a million Europeans taken as slaves by Islam. We do not teach the history of the jihad against Hindus, Christians, or Buddhists.

Humiliation: the victim feels shamed. The things that led to the abuse are hard to talk about.

The victims of jihad in the American immigrant community do not want to talk about the brutality that made them flee to America. Survivors are not bold. They are a beaten people.

Lack of control: during the attack the victim was helpless. This helplessness extends to dealing with the problem.

Where is the person who is optimistic about what can be done to deal with political Islam?

Anger: anger toward the attacker can be healthy. But frequently the anger turns inward.

Notice the rage and hatred in politics since 9/11. Everything is personal, hateful, mean, and spiteful. We don't discuss ideas; we assassinate character.

Powerlessness: things will not get better.

Pessimism about dealing with Islam is the prevailing attitude.

The Abuser

The traits and characteristics of the abuser are well documented.

Denial: the abuser denies that the abuse ever took place.

Muslims do not acknowledge any of the crimes committed in the name of Islam. Anyone killed by jihad was killed in self-defense.

Inadequacy: Abusers are arrogant and overly self-confident.

Islam is never wrong. Muslims are the best of people according to the Koran.

Domination

The word islam means "submit." The abuser expects submission on the part of the victim, the kafir.

Inability to understand or recognize the problem: the abuser is the last person to admit he has a problem.

Islam has never accepted any responsibility for its 1400 year history of slavery.

Manipulation: the abuser wants to make the victim feel guilty.

Islam is presented as the victim. As an example, all of the Palestinians' problems are caused by Israel.

Obsessed with weapons

Have you ever noticed all the swords on Islamic flags and seals? The AK-47 rifle thrust in the air is a symbol of Islam.

The kafir world, in particular its intellectuals, are classic manifestations of the abused wife and the abused child. The dhimmi is a broken person and doesn't even know it.

Can we say that we fit the abused child profile? Let's look at Islam's children one at a time and see how they manifest their abuse.

CHRISTIANS AS ISLAM'S MOLESTED CHILDREN

Political Islam used the sword to take over Syria, Egypt, North Africa, the Levant, and Turkey. Before jihad all of this territory was predominately orthodox Christian. The victims could convert or become dhimmis. This is still going on today. Over 2,000,000 Christians were killed and enslaved in Sudan in the 20th century alone.

What has the rest of Christianity had to say about the slaughter of the orthodox Christians? *The great stain on Western Christianity is its denial of the suffering of its Orthodox and African brothers and sisters in Christ at the hands of the Muslims.*

If you're a Christian, do you know what happened to the Seven Churches of Asia mentioned in Paul's letters? They were all destroyed by political Islam.

Christians are the abused children of Islam, due to their denial of suffering and apologies for Islam.

JEWS AS ISLAM'S MOLESTED CHILDREN

When you read the Islamic accounts of jihad today it is very clear that jihad is happening in Israel, Iraq, Kashmir, Sudan—but the Jews don't see it that way. They just have a "Palestinian problem," not jihad.

Mohammed took the Jews' god and their children. He murdered, enslaved, assassinated, and raped them. He exiled them, took their wealth, and then made the remaining Jews work the land that he stole from them. They also had to give him half of their profits. The Jews were the first dhimmis, semi-slaves.

The Jews have amnesia about the Islamic destruction of the Jews in Arabia. The amnesia extends to life as a dhimmi under Islam. They were the best second-class citizens in all of Islam and willingly submitted. Many Jewish intellectuals are the chief apologists for Islam today. Jews are the molested children of Islam.

HINDUS AS ISLAM'S MOLESTED CHILDREN

In the first 6,000 years of Hindu culture, there was never a religious war. In about 1000 AD Islam started its massive campaign killing, rape, theft, and cultural annihilation. Half the Hindu civilization was destroyed by Islamic imperialism.

In 1977, 2,000,000 Bengalis were murdered and 100,000 Hindu women raped. There are regular jihadic killings in the Kashmir region of India today.

Gandhi, the Hindu saint, showed himself to be a dhimmi in the partition of India. Much of India's Muslim politics come from Gandhi's idealistic pacifism and will result in the final collapse of India.

Most Hindus don't want to talk about political Islam and struggle to make Gandhi's pacifism work. Hindus are in a state of denial and are another of Islam's molested children.

BUDDHISTS AS ISLAM'S MOLESTED CHILDREN

Buddhist cultures do not survive when attacked. As a result, Buddhism is a very small religion. Buddhism would be the world's second largest religion if it could resist aggression.

The first Western Buddhism was in what is now Afghanistan. The Buddhism in Afghanistan was practiced by Greeks who had come with Alexander the Great. There was also a strong Buddhist presence in Turkey and a Buddhist monastery in Alexandria, Egypt.

At one time the entire silk route was Buddhist. Political Islam struck and killed each and every pacifistic Buddhist. But do Buddhists remember? No. Do they want to know? No.

Currently Islam is destroying Buddhism in the Himalayas and mountainous areas northwest of India, in Bangladesh, and southeast Asia. Western Buddhists neither know nor care about this loss of Asian Buddhist culture. Knowing about it would only produce a helplessness since Buddhism limits what can be done against Islam or any other aggressor. In the political arena, Buddhists are all compassion and no wisdom.

Buddhists are profound deniers of jihad. Their pacifism will lead to the annihilation of Buddhism in the face of Islam.

INTELLECTUALS AS ISLAM'S MOLESTED CHILDREN

The Western intellectual has always been ineffectual in resisting Islam. The roots of Western thought about Islam are found in the rapid conquest of half of Western culture 1,400 areas ago. Jihad exploded when the Roman/Byzantine empire was in decay. The West, weak and enfeebled, reeled from overwhelming shock when its culture was destroyed, creating a foundation of fear and denial. This fear manifested in the failure of the Western intellectual to even name the enemy. When you read early Western accounts of that time, you never read of Islam or jihad. All references are to Arabs, Turks, and Moors. There was never a real understanding of political Islam's foundations.

Ignorance

In the late 18th century, scholars studied a weakened Islam that was exotic and romantic. Modern historians shows no horror at Islam's bloodshed, rape, enslavement, and destruction of cultures. History almost seems written with the assistance of opiates; all the victims' suffering is vague. The intellectuals are disconnected and in total denial. The Western attitude towards Islam results from an intellectual molestation.

In *Foreign Affai*rs and other intellectual journals, the analysis of Islamic politics is devoid of any reference to the foundational documents of Islam, the history of jihad, and Islamic foreign policy. All the analysis is purely Western in nature and completely disregards the core values of Islamic politics. The only intellectual criticism is self-criticism, never criticism of political Islam.

Imbalance

Why have intellectuals sliced-and-diced the Bible and Christ but uttered nary a critical word about the Koran and Mohammed? Where is the technical and systemic analysis of the Koran as though it is just another historical document? Find one critical paper of thought about Islam at Harvard. Why are all university opinions of Islam written or vetted by Muslim scholars?

Fear

Every single artist and intellectual who opposed Mohammed was killed or fled Arabia. Intellectuals in both Europe and America have been threatened and murdered. Theo van Gogh, Pim Fortuyn, Salman Rushdie, the Danish cartoonists who lampooned Mohammed and Ayaan Hirsi Ali are forgotten victims.

How refreshing it would be if even one college professor or media writer ever hinted that this type of action was wrong. How remarkable it would be if media criticized the Islamic threats and murder of intellectuals. The Mohammed cartoon riots showed how afraid intellectuals are of Islam. They are willing to do anything to appease the abuser. If Islam objects to political cartoons, then the media will find some imagined high moral ground in submitting to Islam's demands to end freedom of the press.

The kafir intellectuals are the molested children of Islam who deny the history of Islam and are ignorant of the doctrine of political Islam.

BLACKS AS ISLAM'S MOLESTED CHILDREN

The accepted history of race in the U.S. is that white men captured Africans, brought them to the U.S. and sold them as slaves. This is wrong. When the white slavers showed up on the west coast of Africa, they didn't capture Africans. They looked them over in the pens, gave the African slave traders their money, took their bills of sale, and loaded their purchases into boats.

The African slave traders were Muslims. Their ancestors had been plying the trade of war, capture, enslavement, and sale for a thousand years. Mohammed was a slave trader. Long after the white slave traders quit, the Muslims continued their African slave trade. It still exists today.

Blacks define themselves on the basis of slavery. They will not go beyond the white, Christian version of slavery. There is only one theory of history in the black community—the West African Limited Edition version of history. Blacks will not admit the broad scope of slave history. Hindu slavery? It never happened. White and European slavery? It never happened. Slavery on the East coast of Africa? It never happened. A massive slave trade through the Sahara into North Africa? It never happened. Black, eunuch slaves at the Medina mosque? It never happened.

What about modern Africa? How can black leaders not see how Islam carries out its sacred violence? Why aren't the black columnists, writers, professors, or ministers speaking out? They are in total denial. They are the molested children of Islam.

There is a small modern story that illustrates the black, molested mind. A black man was born and given the name of his father, who was named after a white slavery abolitionist, Cassius Clay. After Cassius Clay became the world's heavy-weight boxing champion, he became a Muslim. He then took the name, Mohammed Ali. He dropped the name of a white abolitionist to take the name of two Arab slave traders, Mohammed and Ali. Only a molested mind would be so proud of so great an error.

Blacks are dhimmis and serve Islam by being quiet. There is a deep fear of Islam that makes them overlook and placate Islam. Arabs are the master of blacks.

One thing whites and blacks have in common is that their ancestors were enslaved by Islam, and both are too ignorant to admit it. Molested black and white children of Islam have a secret shame.

FEMINISTS AS ISLAM'S MOLESTED CHILDREN

Western feminists are the abused children of Islam. While jihadists in Africa rape women, cut out the clitoris of the new slave women, our feminists say little.

They deliberately ignore the Islamic doctrine of women and do not teach it in any courses. Feminist professors rarely study wife beating in the Muslim immigrant community.

As the number of Muslims immigrate into Europe, the rape of European women goes up. But it would be racist to attack this problem.

Our feminist, gender intellectuals are the abused children of Islam. They are quiet, don't complain and placate the abuser.

OUR IGNORANCE

Blacks, whites, Christians, Jews, atheists, Buddhists, Hindus, artists, intellectuals, and animists have all been brutalized by jihad and political Islam. Their reactions have all been identical to that of an abused child. Each and every one denies the events, refuses to teach the history, are profoundly ashamed, and try to placate the abuser—Islam. The doctrine of political Islam is not taught in any institution. Each group of victims knows almost nothing about the other's suffering. All are afraid and even more afraid to admit it.

People from a culture with an ethics of unity find it almost impossible to understand Islam with its dualistic ethics.

DHIMMITUDE

When Mohammed conquered the Jews of Khaybar, they became the first dhimmis. They remained Jews, but had no political power, few legal rights, and gave their wealth to Islam. This political state ruled the Christians and Jews under Islam until modern times. You could be a Christian or Jew, but only in your home. Every pubic detail was determined by Islam.

This is our history today, but we refuse to look at it. It is too painful and shameful. We have historical amnesia, but we pay a terrible price for the balm of our ignorance.

Beneath the ignorance is fear. We think that we are free, but our minds are in servitude to Islam. This intellectual submission makes minds dysfunctional. We suffer from the mental state of dhimmitude, a form of social psychosis.

But dhimmitude is easily cured. Knowledge of political Islam and its history cures dhimmitude. And where are our professors with the knowledge to cure dhimmitude?

The Middle East departments are dominated by Muslims and their apologists. No university teaches the Trilogy or confronts the deaths of 270,000,000 victims of jihad. The university curriculums study Islamic art, architecture, history without victims, literature, poetry and derivative comments that put a gloss on the doctrine. You can get a degree in Islamic studies and never have read life of Mohammed, the Sira. That is the training our professors give students who go off and become diplomats, reporters and teachers.

The professors have a special moral task. They are supposed to be thinkers devoted to improving our civilization and giving guidance to the young. That is their job. They have refused their moral responsibilities.

Hence this condemnation: the liberal arts professors are moral cowards who are deliberately ignorant. They are tyrants who suppress thought and questions. They are narrow minded bigots and are culturally self-loathing. They are not just ignorant, but arrogantly ignorant. They ignore the suffering of their own people. They refuse to make fact-based decisions. They are traitors to their own civilization and they are politically correct useful fools serving Islam. They are intellectual eunuchs who serve evil.

How do the professors justify such casual, massive ignorance of both the doctrine and history of political Islam?

Well, it turns out some do have a justification. Money. Money that the Saudis pump into every Middle East department in our universities. In the late 1940s, the Arabs started their program of using money to found professorships and to position Muslims in charge of these departments. For instance, at Harvard, the Saudis built the building that the Islamic studies programs are in. They even fund the professors. The Saudis own Harvard to the degree that a Saudi sits on Harvard's board.

So how do the professors justify their ignorance? For some it is cash. But for others, it is just dhimmitude.

REFORM

The dhimmi argues that Islam is good, but just needs a reform. After all, Christianity reformed, so can Islam. Any analogy between any religion and political Islam is a false analogy, in particular any ethical comparison.

Let us look at Islam from its own doctrine, instead of our intellectual doctrine. Here is the Sunna:

B9,88,174

[...]

Mohammed said, 'There is no mercy for those who change the religion of Islam after me! Islam cannot change!'

What does that say about reform? And here is one more quote from the man who defines Islam:

B2,24,555

Mohammed said, "Allah has hated for you three things:

1. Vain and useless talk about others.

2. Wasting of wealth by extravagance.

3. And asking too many questions about disputed religious matters or asking others for something (except in great need).

Muslims are not supposed to criticize other Muslims or question their religion. Only Muslims can reform Islam. So how can they reform what the Sunna and Koran forbid? They cannot and will not. Islamic reform is a dhimmi illusion.

The Koran is perfect, eternal, universal and complete. How do you reform perfection? Why would you want to reform perfection? What does eternal mean? Eternal means no change. What is hard about this?

"If it ain't broke, don't fix it." Why would Islam want reform? They are winning along all fronts across the globe.

THE CIVILIZATION OF ISLAM

The biggest single mistake that a kafir makes is to consider Islam as a religion. Nothing about the religion of Islam affects the kafir, except the kafir does not get to go to Islamic Paradise. Islam is much more than a religion. Islam is an entire civilization—politics, law, ethics, philosophy, logic, art, culture and religion.

It is the politics of Islam that impacts the kafir, not the religion. The September 11 attack on the World Trade Towers was a political act of jihad. The attack had a religious motivation, but the act itself was a political act. As a matter of fact, the Islamic religion explicitly forbids a Muslim ever taking part in in any religious act with the kafir. Politics is what Islam does to the kafirs, how it views and treats them.

A WAR OF CIVILIZATIONS

Islam is a civilization of dualism and submission. Ours is a civilization with a unitary ethical ideal. We fall short, but our ideal can be used to judge and guide us. The Golden Rule leads us to equality and freedom.

Equality and freedom have no basis in duality and submission. You can't submit and be free. There is no equality in submission.

The vision that humanity is one spirit has no compromise with the vision that all the world must submit to Islam. One or the other must triumph.

For 1400 years Islam has triumphed over the kafir, the Christian kafir, the Jewish kafir, the Hindu kafir, the Buddhist kafir, the atheist kafir and the African kafir.

Today our culture stumbles in the darkness of dhimmitude. But the light of knowledge of the doctrine and history of political Islam can dispel this darkness of dhimmitude.

Once we understand the true nature of the civilization of Islam, we can unite and overcome dualism and triumph over submission.

BIBLIOGRAPHY

DOCTRINE—THE SUNNA

Sira—the life of Mohammed

Mohammed and the Unbelievers, Center for the Study of Political Islam, 2006.

Spencer, Robert. ***The Truth about Muhammad.*** Regnery Publishing, 2006

The definitive work:

Guillaume, A. ***The Life of Muhammad***, (Ishaq's—***Sirat Rasul Allah***). Karachi: Oxford University Press, 1967

Hadith—the Traditions of Mohammed

The Political Traditions of Mohammed, Center for the Study of Political Islam, 2006

The Hadith of Abu Al-Bukhari, ***Sahih Bukhari*** is best found on the internet. The University of Southern California (http://www.usc.edu/dept/MSA/fundamentals/hadithsunnah/) is one of the best sites.

DOCTRINE—THE KORAN

A Simple Koran, Center for the Study of Political Islam, 2006.

HISTORY OF JIHAD

Bostom, Andrew. ***The Legacy of Jihad.*** Prometheus Books, 2006.

GOOD PRIMER

Davis, Greg. ***Religion of Peace?*** World Ahead Publishing, Los Angels, CA.

BEST ONE BOOK SOURCE

Warraq, Ibn. ***Why I Am Not a Muslim.*** Prometheus Books, 1999.

DHIMMITUDE

Ye'or, Bat. ***The Dhimmi.*** Associated University Presses, Cranbury, NJ, 2003

Printed in the United States
216259BV00001B/35/A

9 780979 579400